MARVELOUS

THE MARVIN HAGLER STORY
MARVELOUS

BIOGRAPHY BY DAMIAN AND BRIAN HUGHES MBE

Pitch Publishing
A2 Yeoman Gate
Yeoman Way
Durrington
BN13 3QZ
www.pitchpublishing.co.uk

A CIP catalogue record is available for this book from
the British Library

ISBN-13: 978-1-90917-885-4

Typesetting and origination by Pitch Publishing.
Printed and bound by
CPI Group (UK) Ltd, Croydon, CR0 4YY

Contents

Acknowledgements 8

Introduction 9

The Marvelous Marvin Hagler Story 20

Teaming Up With The Petronelli Brothers 25

Turning Professional 29

The Philadelphia Experience 37

The Cockney Invader, ... 49

Meeting 'Bad' Bennie Briscoe 53

Robbery In Las Vegas – Another Huge Disappointment
   For The Marvelous One 67

Defending His World Championship At Home 82

A Blood Bath In Boston 89

Mustafa Hamsho v Marvin Hagler 93

Caved In 101

San Remo, Italy – Return With Obelmejias 110

A Winter's Night In Worcester 122

Entered The Ring Frozen – The Woeful Wilford Scypion . . . 128

The Build-Up To The Duran Confrontation 136

The 'Bore' Against Hands Of Stone 150

Juan Domingo Roldan 157

Hagler v Hamsho II 168

The Marvelous One v The Hit Man 176

The Penultimate Fight – The African Lion 194

Hagler – Leonard 208

Ring The Bell 229

Aftermath 243

Retirement 250

Epilogue 256

The Authors

Brian Hughes was born and raised in Collyhurst, Manchester. He attended St. Patrick's School in Collyhurst, the playground of former world champion boxer, Jackie Brown and future United heroes, Nobby Stiles, Brian Kidd and Carlo Sartori.

Hughes was a keen amateur boxer, who founded the Collyhurst Lads Club in 1964. Within two years of opening, the club had won the first of over 30 National Schoolboy titles, National Junior ABA titles, England Schoolboy Internationals, Junior England Internationals, Senior champions and internationals. The Daily Mirror dubbed him, "the Pied Piper of Collyhurst" for the positive impact he had on the young people in the area.

During this time, Hughes was mentored by Sir Matt Busby's assistant, Jimmy Murphy, who urged him to "forget what the coaching manuals say. Use your own common sense."

In the early 1970's the Collyhurst Lads Club was demolished along with the Collyhurst Flats and the club moved to its present premises in Moston. Hughes achieved even greater success, producing several British, European and World boxing champions, becoming the first Manchester man to achieve the honour since Jack Bates in 1930s.

During this time, Hughes has authored over a dozen books, which have helped to raise money for his voluntary-run club. These biographies have included United greats, such as Tommy Taylor, Dennis Viollet, Denis Law and his old mentor, Jimmy Murphy.

In the Millennium honours list, Hughes was awarded an MBE for services to the community. In 2012 he was given the award for the 'Outstanding Contribution to British Boxing.'

Professor Damian Hughes is the author of six best-selling books, including *Liquid Thinking*, *Liquid Leadership* and *How to Change Absolutely Anything*, as well the founder of the LiquidThinker Company which takes the psychological methods used by great achievers and shows, in easy steps, how you can adopt them into your own life and business.

He works as a change management consultant and sports psychologist for Sale Sharks, Warrington Wolves, England and GB Rugby League team.

He also runs a Manchester inner-city youth club, Collyhurst and Moston which has helped reduce crime and help many kids find a purpose in their lives from stopping crime to winning Olympic medals. He has also been nominated for the 2007 William Hill Sports book of the year award for *Peerless*, his biography of boxing great Sugar Ray Robinson. In 2009, he co-authored a critically acclaimed biography of boxing legend, *Thomas Hearns in Hitman: the Thomas Hearns Story*.

He was appointed as a Professor of Organisational Psychology and Change for Manchester Metropolitan University in September 2010.

His innovative and exciting approach has been praised by Sir Richard Branson, Muhammad Ali, Sir Terry Leahy, Sir Roger Bannister, Tiger Woods, Jonny Wilkinson and Sir Alex Ferguson.

"There's a monster that comes out of me in the ring. I think it goes back to the days when I had nothing. It's hunger. I think that's what the monster is, and it's still there."

Marvin Hagler, 1981

Acknowledgements

W E WOULD both like to acknowledge our respective corner teams, without whom this book would never have been written.

Brian – I would like to pay tribute to my wife Rosemarie, my sons – Anthony, Damian and Christopher and my daughter Rachael, along with my beautiful grandchildren – Joseph, George, Joshua and Rose. You are the best team in the business.

Damian – I would like to thank Geraldine, George and Rose for their continued inspiration, encouragement and support in letting me pursue my dreams.

Introduction

WHEN A boxer steps into a ring, there are a number of different motivations which propel him into action. Some fighters box through inspiration, a passion to push their abilities as far as possible. Other fighters use rationalisation, an understanding that this is what they are best equipped to do. Others, however, box out of desperation, a primal urge to fight their way past an opponent and past the hand that life has dealt them.

As he looked out at the thronging mass of 12,000 British supporters, waving their Union flags and screaming themselves hoarse, aiming their insults and profanities in his direction, Marvin Hagler danced lightly on his toes and remained sphinx-like in his demeanour, yet inside, "the Monster that lives inside me", as Hagler had explained it, absorbed it all. It stored up all grudges and slights, perceived or otherwise, as a primal fury, ready to explode.

There was a buzz of expectation. There is something special about a world championship fight. As the Wembley Arena arc lights were dimmed the spotlight searched for the lone figure of Alan Minter, the undisputed world middleweight champion, who had begun to snake his way towards the ring. He was flanked by Doug Bidwell, his manager, Kevin, Bidwell's son and Bobby Neil. The crowd, many with National Front leanings, carried him along on a wave of unabashed patriotic fervour. Dancing alone in the

9

ring, Hagler remained impassive to the blanket of noise and hatred which remained unabated even when the Panamanian referee Carlos Berrocal beckoned both men towards the centre of the apron to administer his final instructions as the huge partisan crowd awaited for the opening bell to ring.

While he spoke, Hagler returned the fierce glare of his foe. His monster gathered together the fuel to drive him on towards his destiny of the undisputed world middleweight championship. The build-up to this fight provided it with plenty of ammunition.

He recalled how when he had arrived on English soil, he was met by the British press contingent and plunged into immediate controversy, including being forced to deny that he was a racist.

Peter Moss, a *Daily Mail* journalist, was among a throng of press men lying in wait at the airport. Moss suggested that, "despite wearing a baseball cap, it doesn't hide his image as the ugliest American alive". Hagler incensed the press corps by refusing to sign any autographs or pose for any photographs. His attempts to explain himself, blaming the long flight and a desire to do himself justice when he spoke to them, did not offer any appeasement. Several of the following day's reports offered the contrast to "truly great fighters, like Muhammad Ali, who have emerged dancing and singing from journeys which are twice the distance". He was also bombarded with questions about his racist instincts.

The race claim had gained publicity when Minter gave an interview in which he alleged that the American had refused to shake hands with him when they met in Las Vegas a few months previous. The bluetouch paper was lit when Minter recounted that Hagler had explained, "I don't touch white flesh." The challenger attempted to defuse this powder keg by emphasising why he had come to England. "I am not here for a race fight," he said. "I am here to show people that I'm a champion. And, I am going to do a job to take the world championship belt back to the United States." He denied the remarks by offering the defence, "I'm not a racist. I live in a white neighbourhood and I have lots of white friends." His monster was aggrieved by the slur. Hagler allowed it to find its voice. "There is no love in this game," he said. "Before a fight there are no friends. You aim to destroy each other. Maybe after the fight is over, I will shake hands with my opponent."

The following day, The Casanova Club in London's West End was at bursting point with a phalanx of press, photographers, radio and television representatives for the fight's first official press conference. Minter's crude attempts to build up the fight, choosing to cast Hagler as a force of evil, coming from Boston into London to steal his championship crown had been successful. It was announced that all 12,000 seats had been sold.

Hagler, dressed like a city gent in a smart blue pin-striped suit, wore dark glasses to protect himself from flashbulbs and intense media lights as much as from the glare of the four chunky gold rings adorning his fingers. He continued to project the image of malevolence by refusing to comply with requests to answer questions and chose instead to simply read a statement. He repeated his earlier claims, "I would like to tell all you people straight. This is not a racial fight." He also chose to remind the press of Minter's own dubious stance on racial issues. "Minter, being the champion, should not have made the remark that he would not lose his title to a black man." He made an attempt at conciliation by explaining, "My aim in life is to see the racial barriers broken down. In my neighbourhood, when I play with the kids, I don't see them as black or white, just kids." He finished his statement by reminding the attendees of his Hagler Trust Fund which helped youngsters from his home town of Brockton go to school: "If you're gifted enough to be up here, you should help others who are not so well off." Finally, he signed off by allowing his monster the final word, "I've never shaken hands with an opponent, black or white, amateur or professional, before a fight. I'm getting physically and mentally ready to tear the man apart. Afterwards, I will think about whether we can become friends." With that, he walked out of the conference leaving the press to digest his words.

As the crowd's lusty version of 'Land of Hope and Glory' began to cascade in waves from the back of the arena, Hagler continued to stare through Minter's eyes and into his soul. His monster recounted the words of Kevin Finnegan, another source of motivation.

Finnegan had shared the ring for 61 rounds during five dramatic fights against both Alan Minter and Hagler and so was considered sufficiently well informed to give an opinion on the merits of both men. Despite losing on three occasions to Minter, his ire was solely reserved for the American. He conceded that Hagler was "one of the five toughest fighters I have ever boxed in the ring" and he nominated him as the sole representative in his list of fighters "I have ever truly disliked during my boxing career".

He explained, "I hate him, I really do hate him. He is a bully and one of the dirtiest boxers alive," claiming that Hagler's two victories had been due, in no small part, to his blatant use of the head and other nefarious means. He tipped Minter to emerge victorious inside the 15-round distance but he sounded a note of caution: "Alan has to be careful. Because Hagler is shrewd, strong, mean, and he wants that title badly."

Hagler publicly dismissed his opinion and declared to the press that, "Kevin Finnegan is a cry baby." Privately, he was angry at the allegations of foul play, believing that it would influence the referee and judges. "It is unprofessional of Finnegan to make allegations like that. I was big enough to praise him after the fights because he was a tough son-of-a-bitch but I can assure you that all those cuts he suffered were made purely by my fists – not my head."

He offered the example of Vito Antuofermo, who had required 45 stitches after their fight, "I suppose Finnegan will say those cuts were made by my head but Antuofermo had some class and he certainly didn't." He concluded his defence by suggesting that Finnegan's outburst had been fuelled by something other than hate. "Maybe he'd had too much of that stout when he made his claims. He's certainly fond of the stuff," concluded Hagler.

As he retreated back to his corner, where his long-time trainers, the Petronelli brothers, Goody and Pat, and his attorney Steve Wainwright were waiting, Hagler's unblinking glare didn't leave his opponent, who was dressed in bright red shorts and matching boots. It took in every detail which could prove valuable in wrestling the crown from the head of Minter. The predator Hagler noted that despite the layers of grease on his face, Minter appeared to be dry-mouthed and nervous. The monster added the fuel from two days ago to the mounting fire of rage.

At the final press conference, which took place in the Wembley ring, the two combatants met face to face and the mutual antipathy was palpable. Harry Mullen, the esteemed boxing writer, suggested, "If the action in the ring turned out to be as ferocious as the words preceding the fight, it will be something really special."

Despite his earlier statement and to his intense irritation, Hagler was required to explain on a number of occasions that he had been misquoted about his reluctance to touch white flesh. He did clarify, however, that he "would have no problem hurting it in the ring".

He explained that his real resentment against Alan Minter was because Minter held the world title, which Hagler considered his property. "I won the right to be called the middleweight champion of the world when I beat Vito Antuofermo last year in Las Vegas. I won 12 of the 15 rounds and they only gave me a draw. That should have made me the number one contender and receive an immediate return fight against Antuofermo, but instead, Minter was given the championship fight against Antuofermo. He didn't beat the Vito Antuofermo who I fought. He beat what was left of him."

His monster betrayed the desperation which drove him on, "It should have been Marvin Hagler, who got the second chance at Antuofermo, not Minter."

Minter's response was sharp and straight. "Hagler should not moan about not getting his chance. He had it against Antuofermo and he blew it. He forgets that I was kept waiting and hanging around for two years as the number one contender." Minter continued, "I was sat ringside when Hagler fought Antuofermo and I genuinely thought Hagler just about deserved to be declared the winner. But he didn't get the verdict. He didn't get the championship. I did – and there is no way he will take it from me. I beat Antuofermo far more clearly than he did. I know that in boxing that may not account for everything, but I am quite sure I will beat him and leave him with nothing else to complain about."

Before he left the corner, Hagler said to Goody Petronelli, "I'm ready to die for this. Don't stop it." When the first bell sounded, the two southpaws made good on their promise to bring the bitter war of words to life. Hagler was first from his corner, his monster spitting out the words "seek and destroy" as a final reminder of his intent, and his sharp and aggressive attack seemed to take Minter by surprise. His own strategy appeared to be to keep the challenger at long range, as he had successfully done against Vito Antuofermo, when winning the title. Hagler refused to yield to this plan.

After the initial opening skirmish, both men chose to adopt a jab-and-move approach but Minter's desire for serious action caused him to try and tempt his opponent into a punch-up. Hagler resisted and maintained his discipline. His slashing, scything punches were thrown with a radar-like accuracy and started to cause damage for Minter and consternation for his corner, which had sought to assuage their doubts about Alan's tendency to cut easily and employed the veteran American Jackie McCoy, as a specialist cuts man. By the time the bell sounded to signal the end of the first three pulsating minutes Minter returned to his corner red-faced and with two seeping cuts around his left eye. This would prove a huge hindrance to his battle plan of winning from distance.

Minter was forced to engage at close quarters and when he launched an opening salvo in the second round, he caught Hagler with a few lefts to the head followed by a pumping right jab into the American's face. The increase in the volume of the partisan crowd mirrored the confidence levels of the champion but it merely proved illusory.

Hagler marched on with a demonic intensity, impervious to the attack, and rained a fusillade of punches on to his target. The tissue-thin skin was unable to resist and soon blood began to cascade down Minter's face. Many of the crowd refused to accept that this vulnerability had been legally exposed and echoed Kevin Finnegan's claims that Hagler was liberally using his shaven head to inflict the damage. The mood within the arena started to turn decidedly sour.

Minter drank deep from his well of courage and despite Hagler opening a jagged cut beneath his nose, he attempted to ward off his foe. One observer later described it as "like King Canute vainly trying to turn back the tide" as Hagler swept over him like a tidal wave, crashing both of his fists with an unrelenting fury, ripping open another cut over Minter's eye.

It was starting to become increasingly obvious that the champion's bravery would not be enough to stand between Hagler and his much-coveted title and the Panamanian referee, Carlos Berrocal, focused intently on the British fighter, mentally weighing up the right moment to intervene. He later admitted that he was worried about the wounds which rendered Minter's face into a grotesque red mask as well as the venom which was dripping from Hagler's unceasing assault.

Every punch he delivered landed with a terrifying thud. Hagler helped to finally make up his mind by delivering a brutally accurate right hook on to the unguarded jaw of Minter and when the referee stepped between them and waved his hands to signal the end of the contest, he administered what Hagler described as "the final act of justice by sending the world middleweight championship across the Atlantic to Brockton, Massachusetts, where it should have been in the first place".

There was a momentary silence in the arena as spectators attempted to come to terms with what had just happened. It seemed that after registering that the American was holding his arms aloft, the nationalistic fervour, the racial undertones and the bad blood which had all been prevalent in the build-up, created a powder keg, which exploded.

A shower of detritus descended on the ring, forcing all of those present to run for cover. Harry Carpenter, commentating at ringside for the BBC, was hit by a bottle yet continued his condemnatory commentary of the crowd's antics. Vito Antuofermo, the Italian-American who lost his world title to Minter, was covering the fight for US TV and he also took flight. He was attacked by a drunk, who was swiftly despatched by the former champion. Hagler was forced to take cover in his corner before being hurriedly escorted by the police to the sanctuary of his dressing room, where he was finally presented with his newly acquired championship belt.

Bob Arum, Hagler's promoter, was incensed by the crowd's behaviour. He expressed his incredulity that the "home of sportsmanship" would respond in such a manner. His main gripe was the fact that it denied his man the honour of receiving his belt in the symbolic fashion of a champion. "It is unacceptable that Marvin had no chance to bask in his triumph and enjoy becoming world champion and was not allowed to be interviewed for American television," said Arum.

Hagler was sanguine about it. He had the title, which was all he cared about. He held up his two fists and marvelled at them while telling the press, "I made these my referee and judges. That is all that counts." He would allow the monster to store any grudges for future occasions.

———

After the mayhem had subsided, Hagler and his corner team retreated to the safe haven of their Bailey's Hotel base. Waiting for him were 20 of his friends and family from Brockton who were enthusiastically recounting the nine blood-spattered minutes of ferocious fighting and trading.

When the new champion entered the room, wearing his smart three-piece pin-stripe suit and looking like an incongruous city gent who had completed a day's work on the trading floor, he moved around the room to shake hands and accept the congratulations while Bob Arum started singing "God bless America, the land that I love" as Hagler's sparring partners, Robbie Simms and Danny Snyder, danced beneath the American flag they had clumsily hung.

The next day, Hagler sat in silent contemplation as the plane circled Boston's Logan Airport, wondering what kind of a reception he would receive. He reflected on his arrival home from Las Vegas just 12 months earlier, frustrated by a disputed draw against Vito Antuofermo, and greeted by a handful of the faithful fans who had waited at the airport. "Would today be any different?" he debated with Bertha, his wife. "Will I finally get the respect I deserve?"

Shortly after clearing customs, he received his answer as he was besieged by fans who wanted to acknowledge his new status as world champion, along with the blinding flash of paparazzi who wanted to capture his image. Hagler stood, seemingly shocked by the scene until the state police cleared the way for him to jump inside a waiting limousine.

The ensuing motorcade snaked its way through the rush-hour traffic clogging the Southeast Expressway. When it entered the city limits of Brockton, Hagler switched cars, being driven into his adopted home town in an antique Ford Model T, which had the licence plate HAGLER. As he drove through the streets which were thronged by an estimated 35,000 locals, Marvin waved to the crowds with one hand while waving a small American flag with the other, telling his wife, "This whole thing feels like a dream."

When he arrived at the 80-year-old Brockton City Hall, the band greeted him by playing the National Anthem. City mayor David Crosby warmly embraced him before offering a speech which culminated in the presentation of the keys to the city.

Hagler began his acceptance speech by declaring, "It feels good to be home and it feels good to be an American." He then paid tribute to the city's first world champion, Rocky Marciano, for putting Brockton on the map and promised that he would respect his legacy by keeping it there. He embraced Marciano's aged mother who was sitting nearby. He then reminded them all of his own journey to the summit. "I'm the world champion," he declared. "And I've got here by believing in myself and fighting the hard way to the top. I have earned this title the hard way and I don't intend to give it up."

The Marvelous
Marvin Hagler Story

MARVIN HAGLER was born on 23 May 1954, in Newark, the first child of Ida Mae Hagler and Robert Sims (who weren't married at the time, hence Marvin's surname). The latter abandoned the family when Marvin was a child, leaving Ida Mae to raise Marvin and his brother, Robbie, and their four sisters, Veronica, Cheryl, Genarra and Noreen, on welfare. Hagler grew up in the playgrounds and the streets: cruising sidewalks, hanging out, playing sports, boxing shadows, dreaming big.

"I always wanted to be somebody," Hagler said. "Baseball, I played like I was Mickey Mantle or Willie Mays; basketball, I'd be Walt Frazier; boxing, I'd pretend I was Floyd Patterson or Emile Griffith." Hagler first put on gloves when he was ten for a man he knew only as Mister Joe, a social worker.

By then, Hagler was a fatherless loner who turned Ida Mae's back porch into a clinic for wounded birds and a coop for raising and training pigeons. A turtle lived on the fire escape, and to Ida Mae's dismay Marvin even let it swim in the family tub. "They were the only friends I could relate to," Hagler said of the animals. "Maybe the only friends I really liked. I was always by myself."

Hagler was reaching out when Mister Joe reached in. "He helped me with any problems I had," Hagler recalled. "He taught me sports. We went to the park to fly kites. He'd call up, 'What's the problem? You gonna be at the club?' He kept me out of trouble. He got me involved in counselling other kids. I haven't seen him since I was a kid, and I've been trying to find the guy again for a long time. I do believe that one day he'll show up."

Mister Joe gave Marvin his first set of gloves, and his uncles began to teach him how to use them. "A rough bunch," Hagler laughed.

"He always said he wanted to be a boxer," Ida Mae recalled. "I didn't believe him. He said he wanted to be like Floyd Patterson. 'When I get grown,' he'd say, 'I'm gonna buy you a home.' I thought he'd be a social worker. He loved little kids."

The uncles came and went, as did the broken-winged birds, the pigeons, Mister Joe. The one constant in Marvin's life was his immediate family: his grandmother, Bessie Hagler, his brother, his sisters and Ida Mae. "We were close, very close," said Cheryl. On birthdays and holidays they came together to celebrate.

Ida Mae – a bright, jovial woman of exceptional strength and vitality who kept the kids on a short rein – worked as a caterer and housekeeper. When Marvin was 14 and a freshman in high school, he dropped out of school to work in a toy factory to help support the family.

"As long as we have each other, we can make it," Ida Mae used to tell them. And, "Don't get on the wrong track: No drugs, no prisons for us." And, "Stay away from strangers. Mind your own business." And, "Come straight home from school. Stay home until I get home."

Ida Mae's word was law. "That's what brought us up to be the way we are," said Marvin. "Everybody that came into the house, you better make sure it was 'miss' or 'mister' when you spoke. That's the way she was."

Although they were poor, at Christmas there was always a tree, at dinner-time there was always a meal. If the clothes weren't new, they were always clean. "We took care of what we had," Veronica said. And when there was a race riot, Ida Mae was there, her voice a broom that whisked the kids under Veronica's bed. That's how they survived the first riot, living close to the ground. It began on 12 July 1967. For five days Newark was a battleground and the Haglers were caught in the crossfire. They lived on the top floor of a three-story building. Looking down on the streets at the looters, Marvin says, was like watching ants on a picnic table.

"People were running out of stores," Marvin recalled, "carrying big TVs on their backs, and couches. You'd see little guys trying to carry things they couldn't even carry."

"Really terrifying," Ida Mae shivered. At night, she drew the shades, turned off the lights and double-locked the door, securing it further by jamming the back of a chair under the knob. For three days no one left the apartment. "She'd have killed us," Hagler says. When uncle Eugene, who had been visiting, tried to leave the apartment to get home, a burst of gunfire chipped the facade above the front stoop and drove him back inside. The Haglers lay that night under Veronica's bed. One night, two bullets smashed through the bedroom window and shattered the plaster above the bed.

"Stay away from the windows," Ida Mae told her family. Police and National Guardsmen were everywhere – on the street, on the rooftops, chasing looters, searching for snipers. "You could hear them running across the roof above us," Ida Mae recounted. "There was running and cussing and policemen outside." Ida Mae forbade any of the kids to stand up. For three days they went about the five-room apartment on all fours, sliding around on cushions to get to the bathroom and the kitchen.

"It was like the end of the world," Veronica said.

By the time it was over, 26 people had died, and whole ghetto neighbourhoods of the once vibrant city lay in ruin: Buildings were abandoned, garbage and mattresses were strewn in the streets, and countless cars were stripped.

"It was scary," Marvin said.

Ida Mae thought, "I never want to go through that again."

Nearly two years later there was another riot. A thousand angry blacks roamed the streets, smashing store windows, looting and throwing bottles at police cars. Once again, the Hagler kids weren't allowed outdoors. The 1969 riot lasted only two nights, and no one was killed, but Ida Mae called a relative in Brockton, Massachusetts, 20 miles from Boston, and asked her to help find the Haglers a place to live.

So, with the help of friends, a few weeks later she filled a U-Haul truck with their belongings and moved the family to Brockton, once renowned for its shoe factories, later as Rocky Marciano's home town, a city that hadn't seen much social unrest since militant townsmen with hunting rifles took to its streets to support Shays' Rebellion in 1786. An old blue-collar town, it is also a mixed ethnic salad of Yankees, French Canadians, Lithuanians, Italians and Irish, with a small percentage of blacks and Puerto Ricans.

"What a relief," Ida Mae sighed. "It was wonderful. I could leave my doors unlocked. The kids could go outside and sit on the porch. I was strict in Newark because I had to be; here I let up a little."

In culture shock, Hagler didn't adjust so readily. "I felt out of place, going from an all-black society to a mixed society," he explained. "The only place I'd run across whites was in stores. They were always behind the counter, taking the cash. School principals. Police. The post office. I really didn't trust them. If they were nice, I thought, 'What do they want from me?' I had to learn for myself how people really were. When I found out all white people weren't bad, I started to relax around them. It took me a long time. Goody and Pat had a lot to do with that."

Teaming Up With The Petronelli Brothers

FROM THE age of 15, Hagler started to visit some of Brockton's boxing gymnasiums. Vinnie Vecchione, who in later years became well known when he pulled his fighter Peter McNeeley out of a one-sided mismatch against Mike Tyson, recalled that the quiet young man would sit on the sidelines, resisting offers to join in, and instead would watch fighters including Angie Carlino, who would later become Hagler's personal photographer, going through their work-outs.

Two brothers, Guerino, who was more commonly known as Goody, and Pasquale, nicknamed Pat, also ran a boxing club. The pair were partners in a small construction company. They had both boxed as amateurs and had been close friends of the late world heavyweight champion Rocky Marciano. After Goody had left the US Navy, following 27 years of service, in which he had served in the medical corps and had also been the division's boxing coach, he persuaded his brother to join him in continuing to develop young fighters.

Hagler was drawn back to their gym on a number of occasions, continuing his practice of sitting quietly and diligently observing the fighters' every move. After a while, Goody approached him and asked him if he wanted to learn how to box. Goody, the recognised trainer of the two brothers, recalled years later that he had not approached the shy young man earlier because, "I recognised that it would take time to cement and mature a trust and friendship with him. Marvin seemed to have a deep distrust about white people and so I took my time."

After his first week of training with the Petronelli brothers, they both noticed his fierce desire and eager willingness to listen and learn. "His passion for boxing was intense," Goody recalled. "He appeared fascinated with boxing and seemed to love everything about it from the smell of the liniment and the rich leather of the boxing gloves through to the different techniques he saw the other boxers practising. I vividly remember on one occasion when he came and spoke about a green pair of gloves he had seen Emile Griffith wearing in one fight. He told me that he favoured red gloves. 'They are my favourite colour,' he said, 'because that's the colour of blood'."

Hagler soon became a regular face at the gym, turning up every single day. Goody Petronelli recalled, "Like most kids who start off, he received a black eye, a swollen nose or cut lips. All of the little knocks and bruises. Unlike many kids, he never lost interest and it never put him off. He would be back in the gym the next day."

Petronelli was impressed that his learning curve was in such a steep ascent. "After a while, I told Marvin how pleased I was with his development. His eyes lit up with delight. He confessed that when he went home, he continued to practise his moves over and over again in a big mirror. 'One day, I want to be somebody famous,' he said."

The brothers registered Hagler for an amateur card and were unaware that he had lied to them about his date of birth. He claimed to be two years older than his 16 years in order to be allowed to box in sanctioned tournaments much sooner.

Hagler was also given a labouring job with the Petronellis' construction company. His attitude towards his tasks, including digging ditches, mixing cement, cutting down trees and other hard labouring jobs, also impressed the trainers. The experience also proved to be an education to Hagler. Much of the work was situated across town in Brockton's affluent white West Side. Hagler later recalled, "Those areas were always nice and the people there were courteous and friendly." He told his mother that this was the place he wanted to live when he had made the big money. His trust in Pat and Goody was also built in these early days. "They taught me a trade and matured me. I found out that I could trust these two people and I intended to repay that."

Hagler's early amateur days initially found him searching for his ring persona. He first attempted to showboat and imitate Muhammad Ali's theatrics, which earned him the nickname 'Marvelous' after a local reporter in Lowell, Massachusetts, commented on his spectacular fighting style. As he progressed, he adopted a southpaw stance despite being a natural orthodox and dispensed of the showboating and adopted instead a serious, no-nonsense demeanour, focusing on utilising his natural strengths, including his balance, poise and stingingly accurate two-handed punching power.

His amateur career was brief and relatively unspectacular. He won 50 of his 52 contests, the highlight being his victory as a middleweight in the 85th National Amateur Athletic Union Championship in 1973. His opponent was Terry Dobbs, a durable Marine. Goody Petronelli recalled that this was his finest moment in the ring to date and compared him to a young Henry Armstrong. The officials were equally impressed by his stylish combination punches and voted him as the tournament's 'Outstanding Boxer'. This achievement was even more impressive when the list of other fighters included light-welterweight champion Aaron Pryor, imminent Olympic gold medallist and world heavyweight champion Leon Spinks (who was flattened in one round), and a young boxer named Randy Shields who beat one Sugar Ray Leonard. "Marvin showed that he had something special that night and for the first time, he made people sit up and notice him," commented Goody Petronelli.

Hagler watched the television executives who covered the championships woo these various fighters, especially the Spinks brothers, Howard Davis, and the young Sugar Ray Leonard, grooming them for the next Olympic Games, following the country's meagre return of one boxing gold medal in Munich. Petronelli said that he felt some resentment that despite his showing, he didn't receive the same kind of interest.

Within weeks, he spoke with the brothers who had guided him and asked whether he could turn professional. "I had just become a father for the first time and realised that you can't take a trophy and exchange it for a bag full of groceries," he later said.

Turning Professional

ON FRIDAY 18 May 1973, just one week after Marvin Hagler joined the professional ranks, 'Subway' Sam Silverman, Boston's premier boxing promoter, took Goody Petronelli into a quiet corner of Brockton High School's corridors and counselled him that he should turn his latest young fighter orthodox, "I've had real problems getting him this fight and it won't get any easier."

Two hours later, after watching the ferocious apprentice dominate the opening two rounds against the wily Terry Ryan before winning on a technical knockout to send his foe into a permanent retirement, Silverman followed Petronelli back into the changing rooms. "Forget what I said," he waved his hand with a theatrical flourish. "Keep him as he is. He'll be more devastating that way."

Under his promotion, Hagler followed up his opening victory by recording two quick wins, on points and with a second-round knockout, before he was pitched in against a local fighter, Dornell Wigfall, where he would receive his biggest purse of $1,000. Most significantly, it was also the fight where the monster would first rear its head and prove its devastating ferocity.

Hagler had first encountered Don Wigfall nearly three years earlier at a party in Brockton. Hagler was entertaining a young woman when Wigfall, fresh from prison and eager to embolden his local notoriety, attempted to steal her away.

Rather than back down from this challenge, Hagler agreed to step outside the party and settle the difference. When he was removing his new leather jacket, Wigfall, unaccustomed to such niceties, seized his opportunity and butted Hagler before pinning him to the ground and pummelling him. Hagler's only refuge was to roll under a parked car and wait until Wigfall had gone. He remembered nursing his bruised jaw but being unable to salve his equally damaged sense of pride. On the evening of 6 October 1973, he would have his moment.

It was a full house once again for Sam Silverman's latest promotion at the Brockton High School Gym and they witnessed a cold fury descend upon the dead-eyed Hagler. He set a relentless pace and appeared to have Wigfall in trouble on numerous occasions, only to pull set back and allow him to gain some degree of composure, before continuing his assault. After eight rounds of one-sided battery, Hagler was awarded a unanimous points decision. In later years, Hagler explained that his strategy had been executed flawlessly. "I could have stopped him on several occasions during the eight rounds but I held back purposely so I could teach him a lesson." He took pleasure in knowing that there were witnesses present for both of their clashes. "It might have taken me three years to catch up with him," he asserted, "but when I did, I hammered him."

The Petronelli brothers were eager to continue his apprenticeship and just 20 days after his most satisfying victory, he was pitched in against Cove Green, who he stopped after four one-sided rounds. He fought twice more in November, winning both inside the distance, before he closed his first year as a paid fighter with a fourth-round knockout of New York's James Redford.

Before he faced off against his old foe Wigfall again at the start of 1974, he decided that he needed an image that reflected his alter ego, the monster. He decided to start shaving his head. Pat Petronelli declared, "It made him look evil." He certainly showed those characteristics when he showed no mercy to the hapless Wigfall and stopped him in six rounds to record his ninth consecutive victory.

Recalling the names and career highlights of Bob Harrington, Tracy Morrison, Jim Redford, Curtis Phillips, Robert Williams and Peachy Davis would trouble even the most ardent of boxing fans as although they were regarded as durable, middle-of-the-road fighters they would never trouble the boxing elite. Nevertheless, they were all despatched with clinical precision during the first half of the year. Sam Silverman liaised with the canny Petronelli brothers to determine a sterner challenge for Hagler to surmount.

Sugar Ray Seales had been born two years earlier than Hagler in Saint Croix, on the United States Virgin Isles. As a young man, he moved to Tacoma, Washington, from where he had represented the United States as a light-welterweight in the 1972 Munich Olympic Games. By winning all five of his bouts by points decisions, he became the only American boxer to win gold in what would be a forgettable tournament for the proud boxing nation. His rangy southpaw style had transferred across to the professional ranks with equal success and he boasted an unbeaten record of 21 fights when Sam Silverman offered him a headline slot on the weekly televised Channel 7 boxing show.

Seales arrived in Boston a week before the August event and he did his best to hype the match. He dressed in wide-lapel suits, two-tone shoes and an ever-present black bowler hat for all public appearances. He also wore his Olympic gold medal as a potent reminder of his impressive achievement in Munich.

Hagler said, "Everywhere we appeared together, Seales tried to out-talk me. I'm not much of a talker, so I just let him carry on spouting off about what he was going to do to me when we got into the ring. He told me that he planned to teach me a lesson and would beat me so decisively there would be no arguments. He tried to show me that he wasn't scared but I knew, deep down, that he was just like me. He knew he was going to be in a real fight. I would do my talking with my fists!"

The contest was an absorbing encounter in which referee Billy Connelly hardly had to intervene. Hagler started fast and offered a reminder of how he had stopped 12 of his 14 opponents by dropping Seales in the first round. The Olympian used all of his wiles to nullify the immediate threat but when he retreated to his corner, blood oozing from his nose, he knew that the threat was real.

In the second round, the Brockton prospect opened up with series of whiplash combinations which caught and startled Seales. By the time the bell signalled an end to the round, his left eye was almost closed and welts had begun to pock-mark his face. The fight didn't improve for Seales as Hagler hunted him down with laser-like accuracy and made the pre-fight favourite look bewildered.

When the tenth round finished, Hagler was declared the unanimous winner, while Seales was adjudged not to have won a single round. In the dressing room after the fight, Hagler told reporters, "I warned him that if he went ten rounds with me, he would take a beating. You all saw what happened. Did he take a beating?" The assembled press pack nodded their assent and Seales offered no excuses about his defeat. Hagler also claimed that the victory was doubly sweet as it helped avenge an amateur loss to Seales's brother in the Golden Gloves Championship.

His boxing education continued at some pace as he fought and defeated Morris Jordan and George Green over the next two months. These were seen as opportunities to retain his sharpness before he had agreed to box a return against Seales, who vowed to avenge his loss and continue with his stellar career.

When Hagler entered the ring of the Seattle Center Coliseum on 26 November he noted that Seales appeared to be a lot fitter on this second occasion, starting fast and demonstrating the boxing prowess that had been so notably missing in August. His most powerful weapon was a long, stinging jab that he landed repeatedly. Hagler contented himself by staying out of range and looking to counter when opportunities presented themselves.

By the start of the fifth round, Hagler seemed to have solved the conundrum he had been posed and increased the pace and pressure of his power punching. His trademark aggression began to tell and the momentum of the fight began to turn. Hagler targeted Seales's right eye, which soon began to swell and close, forcing him to stave off the two-handed assaults for the final six rounds.

Hagler finished the tenth round in some style, unleashing a combination which visibly stunned Seales. The Seattle sportswriters sitting at ringside viewed this as significant, awarding Hagler their vote as the winner by the narrow margin of 97 to 96 points. Clay Nixon, one of the official judges differed and scored the fight 98-96 for Hagler. His colleagues, Frank Pignataro and William Kidd felt that eight of the ten rounds had been even and both scored it 99-99.

Hagler, nursing a bruise under his eye and a deep cut inside his mouth, couldn't hide his disappoint when the drawn verdict was announced. He shook his head in disbelief. "I can't believe that people could do this to me," he told the ringside interviewer. Seales declared himself satisfied with the draw but promised Hagler a return within six months.

Hagler took the frustration of seeing his perfect professional record blemished out on D.C. Walker during two brutal rounds in December to complete a year of promise.

In an attempt to satisfy Hagler's yearning for progress and also to bolster the burgeoning public awareness of the undefeated tyro, the Petronelli brothers offered a $10,000 guarantee to experienced fighters such as Tony Licata, Vito Antuofermo, former world champion Emile Griffith and Vinnie Curto to face Marvin in any location they chose.

It was a calculated display of confidence in Hagler as both Licata and Antuofermo were looking for fights with the world middleweight champion Carlos Monzon and the WBC title holder, Rodrigo Valdez. The Petronellis' offer along with the risk of fighting a comparative unknown was unthinkable. The Petronellis didn't receive a public or private response to their proposal.

It did prompt the normally taciturn Hagler to speak about the loyalty he felt to his trainers, "They have taken really good care of me since the day I arrived in the gym and I appreciate that." He revealed that they had refused to take any money from him in his early fights. "They knew I needed the money, and helped me a great deal. Of course they have got a fair cut out of my recent fights when I have started to get decent purses."

———

In 1975, Hagler started his fighting year in February, bettering his previous two fights by disposing of Don Wigfall in the fifth round in Brockton. He then reeled off a further six victories before bookending his year in Boston with a ferocious fight against John 'Mad' Baldwin, an Olympic bronze medallist from 1968 and unbeaten in 20 professional bouts. This fight was voted one of the best of the year.

During this year, Sam Silverman expressed his growing frustration about the increasing difficulty and associated costs of trying to make matches for Hagler. He attributed to three factors, which Joe Frazier would later repeat, "You have got three things going against you. You're black. You're a southpaw and you're good", and the wily promoter was finding these barriers increasingly insurmountable.

Pat Petronelli was a frequent conduit for these Silverman soliloquies. He turned the frustration on its head by suggesting that he find an opponent who could beat his young charge instead. Silverman, before his sudden death in 1977, recalled being instructed, "Why not try and get Hagler licked if you can?"

On Saturday 20 December 1975, Silverman staged an "all-star-Christmas Boxing Tournament" at the Prudential's Hynes Auditorium. Facing Hagler in the ten-round headliner was Houston's Johnny 'Mad' Baldwin in what was unofficially dubbed the "black American middleweight championship".

Despite weighing in an astonishing 18 pounds heavier than his opponent, Baldwin had no answers to the questions which Hagler posed. After a ferocious first two rounds, his default setting was set merely to survive and he looked visibly relieved to make it to the end of ten, one-sided rounds still on his feet. Sam Silverman, promoting Hagler for the last time before his death, paid him a career best purse of $2,000 and admitted defeat to the Petronelli brothers. "'You win', he told me with a big grin," recalled Goody. "It helped us make a decision about where we went next."

"Rocky Marciano eventually had to leave New England in order to get the opposition and publicity he needed in order to make the big money," Hagler explained to local journalists early in 1976. "I love Brockton but in order to make it big in boxing, I gotta move out."

Following the Baldwin fight, Hagler and the Petronellis had been increasingly aware that they had become too big a fish to swim in the local ponds of New England. "Bennie Briscoe, Willie 'The Worm' Monroe, Eugene 'Cyclone' Hart and Bobby 'Boogaloo' Watts were some of the meanest, baddest middleweights in the world," Goody Petronelli recalled. "We knew if we were going to get anywhere we had to fight 'the iron.' So we went to Philadelphia, to their backyard, to fight them."

The Philadelphia Experience

IS FIRST test came merely three weeks after his masterclass against Baldwin when he was pitched in a ten round fight against the teak tough veteran Bobby 'Boogaloo' Watts.

The 35-year-old Watts was born in Sumter County, South Carolina, but came to Philadelphia at the age of ten. His cousin, future heavyweight contender Jimmy Young, had urged him to try the sport and after his early career fighting out of the same 23rd PAL gym as Joe Frazier and Gypsy Joe Harris, he had become a boxing nomad, travelling the country, dancing his way to the ring (hence his nickname) and establishing a deserved reputation as an awkward foe.

When Hagler strode down the aisle of the Philadelphia Spectrum for the very first time, Watts was waiting for him. A tall, rangy scrapper with quick hands and a sharp jab, he was five years older and more experienced. Philly fight fans demanded action and they got it as both men staged a fast-paced and bruising battle. It was clear Hagler had the edge in terms of aggressiveness, strength and power, but Bobby Watts's preferred style was to draw and counter and he never veered from this tactic.

"I had been sparring with light heavyweight Wayne McGee and he had been wearing me down," Watts later recalled. "I felt I had overtrained and only weighed 155 on the night and so didn't have the strength to match Hagler. He kept walking in but didn't throw that many punches when he got inside."

The Philadelphia judges agreed and despite most observers believing that Hagler had clearly deserved the win, after ten rounds they awarded the decision to Boogaloo. J. Russell Peltz, the Spectrum's boxing promoter, actually went over and apologised to Hagler's people. "It might not have been the worst decision of all time," Peltz would say later, "but it was pretty bad." In the next morning's *Philadelphia Inquirer*, the headline read, "Welcome to Philadelphia, Marvin Hagler!"

Hagler writhed in rage and bitterness on the journey home. "He begged me to get him a return fight against 'Boogaloo' Watts as quickly as possible," Pat Petronelli recalled. "He could not accept that he had been beaten. The injustice seemed to touch him at a deep level." Hagler's alter ego, the monster, absorbed it all and stored it as a source of motivation.

Attempts to entice Watts back into the ring as quickly as possible stalled so Hagler was pitched in against Trinidad's Matt Donovan just three weeks later in an attempt to wash the bitterness of defeat from his mouth. Referee Tommy Rawson moved swiftly to stop the fearsome slaughter after just two rounds.

Within a month, he returned to the City of Love in a match against another local favourite Willie 'The Worm' Monroe.

Monroe had begun his boxing career as an amateur in Rochester, NY, where he relocated after finishing high school in Florida. His fighting style, which combined head movement with swift hands and nimble feet, allowed him to compile 43 straight wins as an amateur. Monroe came to

Philadelphia to visit friends one summer and was awed by the city's boxing history. He met some of the fighters he had idolised, including Gil Turner and Harold Johnson, Georgie Benton and Gypsy Joe Harris, whose sister he would later marry.

"Willie would tear you up," recalled Joe Frazier, who also trained in the same gym, a school of hard knocks. "You were either gonna learn, not gonna learn, or get out of the ring."

Monroe agreed with this assertion and warned the press before his fight against Hagler, "I was taught that way. It's my upbringing as a fighter – the way I am trained, the way I am taught. You know, 'Don't go for nothin'. You gotta be nasty.' This is the profession we are in."

Yank Durham, Joe Frazier's manager, and the man who christened Monroe with his nickname, also managed the Philadelphia man and he was dismissive of Hagler's chances. "He's coming back to Philadelphia seeking vengeance and he thinks he'll get it against Monroe. We'll send him back to Brockton a broken man."

From the opening bell, Monroe, who stood just over six feet tall, used his greater range and experience to dominate the proceedings at the city's Spectrum Arena. "He had something to prove. He wanted to come back and prove it," said Monroe after the absorbing ten-round contest. "He was gonna get even, so they brought him back to fight me. And I busted a vessel in his nose and he just bled, bled, bled. He wouldn't stop bleeding. Both eyes closed. They had to lead him back to the dressing room. He couldn't see nothing."

The judges agreed and made Monroe the unanimous winner. Referee Tommy Reid scored it 48-42, Judge Dave Beloff had it 47-44, while judge Lou Tress 49-41. Before the result was announced, a humbled Hagler told the 31-year-old Monroe, "Man, you taught me a lesson. I thought I could fight, but you showed me something." Goody Petronelli recalled that neither he nor Hagler had any protest about the result. "He beat us fair and square," he claimed. "The one thing that sticks in my mind from that miserable evening, though, was a quiet promise Marvin made to us that he would get his revenge over Monroe."

The Petronelli brothers decreed that the best way to recover from a potentially devastating loss was to remain active and in June, they pitched Hagler in against a southpaw named Bob 'Natchez Lightning' Smith from Natchez, Mississippi. Marvin conceded weight to the big light-heavyweight yet despatched him in five one-sided rounds, forcing referee Billy Connelly to dive in and call a halt. Two months later, he appeared in Providence, Rhode Island, against Bobby D.C. Walker where he applied relentless pressure to terrorise the out-gunned Walker, who looked relieved when the referee, Larry Bolvin, stopped the bout in round six.

Watching this fight with interest was Eugene 'Cyclone' Hart, another of Philadelphia's grizzled veterans and the next opponent who vowed to add his blemish to Hagler's record. He was unimpressed by Hagler's pedigree.

Hart had been a gang member in his youth before stumbling into the city's Police Athletic League Center gym. He earned 28 of his 30 professional wins by knockout or technical knockout and garnered a reputation as a knockout artist. "When I started, I went home with headaches from having to fight guys like Georgie Benton in the gym," Hart says. "Guys that I had to spar in the gym are rough and rugged. They have helped me a great deal."

Promoter Peltz agreed, "Hart is probably the best one-punch puncher I have ever seen. He can knock your head off with one left hook. I have never seen a puncher in my life as dangerous." He pointed towards his first 19 victories, which had all ended in knockout and the eventual career statistics that 25 of Hart's knockout victories had come before the sixth round and 18 in the first three rounds. "His left hook is lethal."

In their September meeting, Hart seemed intent on ending the fight early as he stormed out of his corner and attacked the Brockton fighter aggressively. Hagler kept calm and moved backwards to neuter Hart's powerful left hook.

In the second round, Hagler assumed a more offensive stance and got behind his southpaw right jab, mixing in two-handed combination punches. In the next round, the shaven-headed visitor caught the 'Cyclone' with an accurate left cross that stunned him and then dropped him heavily to the canvas, where he received a count of eight.

Hart looked rattled by the turn of events and attempted to drag Hagler into a street fight. After the bell to signal the end of the fourth round had sounded, Hagler dropped his hands and ventured towards his corner. Hart threw a sneak punch and earned an admonishment and a point deduction from referee Tom Reed. He repeated the foul again at the conclusion of the fifth round and received the same punishment.

Hagler remained in total control of his emotions and his game plan throughout the rounds but Hart left his corner for the eighth round with an added buoyancy in his manner. He seemed rejuvenated and caught the evasive Hagler with two hard left hooks, which he absorbed before ploughing on relentlessly.

As the two fighters returned to their corners and sat down, ringside commentators predicted an explosive final two rounds. Hart had other plans. He wilfully ignored Sam Solomon, his trainer, who tried to encourage him and when the bell for the ninth round sounded, Hart simply shook his head and refused to leave his stool. He later claimed that an ankle injury had prevented him from continuing.

Just four days before Christmas, Hagler returned to Boston to headline at the Hynes Auditorium against Oakland's George 'Indian' Davis. Hagler, displaying the poise and control he had used to such devastating effect against Hart, stepped through the gears and forced an end after two minutes and 56 seconds of the six, one-sided rounds. Davis, who would box just once more before announcing his retirement, declared that he had been beaten by "a future world champion". He was the first of Hagler's opponents to recognise the seeds of greatness in the unsmiling, ferocious manner of the Brockton fighter.

1977 brought some welcome news for Hagler. Goody Petronelli confirmed that he would compete for his first professional title, the vacant North American middleweight championship. As a bonus, he would be granted his desire for vengeance by facing Willie Monroe.

Hagler trained with a monastic zeal for this match. His only public comment was, "I cannot wait for the opportunity to win my first title and avenge the loss on my record." In contrast, Monroe remained active and scored a three-round technical knockout over Lenny Harden in Rochester, NY, just three weeks before his encounter in Boston. He simply commented, "I had such an easy time [with Hagler] the first time, I'll beat him again. I beat him badly the first time and I'll beat him badly again."

Boston's Hynes Auditorium was packed on the freezing cold evening of 17 February as people came to see whether Hagler could make good on his quiet declaration that he had learned from his bruising experiences in Philadelphia.

Both fighters put on a thrilling display of all-action boxing that had the crowd in raptures. "Hagler had done his homework and came back strong. He surprised me and I struggled to hold him off," Monroe later reflected.

"I had to be up there in Boston for two weeks before the fight," Monroe says. "It was cold and snowing. Man, I got sick. I caught a cold, but I went through with the fight anyway. I had such an easy time the first time."

The virus would prove a debilitating factor in Monroe's vain attempts to stem the relentless swarms of Hagler's punches. "I got weak in the later rounds and in the 12th round, he knocked me down." Monroe attempted to get up but his rubbery legs defied his will and referee Tommy Rawson ended the attack.

Hagler was jubilant while Monroe was sanguine about his defeat. "It's one of those things. I have two babies in a private school and I am trying to get what I can get."

After this fight, Hagler visited Philadelphia and was granted an audience with Joe Frazier. Hagler was impressed by the former heavyweight champion's style. "Somebody had told me that he owned eight cars, and he wore a special outfit to match each one. I wasn't sure whether to believe this but on the day I met him, he was driving this long maroon Cadillac and he was wearing a maroon suit, a maroon hat and a maroon and white shirt," he noted. "The man looked like a champion and he acted like one."

It was Frazier's advice, delivered in the same straightforward manner he fought, which resonated with Hagler. "He brought me into his office, which was beautiful. He had a big boxing glove sewn into the carpet. We talked and I'll never forget what he told me. 'You've good, very good,' Frazier said, 'but you've got three strikes against you. You're black, you're a southpaw, and you can fight.'"

Just five weeks after hammering Monroe to defeat, Hagler ventured back in the ring to face Guyana's Reggie Ford, who fought out of New York and came with a reputation as a durable southpaw. His first fight had been a loss to the common foe Bobby Watts over ten rounds. His second professional fight was not to be any easier.

Ford was unable to withstand the frenzied pace which Hagler set from the first bell and succumbed to his second defeat after three, one-sided rounds. Hagler declared himself pleased with the workout, which looked far better in hindsight as Ford subsequently enjoyed a respectable career, beating Dave Boy Green, Kirkland Laing, Hunter Clay, and John LoCicero before retiring.

Three months later, Hagler headlined the Civic Centre in Hartford, Connecticut, where he boxed Las Vegas's Roy Jones Snr. Jones entered the ring having emerged victorious from 13 of his 15 fights, drawing once and losing to Hagler's stable-mate, Tony Chiaverini, inside six rounds.

The monster was determined to go one better than Chiaverini and he pawed his way through the first round before opening up to deposit Jones on the canvas in the second. When Jones got back up, he was saved by the bell but his respite was brief. Hagler leapt from his stool and mercilessly blasted away with both hands moving with metronomic precision until Duke Lawson, the referee, stopped the slaughter.

Hagler, pleased to be active, asked his trainers to ensure that this remained the case. Willie Monroe was offered the opportunity to avenge his February defeat in a third rubber match during the baking August summer in Philadelphia.

Monroe insisted that it was a virus that had defeated him last time and attempted to unsettle Hagler by trying to intimidate him at the weigh-in. Hagler retained a Sphinx-like demeanour but privately conceded to Goody Petronelli that he would "make Monroe suffer for his behaviour".

When Tommy Reid heralded both fighters into the middle of the ring, the precedent of previous fights went out of the window. Hagler showed how his talent was developing at a frightening rate. He came into the centre of the apron, feinting and on the move before Monroe came into his range. He pounced on him and then hammered away, his punches like pistons until the action was stopped within one minute and 46 seconds of the second round.

Watts reflected on this loss. "I think I was born too soon," he said. "I have been denied [opportunities] because I am a fierce, fearless middleweight and nobody wanted to fight me. Unfortunately, one of those that did was Marvin Hagler. Simple as that."

Hagler was determined to continue the momentum he felt his career was enjoying and just four weeks later, he returned to Boston to face Ray 'Sugar' Philips, who hailed from Dallas.

Philips, the 1975 National Golden Gloves Light middleweight champion, came into the fight boasting an unbeaten 11-bout record supplanted by an amateur pedigree that included six Fort Worth Golden Gloves championships and a record of 145-6.

Goody Petronelli urged his charge to use the contest as an opportunity to showcase his skills rather than just his power. Hagler did as requested and boxed carefully. Philips had enough confidence to try and match his foe but was frequently beaten to the punch. The demoralising effect of this eventually started to tell and Billy Connelly, the referee, stepped in and ended the bout after seven rounds when he felt that Philips was failing to defend himself adequately.

In October, he headed to Rhode Island to meet Toronto's Jim Henry, a modest fighter coming into the bout on the back of eight consecutive defeats. Hagler viewed this match as another opportunity to hone his craft and practise on a real-life target. Henry understood his part and gave a spirited showing over ten rounds.

Pat Petronelli wanted to end the year with a tougher test than Henry and he campaigned to get Mike 'Cobra' Colbert into the ring in November. Portland's Colbert had an unbeaten 23-fight record but most importantly, had established a worthy reputation as a tough and durable brawler.

He had been named as *The Ring* magazine's Progress of the Year fighter in 1975 and having won the National AAU Welterweight title in 1968 as an amateur he then turned professional six years later. Colbert had participated in the controversial ABC US Championship tournament that was part of the infamous *Ring* scandal, where he was attributed with fictitious wins in the 1977 *Ring Record Book*, occurring on 8 September, 8 November, and 11 December 1976. Colbert had won both of his bouts in the tournament, beating Jackie Smith and Rocky Mosley Jnr. before it was cancelled after the scandal was uncovered.

Hagler, who nicknamed himself Mongoose for the bout so he could joke about eating the Cobra, was determined to enhance his leading challenger status before the sparse crowd of 3,911. The pattern of the bout never varied. Hagler depended on his jolting left hooks to turn the fight his way. But Colbert made use of the ring and circled and back-pedalled, stopping short occasionally to fire jabs, sneaky right leads and rapid combinations. He was encouraged in this approach by his cornerman Al Braverman.

Hagler carried more early rounds because he pressed the action and scored solidly several times in each of the rounds, with crisp left hooks. The powder-puff punches Colbert used were blocked by the high guard Hagler used. He seemed to be deliberately pacing himself.

While the crowd constantly yelled for Colbert to get off his bicycle, he kept darting inside to score weakly with his slappy punching style. Hagler was anything but marvelous as the bout progressed. He took too much time getting off and missed far too often while his busy rival kept scoring with his assortment of patty-cake punches.

Hagler became increasingly frustrated by his inability to land a damaging blow and seemed bewildered by the speedy footwork. Several times he stood off and beckoned the light-punching Oregonian to use his hands instead of his feet.

Colbert was using his hands, plenty in fact, but he never hit hard enough to make Hagler realise this.

His downfall occurred because he lacked even minimal punching power.If the bout had been a bore then the climax was spectacular. Hagler's cornermen sent him out for the kill and as the 12th round opened, Hagler, snarling with genuine anger, stormed across the ring and unleashed a barrage of his best punches. Colbert did not get a chance to get off the ropes.

A left to the head staggered him, and a right to the ribs doubled him up. He went down from the cumulative effect of those withering shots.

There was no doubt which punch put Colbert down for the second time. A terrific right to the jaw dropped him flat on his stomach. Colbert raised himself to his hands and knees and was counted out in that position at one minute of the round by referee Tommy Rawson. Because the fans had not seen the knock-down punch and because Colbert looked at the referee while being counted out, some of them accused Colbert of taking a dive.

Hagler was very complimentary to Colbert for his performance. He said, "It was my pleasure, and my privilege, to welcome Colbert here to Boston. He's someone whom

I've always personally admired, perhaps more deeply, more strongly, more abjectly than ever before."

Colbert, who now goes by the name Adolfo Akil and works as a certified public accountant back in Portland, enjoyed a respectable career, going the distance with Thomas Hearns and Curtis Parker. He rated his fight with Hagler as the toughest. "He was one mean bastard."

The Cockney Invader

KEVIN FINNEGAN belongs to the last days of the dark ages in British boxing when titles changed hands behind closed doors at men-only private sporting clubs in the West End of London. He fought at a time when being the best in Britain and Europe was no guarantee that a world title fight would follow. He won the British middleweight title on three occasions between 1974 and 1979 and held the European belt, but he never challenged for a world title.

In 1970, Finnegan followed his older brother, Chris, who had won the Olympic middleweight gold medal in Mexico in 1968, into the professional business. They each fought as amateurs, but Kevin had been banned for 18 months for climbing into the ring to dispute a loss suffered by his brother, whom he always referred to as Christopher. "It was never easy living in his shadow but that doesn't mean I resent his success at all," said Kevin. The respect the two brothers had for each other was suspended for their regular and often brutal sparring sessions at Freddie Hill's legendary Lavender Hill gym in south London.

"I knew from the first punch in a fight if I would win and I also knew that if I was going to lose, then Christopher would be in trouble because we had been having some real wars in the gyms," said Kevin.

When the Finnegan brothers had finished training they would go to the pub below the gym and have a Guinness or three. Hill, their eccentric but brilliant coach, propped up the bar with them, but his methods worked and both brothers adored him.

Finnegan was also a keen painter and the gym was littered with his work. In training camps, he would often speak of his desire to paint full time when he had made enough money.

Finnegan's win in Paris over the French idol Jean-Claude Bouttier for the European title in 1974 was regarded as one of his best performances but he was in a confident mood when he travelled to Boston for his 4 March meeting with the fearsome Hagler.

On the night of the fight, Boston was gripped by an Arctic chill which limited the attendance and just over 5,300 fight fans braved the elements. Promoter Rip Valenti bemoaned the effects and suggested that a sell-out had been expected. Finnegan was greeted by polite applause when he was accompanied by his trainer Hill and cornerman Mickey Duff to the ring. This was a contrast to the rapturous reception which the local menacing-looking Hagler received as he danced to his corner.

Hagler's powerful hooking put him in control early on, but after being cut badly in the second, Finnegan soon discarded his caution and became more aggressive. The Boston crowd rose to him as, blood dripping down his chest, he smashed back at Hagler with right-handers.

Hagler was shaken by rights in the sixth and seventh, but when a head clash in the seventh opened up a gash on Finnegan's cheek it became apparent that he would not be able to complete the ten rounds.

This seemed to stoke the fire of Finnegan's rage and he attacked throughout the seventh and eighth, winning both big but his retirement was almost inevitable as the blood continued to flow. Hagler, in his customary southpaw stance, fought back and he was leading by just one point on the referee's card at the end of the eighth, when Finnegan's cuts over both eyes, on the forehead, and under his left eye, along with the shocking two-inch split on his left cheekbone, compelled cornermen Freddie Hill and Mickey Duff to retire him.

In all, he needed 20 stitches from the physician back in his dressing room. Mickey Duff explained, "His cheek was laid open almost to the bone. He couldn't have carried on."

Duff reflected on the Boston public's admiration for the British warrior. "The fans loved him and they want him back for a rematch as soon as the cuts heal," he suggested, warning, "His purse was £5,000 but we can look for much more in the return." Promoter Valenti agreed and promised that the rematch would happen soon.

Hagler wanted to remain active and resumed the pace of fighting he had kept up in the previous year and within four weeks, was appearing in his 43rd fight on the undercard of the national broadcast of Bruce Curry's fight against Monroe Brooks in a match-up against Minneapolis fighter Doug Demmings.

Demmings had moved from Iowa to Minneapolis as a child. The eldest of 11 children, he established a reputation as a hot amateur prospect, with a record of 65-3, including winning the Upper Midwest Golden Glove championship in 1972 and 1973 and was a national Golden Glove runner-up in 1972.

He finally turned pro in 1973 and earned a reputation for being quick and elusive. Scott LeDoux, the former world heavyweight contender, used Demmings as a sparring partner on several occasions and reasoned, "As a fellow fighter, you know what a guy has. Doug can work with anybody, box with anybody and do well against anybody." He was coming off the back of his second defeat to Sugar Ray Seales but he was never allowed to settle into a rhythm and Hagler forced the pace throughout before stopping him in the eighth round.

Ten weeks after their first collision, Rip Valenti announced that Hagler and Finnegan would resume hostilities at the Boston Garden on 13 May and fans anticipated that Finnegan would give Hagler another tremendous battle.

From the first bell, it quickly became apparent that he would struggle to reproduce that form as he was fighting uphill after a clash of heads reopened the old, newly-healed scar tissue on his left cheekbone. Finnegan maintained his composure and tried to box coolly and countered effectively but the shaven-skulled Hagler was relentless and kept driving him back against the ropes with a two-handed barrage.

Finnegan, who had never been on the canvas as an amateur or pro, didn't look in any danger of being floored here but the decisive flurry came midway through the sixth, when Hagler opened cuts above and below Kevin's left eye.

"The important cut was the one-inch break at the corner of the scar on Kevin's cheekbone," Mickey Duff said. "It was certain to spread further and I didn't want to see him go through that again."

Hagler, who celebrated his 24th birthday after the fight, sportingly declared, "Finnegan is the toughest man I have ever fought." He looked across at the bloody mess that masked the face of the British fighter and mused, "How did he keep going?"

Meeting 'Bad' Bennie Briscoe

I N THE 1970s, the name 'Bad' Bennie Briscoe was enough to send an involuntary shudder through the middleweight boxing fraternity and the local vermin. "He once told me a story about killing rats in abandoned buildings," recalls J. Russell Peltz, Briscoe's former promoter. "I asked if he used poison. He laughed and told me he used a baseball bat. He was an intimidating man."

Peltz should know all about Briscoe and his career after promoting 45 of his fights during the 1970s, plus he is also the brother-in-law of Arnold Weiss, Briscoe's former manager. On 30 September 1969, Briscoe headlined Peltz's first-ever boxing show at the Blue Horizon. That night Briscoe was awarded a first-round KO victory after Tito Marshall could not come out for the second round.

As an amateur Briscoe won all but three of his 73 bouts and began his professional career at the age of 19, going three years without a loss, winning his first 15 fights with ten by knockout. In his pro career, spanning 16 years and almost 100 professional fights, Peltz and Weiss had him face the best available talent. Only four of Briscoe's 96 professional opponents had a losing record.

Briscoe scored victories over such notables as Charley Scott, George Benton, Vicente Rondon, Kitten Hayward,

Tom Bethea, Juarez DeLima, Carlos Marks, Rafael Gutierrez, Art Hernandez (for the NABF title), Billy 'Dynamite' Douglas, Tony Mundine, Eddie Mustafa Muhammad, Eugene 'Cyclone' Hart, Jean Mateo and Tony Chiaverini. He also had one draw and one loss to Emile Griffith.

"Bennie was a good fighter that pleased the crowd. When he came to fight, he came to fight," recalled Bobby Watts. "He was among the toughest fighters ever to come out of Philadelphia, and was arguably the best middleweight in the world in the 1970s."

A bald sanitation worker by day and an intimidating presence in the ring, Briscoe's fists took him around the world. In Monaco, he met Princess Grace. He fought in Paris, Italy, Puerto Rico, Switzerland and Argentina, where he dined with the country's president.

But Briscoe, whose first title shot didn't come until he had fought professionally for ten years, would remain destined never to win a world title.

He did have opportunities. He fought for the world middleweight title three times. In his first fight against Carlos Monzon in Argentina, Briscoe came away with a draw. At the time, everyone felt that getting that draw in Argentina was like getting a victory in the United States. In their rematch, also on Argentine soil, this time for the world title, Briscoe stunned the champion in the ninth round, but failed to score the knockout. End result, after 15 hard-fought rounds, Briscoe lost by decision. Monzon never forgot those two battles and always had the highest respect for Briscoe.

The second and third title fights were against Rodrigo Valdez. The first, on 25 May 1974, resulted in the only knockout of Briscoe's career in the seventh round of a 15-rounder in Monte Carlo. Valdez won the rematch on 11 May 1977, in Lombardia, Italy, a unanimous decision over 15 rounds.

Briscoe was always prepared to take a couple of blows to devise his strategy to defeat his foe. His notoriety grew even more after he would challenge an opponent to take the first punch and then he would give them a wide grin. It was one of those scenarios where he was asking a rival, "Is that all you got?" The tactic often cowered opponents who then got on their bicycle. This reputation was well-merited. In *The Ring 2003 Yearbook*, Briscoe was listed as 34 on its list of all-time greatest punchers.

The highest purse of his career was $75,000, which he earned in the third Valdez fight. Briscoe seethed at seeing less-talented fighters earn higher purses than him. He reflected on what could have been had he been born later: "I think if I had been born ten years later, it would have been different, as the quality of fighters in my era was deep."

When the fight with Hagler was announced for 24 August, predicting a result seemed simple. The New York boxing press, including Johnny Bos, Neil Terrerz, Ray Jocvics, Mike Wool and Alan Hiss, predicted that the wily Briscoe would win. Journalist Eddie Cool reasoned that, "Before he beat Colbert in the 12th round, he looked dreadfully orthodox and mechanical. He's a southpaw who throws his left hooks one at a time."

New York match-maker and booking agent Johnny Bos was similarly unimpressed. "His punching style lacks versatility," he said. "Kevin Finnegan was the aggressor and put plenty of pressure on Hagler which he struggled with in that first fight and Briscoe will pressure Hagler a lot harder."

Promoter Peltz had taken the decision to not televise the fight, believing that it would attract a higher gate. He was rewarded with 15,000 spectators crammed into the Philadelphia Spectrum, a record crowd for a non-title fight in the city's history.

In the dressing rooms before the fight, Peltz discovered that both fighters were planning to wear burgundy shorts. Refusing to cede a psychological advantage, neither man would agree to change. Hagler refused to agree to an arbitrary coin toss to determine a result. Peltz recalled, "I tried to explain to both men that fans in the cheaper seats would have a tough time distinguishing between two black, bald-headed fighters wearing the same colour shorts but they both flatly refused to even listen."

During their respective marches to the ring, there was no doubting who the crowd were backing. Hagler entered the ring first to a low-level reception but when Briscoe followed, one ringside account later suggested, "It sounded like the fans were tearing the place down."

Buoyed by the reception, Briscoe started the fight at a swift pace and both fighters quickly settled into their role. Briscoe marched forward and his first punch was an attempted body shot. Hagler was up on his toes and in perpetual motion, moving swiftly out of danger, choosing to counter Briscoe's aggression with his stinging southpaw jabs. Hagler later explained, "I wasn't punching that hard. I was trying to frustrate him and keep him off balance and confused."

Hagler maintained the same pattern of hit and run in the second round. Briscoe's rising frustration caused him to butt Hagler during one of their clinches and he opened a jagged gash over Hagler's left eye. The blood flowed freely and forced Hagler to keep his distance for the remainder of the round. When the bell sounded, Pat Petronelli was halfway to the ring, ready to address the wound.

"I had 20 years of medical experience from my days in the navy," he explained. "I knew that I could seal it up." However, as Hagler took his seat, Pat spotted the fight doctor approaching. "I knew that as the out-of-town fighter, we wouldn't get any favours here and I thought he might try to stop the fight," the wily trainer recounted. "As the doctor got closer, I pointed to the crowd and shouted to him that they were calling for him to go over as someone might be hurt badly. The distraction worked."

The team also discussed their tactics and urged Hagler to remain calm and measured, waiting for the pace of the fight and Monroe's age to combine and tire him. By the seventh round, the plan began to follow the script. Briscoe abandoned his attempts to hammer Hagler's body and instead, go head hunting, looking for a premature end. The Brockton fighter now controlled the pace of the fight and in rounds eight and nine, he attacked Briscoe without mercy. He maintained a ceaseless stream of southpaw jabs into Briscoe's puffy face and then followed through with hurtful left-handed smashes. The teak-tough Philadelphian offered an easy target until the end of the scheduled ten rounds.

When the formalities were completed and Hagler was declared the winner, Briscoe's trainer, the venerable George Benton, conceded, "We have no arguments. Bennie fought with courage but tired towards the end. Hagler's jab was in his face all evening and Bennie could do nothing about it." Hagler was fulsome in his praise for Briscoe. "The man will go down as a legend," he declared. He offered to take on Briscoe's mantle as "the baddest bald-headed fighter in the world".

Pat Petronelli told the gathered pressmen that this fight confirmed his plan, "to make Marvin Hagler into a world championship contender, was now nearing completion". He said, "It needs just one more fight to cement it."

Russell Peltz echoed the Petronellis' view but made public his frustrations of his role. "I know that many people herald Marvin as the uncrowned world middleweight champion," he said, "but this is a double-edged sword as the managers of the world top ten middleweights seemed determined to sidetrack or avoid dealing with him."

In November, Hagler remained in active duty by whipping the outgunned Willie 'Sweetwater' Warren inside seven rounds at the Boston Garden. In his post-fight debrief, he admitted that the politics of his world title ambitions were frustrating but maintained with a grim determination, "I will continue to do my job and beat anyone I face until I can't be denied."

Pat and Goody Petronelli knew that they had to keep their charge motivated and active while the boxing rulers ceded to their undeniable claims of entitlement to fight for the major championships. They persuaded Hagler to box a third return fight with 'Sugar' Ray Seales, the former Olympic gold medallist, who he had previously beaten on points and then shared a controversial draw. "I figured that the chance to avenge the draw would tempt Marvin and it did, more than I imagined!" Goody reflected.

Hagler prepared for the 3 February 1979 contest by relocating to the Provincetown Inn on Cape Cod, which was eerily deserted during the long winter months. Brooke Evans, the hotel owner, recalled the intensity in which the boxer prepared. "Every morning at dawn, whether it was hail, rain or snow, Marvin would be out pounding up and down the sand dunes, wearing his heavy-duty Army boots which he believed strengthened his legs."

The hotel proprietor asked Hagler if he could join him on one of his morning six-mile runs. "He set a real quick pace and pretty soon, I was doing my best to keep up. All the while he was running, Marvin would be shadow boxing and I could hear him grunting, 'I'm going to kill him. They aren't going to stop me. I'll kill them all.' His intensity was frightening."

Hagler used these lonely sojourns to feed the monster which raged so fiercely inside of him. He would instruct his family that they were not to contact him at all in camp. "I use this time to store my anger and then take it out on my opponent," he explained to Evans one evening.

He would use the long, cold evenings to dwell upon perceived slights, upsets and injustices which would further fuel his rage. Goody Petronelli claimed, "He would talk about his upbringing in Newark and his distress at witnessing the riots which forced his family to flee." He would also talk bitterly about his boxing career. "He had won 42 professional contests, losing only twice to controversial decisions. He had fought number one contenders and proved successful by beating them. He had boxed more top ten contenders than anyone else in the middleweight division. However, he had never been given a world championship opportunity," Petronelli mused.

"He would also talk about the amount of money which other sportsmen, especially tennis players made. 'It's not nearly as tough', he would shake his head in dismay." Petronelli laughed. "However, when he mentioned other fighters like Leon Spinks being given a shot at Muhammad Ali's heavyweight title after just seven professional bouts his ire was evident. 'This is my 45th fight,' he said, 'and I am still waiting to get my chance.'"

The monastic existence of his camp ensured that Hagler was consumed with a red hot fury when he entered the ring at the Boston Garden. Fight referee Tommy Rawson had to stand between Hagler and his prey when he called them together for their last instructions. Just before he had left the dressing room, he told the boxing writer Don 'Sailor' Sauer, "I'll destroy this guy and I'll do it quickly." "The look of menace on his face was intimidating," Sauer said. "He meant business."

When the bell sounded, Hagler, who had been bouncing impatiently, rushed from his corner like a dog escaping its leash. Seales, who had been meditating in his dressing room sanctuary, seemed in a trance as Hagler deployed vicious two-handed combination punches which were whipped with zeal. Hagler was in a spiteful mood and the accuracy of his punches to both head and body meant that Seales didn't stand a chance.

Hagler swarmed all over the 1972 Olympic gold medallist, forcing him to seek some respite by dropping to one knee. When he rose to accept the eight-count, Seales smiled at the referee. A few seconds later, Seales, the WBA's number one ranked fighter, visited the canvas again and accepted a mandatory count. It was a slashing left hook which forced Rawson to step in to halt the slaughter after just 80 seconds.

Frankie Valenti, the son of veteran boxing promoter Rip, later wrote, "If the United States Navy had possessed a destroyer like Hagler, World War Two would have been all over within two years."

Hagler didn't seek to agree a peace treaty when he was interviewed on television afterwards. Instead, he sought another war, challenging Hugo Corro, the world middleweight champion, to accept his right to contest his belt. "Corro," he said to the Argentinean, "I want you."

The dizzying power of Hagler's fists, which he had dubbed 'Destruct and Destroy', was evident an hour later. Seales sat in his dressing room and offered his eyewitness account of the pummelling. "I got up too quickly after that first knock-down," he said. "I had not fully recovered before the referee stopped it." When the gathered journalists explained that he had visited the floor on a further two occasions, Seales shook his head. "Oh my God," he said, "he hits harder than I thought."

The Hagler entourage wanted to maintain the momentum of this stunning win and keep him motivated in training. He was matched against two unthreatening foes within the following eight weeks, systematically taking apart New Jersey's Bob 'The Hunter' Patterson and Ohio's Jamie Thomas, both inside three rounds.

These fights were merely glorified sparring sessions, stepping stones towards the grand prize which became tantalisingly close when Hagler was offered the chance to face Argentina's Norberto Rufino Cabrera in the rich man's playground of Monte Carlo in June.

Bob Arum and the Italian promoter Rodolfo Sabbatini were staging an open-air tournament outside the Royal Palace, with Hugo Corro putting his world title on the line against the Italian challenger Vito Antuofermo. Arum had persuaded the winner to agree to meet the victor of the Hagler-Cabrera contest and wanted both fights to be on the same promotion.

Arum's willingness to engage with Hagler had come about after the Petronellis had taken the extreme measure of writing to Massachusetts politicians – Edward M. Kennedy, Thomas P. O'Neill Jnr., Paul E. Tsongas – and to a Rhode Island Congressman, Edward P. Beard, and asked for their assistance in helping them understand why Hagler appeared to be frozen out from title honours.

The politicians contacted the movers and shakers of boxing, Bob Arum among them, and threatened an investigation. Having been an Assistant United States Attorney in the Justice Department during the Kennedy Administration, Arum was sensitive to Teddy Kennedy's involvement and subsequently guaranteed Hagler a title shot.

Norberto Rufino Cabrera was born and raised in Santa Fe and turned professional at the age of 20. He had a mixed record of six defeats in his first 30 contests. The defeat at the hands of London's Frankie Lucas was of particular interest to Goody Petronelli as he believed that it offered a blueprint for Hagler's tactical approach. "Lucas was an aggressive, hard-punching brawler," the wily trainer said, "and Cabrera wouldn't resist trying to match him. He came off worse inside eight rounds."

The headline fight was the hotly-anticipated clash between the Argentine Corro and the Italian-American challenger, Vito Antuofermo, for the former's undisputed world middleweight championship crown. Hagler, however, felt disdain for the two men who he considered inferior to him and who had denied him his opportunity to stake a claim for the title. He used this emotion to feed his monster, looking for the merest slight to take offence.

His opportunity came at the official press conference which was held in San Remo, Italy. The local master of ceremonies introduced Hagler as "Marvin Hagler of Brockton, Massachusetts". Hagler immediately leapt to his feet and snatched the microphone from the startled MC. "My name is Marvelous Marvin Hagler," he snarled. "Don't forget the 'Marvelous' when you announce me again."

Witnessing the startled looks on the faces of the assembled press corps, he continued. "I am the uncrowned middleweight champion. I'll take care of Cabrera and then I get the first shot at whoever wins the other fight," he said with a disdainful wave of the hand.

He sat in a brooding silence during the rest of the conference. When it had ended, photographers gathered around for the customary nose-to-nose images which would dominate the boxing pages. Both men were initially asked to shake hands and the obliging Cabrera immediately thrust his hand out towards his foe. Contempt dripped from Hagler's face, which inched closer to Cabrera. Without removing his unblinking gaze from his opponent, he snarled, "There are only two things on my mind." He paused. "Destroy and Destruction."

It was left to Goody Petronelli to attempt to salve some goodwill. "Marvin never shakes hands with an opponent until after the fight," he explained. He then expounded upon the reasons for Hagler's sense of injustice. "Rodrigo Valdez, the fighter who Corro beat to become the champ, had continually ignored our offers to fight and so have a number of the top middleweight contenders, including Antuofermo. Marvin feels that he deserves the chance to fight for the title."

Petronelli recounted a story that Rip Valenti, the promoter of several Hagler fights, had shared with him. "Rip told me that he had spoken to Teddy Brenner, the promoter of Madison Square Garden, and assured him that Hagler would accept a meagre $30,000 to fight the Brooklyn-based Antuofermo. 'Teddy laughed,' said Valenti, 'Antuofermo has already turned down twice that amount for the fight'."

The large Argentine press contingent covering Corro's fight were fascinated by their first glimpse of the Brockton fighter. They observed his training schedule, starting with his daily six-mile run on the steep hills outside town. They attended his workouts in the gym, where Hagler had been unable to secure any sparring partners and so watched Goody Petronelli working with him in the ring.

Goody would often stop the session to make points to his charge, who listened intently. He would ask Hagler to use certain combinations by a code they shared. Petronelli continued his charm offensive by inviting the press to listen, saying, "Neither me or Marvin are bothered by the Argentine camp spying on our training sessions. As long as they don't interrupt the work-out, they are welcome." Hagler's only comment was, "They can watch what I do. Cabrera won't be able to stop me doing it anyway."

This quiet certainty transmitted itself through every pore as Hagler walked to the ring in front of the select crowd of 1,000 spectators gathered in the temporary stadium that had been erected for the fight. He dominated every round in every conceivable way. He started the fight at range and walked and sometimes even ran backwards, counter-punching all the way. The ringside stats showed that Cabrera managed to score in every round with big hooks but Hagler was landing five punches to each one of his Argentine opponent.

Hagler closed the bout in the eighth round by coming forward and landing a lengthy series of power punches with nothing in return. He wiped out Cabrera with an avalanche of nearly 50 unanswered punches before the corner mercifully threw in the towel.

When he was back in the safe confines of his dressing room, Cabrera marvelled at what he had been subjected to. "Hagler landed his punches faster than anything I've ever seen before," he said. "When I was expecting two punches, he would throw two, three or even four. He is so quick." When asked about Hagler's chances of facing the world champion, Cabrera was adamant, "He would beat both Corro and Antuofermo in less than seven rounds on the same night."

Hagler agreed. "It wouldn't take me much longer with either one of them than it did with Cabrera," he said. "I didn't train as well as I would have liked, because I lacked sparring partners but when I face the winner, I'll be much better prepared."

The main event was wreathed in controversy, especially about the standard of judging. British judge Roland Dakin gave Antuofermo the victory 143-142, while his countryman Wally Thom favoured Corro 146-144. Mexican referee

Ernesto Magana cast the deciding vote for the challenger, 146-145. This close decision was initially miscounted and the ring announcer was preparing to proclaim Corro the winner when Antuofermo's corner convinced the officials to recount the scoring and award the title to the rugged Antuofermo, who had been cut in the second round and then won a war of attrition, with Antuofermo butting and wrestling Corro into defeat.

Bob Arum announced that the new champion was now obliged to defend his belts against Marvin Hagler in Las Vegas on 6 October. "Destruction and Destroy," Hagler said, unable to conceal the menacing smile that crept across his face.

In September, the Italian-born fighter pulled up in training, suffering from a strained back. Arum had his personal physician, Dr Edwin Campbell, check the injury and he confirmed that Antuofermo had suffered from an acute lumbosacral sprain, requiring two weeks of rest.

The injury fitted into Bob Arum's ambitious plans and he announced that the rescheduled fight would take place on 30 November and would be one of three world title fights that would be televised by ABC from two different locations.

Apart from Hagler's long-awaited title tilt, Sugar Ray Leonard would meet Wilfredo Benitez in the richest non-heavyweight bout ever in Las Vegas, while Victor Galindez would defend the World Boxing Association light-heavyweight title against Marvin Johnson at New Orleans.

In the press conference to announce this mouth-watering line-up, Arum excitedly boasted that Benitez and Leonard would receive $1.2m and $1m respectively, the highest purses ever paid to non-heavyweight combatants. Hagler watched impassively yet privately seethed at the injustice of not receiving similar rewards. He was being paid $40,000 against Antuofermo's $150,000. He told Pat Petronelli that he couldn't understand it. "I explained that Leonard's lawyer Mike Trainer did all the negotiations for him and it was easier because the television people liked Sugar Ray, the guy with the big smile. Marvin sat and listened and then simply shook his head," said Pat.

At the same time as the fights were announced, Britain's Alan Minter gave up his European middleweight title. In a letter to the British Boxing Board of Control, his manager Doug Bidwell explained that Minter's defence of the European title against Frenchman Gratien Tonna, which was scheduled to take place by December, conflicted with his preparations for the prospective world title fight between the winner of Antuofermo and Hagler he had been promised for January or February 1980, leaving him with no alternative than to vacate his belt and prepare for his world title chance.

Robbery In Las Vegas

MEANWHILE BACK in Las Vegas, the bookmakers sensed that the defending champions, Benitez and Antuofermo, were the betting underdogs. The classy, defensive wizard Benitez was regarded as 3-1 but Antuofermo was an even more distant 5-1.

Just days before their meeting, both men gave separate briefings to the assembled press who scoured the city, looking for fresh angles to their intriguing match. Hagler was asked whether the fact that he boxed in the southpaw style was the reason why he had been so resolutely ignored in his quest to fight for honours. The question disarmed Hagler and set him up to discuss his favourite topic, the one area that his monster craved, injustice.

"There have been times in the past when I would get up from my bed and feel like crying," he confessed. "But my desire and determination to beat the system and the boxing politics only makes me try even harder." He pointed out that he had done this the hard way and not been granted any favours. "I am on a three-year winning streak and am unbeaten in my last 20 contests, stopping 18 of them early," he warmed to his point. "I have made it impossible to be ignored."

He turned his attention to the imminent fight and said, "It has taken me so long to get where I am, I don't think I will get another opportunity, so I can't make any mistakes." Hagler returned to his dismay at the inequality of his purse. "The cheque I am receiving may be the biggest of my career but it is peanuts to what I will earn in the future as a champion. God has a reason for making me bide my time," he added. "But I'm much stronger and much smarter for it."

In later years, when Vito Antuofermo had retired from boxing and embarked on his acting career, which included roles as a prizefighter in *Goodfellas*, hit man Anthony (the Ant) Squigliaro in *The Godfather: Part III* and tough guy Bobby Zanone in *The Sopranos*, he shared an anecdote which took place before shooting a scene with Andy Garcia in *Godfather III*. "The director, Francis Ford Coppola told me to 'think back to 1979, to Caesars Palace in Vegas, when you were about to fight Marvin Hagler'. I listened and then hit Andy right in his fucking nose," he laughed.

When reporters met him before the actual encounter, they didn't need any understanding of method acting to see the grim determination etched across his face. He ticked off the many obstacles that should have kept him from success in the ring: his club right foot, a lifelong handicap that he hides beneath bandages; his height of 5ft 7ins, more suited for a lightweight than a middleweight; his double vision, which was only partially corrected after he retired; his unfamiliarity with the sport when he immigrated to Brooklyn from Bari, Italy, at the age of 16; and the fact that he didn't speak fluent English until he was an adult.

Nevertheless, after a cop sent young Vito to a Snyder Avenue gym instead of jail following a street fight, he began boxing and in 1970 won the New York Golden Gloves 147-pound title at age 17. Nine years later, in Monte Carlo, Antuofermo bulled and body-punched his way through 15 rounds with Hugo Corro of Argentina to become the undisputed world middleweight champ. "I have won this title the hard way and there is no way I am giving it up," he said.

When the fight started Hagler's first surprise was to switch from his usual southpaw stance and box in the orthodox style which he used to control the shorter man with consummate ease. Whenever he sensed that Antuofermo had adjusted to his style, he would then switch to southpaw. One ringside scribe later wrote, "Antuofermo could have been excused for thinking he was boxing twins."

Hagler remained strong, winning most of the first seven rounds, but in the eighth round, Antuofermo began to fight his way back into the match and until the 13th, he accumulated points on the scorecards. It seemed that nobody had expected Antuofermo to fight so well. Prior to the bout, a joke circulated that Coca Cola wanted to rent the soles of Antuofermo's boxing shoes. "Good Night" and "Drink Coke" were to be emblazoned on the bottom of the champ's feet.

Antuofermo began to emerge as the star of the evening, simply by finishing on his feet. The champion's gruelling, relentless attack and preternatural capacity to absorb punishment made him competitive against Hagler. Mike Marley from the *New York Post* described Antuofermo as a "human barricade" and wrote, "Antuofermo, the undisputed 160-pound champ, bleeds, but doesn't quit. He bruises, but doesn't bend. He scars, but survives. He is boxing's last Neanderthal man and he was the wall that Hagler could not clear."

Hagler's sharp right jabs, jolting left crosses, and varied repertoire of punches dominated the action when the fighters were at long range and when they were at close quarters, Hagler tended to get the better of the exchanges, beating the champion at his own game by putting punches together effectively and unleashing frequent, flashy uppercuts to the head. Marley wrote, "These two battlers would not go down to anything less than a sledge-hammer or a baseball bat."

When Antuofermo retreated to his corner at the end of the fourteenth round, he was reassured, "Hagler's dead on his feet." Whether this was a psychological ploy to get the champion through the final three minutes or a realistic assessment of Hagler's physical fragility, it was wrong on both counts.

Hagler unleashed a furious assault which culminated in him connecting with a ferocious right uppercut followed by a dizzying left hook which sent the champion staggering backwards. The bell sounded in time to rescue Antuofermo and put the decision into the hands of the judges. Referee Mills Lane, however, was in no doubt who had won. "Stay facing this way," he told Hagler while gesturing to the television cameras. "Until they officially announce the decision and I raise your arm."

Duane Ford agreed with Lane and had Hagler winning by 145-141, Dalby Shirley disagreed and saw Antuofermo winning by 144-142 while Hal Miller's 143-143 scorecard sealed the draw. Antuofermo retained his WBA and WBC world title belts by the slimmest of margins.

Most ringside journalists disagreed with the decision. The special correspondent for the *New York Times* stated bluntly, "The *New York Times* had Hagler clearly ahead." The same correspondent also wrote, "All ten Italian journalists here could not believe the decision of the three Nevada officials. They all thought Antuofermo had been clearly outpointed by the stylish, switch-hitting Hagler."

On the other hand, some reporters favoured Antuofermo. The Associated Press scored 143-142 for the champion. Prominent boxing reporter Mike Marley, covering the bout for the *New York Post*, saw it 144-142 for Antuofermo.

The *New York Daily News* pegged Hagler a winner by one point, but did not argue with the draw. The *Daily News* correspondent, the late Dick Young, wrote, "I had it even after 14 and gave Hagler the 15th by one point; I do not score even rounds. If I had, it would have been a draw. When you score a fight one point either way, you cannot be dismayed over either decision."

Hagler looked momentarily stunned before shaking his head as if to dispel a bad dream. He repeatedly mouthed the words, "I won this fight, I was robbed." The jubilant champion, his craggy face sporting cuts beneath both eyes, disagreed: "I thought I won the fight and I am glad the judges agreed." As Hagler left the ring, Joe Louis tugged at the sleeve of his robe and pulled him close. The 'Brown Bomber' told him, "Marvin, you won the fight. Don't get discouraged."

After he emerged from the sanctuary of his dressing room, the bitterness of the decision spewed through Hagler's analysis. "I knew that the fight was close, but Vito knew that I had won it. I could see it in his face," he claimed. He then turned his wrath towards the judges. "If they knew anything about the skills of boxing, I would be a world champion today. I gave Vito Antuofermo a boxing lesson." His resolve remained strong. "I'll become the world champion eventually because that's my dream and that's my destination," he concluded.

The Top Rank promoter Bob Arum announced that there would be an immediate rematch and Antuofermo magnanimously agreed but the heads of the WBC and WBA quickly moved to quell this argument. Jose Sulaiman said, "There is no doubt that Hagler deserves another chance to fight for the title but Alan Minter has been promised the next championship contest no matter who won in Las Vegas this evening. Hagler will have to wait his turn."

Hagler's mistrust of the boxing authorities and the way that he had been denied his world title tilt for so long ensured that he placed little faith in this promise. Rip Valenti, the Boston promoter, said, "Hagler doesn't believe that there will ever be a rematch." Antuofermo's imposing brother Nicky disagreed but insisted that the return match would happen within the year. Tony Carione, the Italian champion's manager, attempted to reassure Pat Petronelli with the non-committal, "You'll get a shot again sometime."

The only man who would offer a firm commitment was Antuofermo himself. A few days after the fight, he revealed that he had been suffering from bronchitis for a week before the contest. He claimed, "There will most certainly be a next time for Marvin Hagler and me." He explained, "I'm the only fighter to hold both the WBC and WBA titles. And that's the way I want to keep it. I'll fight who they tell me to fight. It looks like it will have to be Alan Minter but once I have dealt with him, I will beat Hagler even more convincingly because I'll be in better condition."

Hagler, meanwhile, had followed through with his own plans and married Bertha Washington, his long-time partner in a small, intimate ceremony before disappearing on his honeymoon.

———

"We needed to keep Marvin active," observed Goody Petronelli, "because we needed to be ready to seize the first opportunity to fight for the title again." This meant that in early January 1980, Hagler signed to fight Frenchman Loucif Hamani in February.

Hamani, the African middleweight champion, possessed an impressive pedigree. He had reached the quarter-finals of the 1972 Munich Olympics where he had lost to Alan

Minter, before he ventured into the paid ranks, achieving an impressive record of 25 victories and one reverse, including the notable scalp of Emile Griffith. Hamani had been promised that he would be entitled to the first shot at the winner of the Antuofermo-Minter fight provided he could get past the snarling presence of Marvin Hagler.

In his preparations for the fight, Hagler had no shortage of anger and fury to feed to his alter ego, the monster. "They want me to get beaten so I lose my number one world ranking," he railed. "I know their game but I'm not gonna play it. I'll clean up the division before I win the title." He had received a welter of support from the boxing public who recognised that he had been the victim of an injustice. "Because of my knockout record (38 in 49 fights), they expected me to knock Antuofermo out'. As long as he was still standing, it was to his advantage," he told the *Portland Telegraph*. "I have now got to forget about it and concentrate on the future. From now on, I am going to let these do my talking for me." He held up his fists.

On the morning of the fight, a fierce snowstorm battered Portland. Hagler arrived at the weigh-in and suggested that the storm was a portent of what Hamani could expect that evening. When Hagler weighed in a few pounds heavier than the agreed 161-pound limit – a pound over the middleweight division limit – he used it as an excuse to "remind myself of what I'm going to do to him" – he nodded at the French fighter and went to shadow box in order to lose the excess weight.

The inclement weather didn't deter 4,306 fight fans from arriving at the Cumberland County Civic Center. "In the dressing room and again in the corner, Marvin kept telling us, 'I'm taking no chances with the judges'," recounted Goody Petronelli.

He rushed to the centre of the ring's apron and immediately began stalking his prey like a panther. He scored straight away with a jolting right cross that sent Hamani backwards. Hagler seized the initiative and opened up with a two-handed barrage of combination punches which were lightning fast and accurate. "He was like a car that can go from 0-60 in a second," Petronelli said. "Hamani hadn't even started his engine."

The second round followed the same pattern. Hagler began by directing a searing left jab on to the forehead of Hamani, sending him into reverse. Hagler, showing no mercy, followed him while throwing a relentless stream of head and body shots that landed with a repetitive thud. It was enough for the African champion to resist let alone respond but Hagler continued to force the pace.

After 80 seconds of this fusillade, Hamani's legs betrayed him and he stumbled backwards. His momentum, aided by a heavy body shot, sent him falling through the ropes. "I saw him fall and moved quickly to prevent him hitting the floor," said Petronelli. "As soon as I saw his eyes, I knew that he was finished. He was gone." Fight referee Rene Laliberte ruled it as a technical knockout. Bob Arum entered the ring and told Hagler that this was the first occasion Hamani had ever been knocked down. Hagler grinned, "Well, he's out now for sure."

Goody Petronelli's desire to keep Hagler's motivation burning bright until he could get his opportunity to fight for the world title was a simple task: offer him the chance for revenge. "I asked Marvin who he would like to fight next and typically, he told me he would fight anyone. When I dangled the name of Bobby Watts in front of him, he started to salivate."

There were three names that were guaranteed to elicit a venomous reply from Hagler whenever they were proffered:

Willie Monroe, Vito Antuofermo and Bobby 'Boogaloo' Watts. "Marvin hated the fact that each of these fighters had beaten him. He soften his stance on Willie after he had avenged his loss but it left a scar that he felt could never fully heal until he had settled the score," the Boston promoter Rip Valenti once suggested.

Hagler didn't take a break from training after his brutal demolition of Hamani. He continued to train for the next seven weeks until the 19 April fight which was staged again at Cumberland County Civic Center. "He was so intense for this fight, it was a tough job to try and get him to rest up," said Pat Petronelli.

At the weigh-in, Hagler came face to face with Watts for the first time in the four years since they clashed. Watts approached Hagler and offered a sporting handshake. Hagler pointedly ignored the gesture, choosing to look deep into Watts's eyes. His voice dripped with poison as he said, "I'll shake your hand after we have fought, not before." Without missing a beat, he added the chilling caveat, "Unfortunately, you won't be in any condition to shake anybody's hand."

Watts was momentarily stung by the icy blast. His conciliatory facade was dropped. He pushed his face close to Hagler and spat, "This time, I'm gonna knock you out." Hagler laughed and backed away, refusing to look away until Watts could no longer hold his stare. Bob Arum later joked, "Trying to intimidate Hagler is harder than selling him shampoo."

The first round was close. Hagler controlled the fight but just before the bell, Watts landed a stunningly effective right cross to the jaw of Hagler. He ignored the blow but it seemed to rekindle the feelings of agony which he had felt on that dark night in 1976 when he sat in the rear passenger seat of the Petronellis' car on the ride back to Brockton, trying to come to terms with the injustice of his loss. The monster's voice, taunting him and reminding him of another unfair obstacle that had been placed in his path, made Hagler demonic.

He rushed from his stool and began hitting the body of his foe like an axeman chopping a tree. He landed his right hook which floored Watts twice. On the second occasion, as the referee Rene Laliberte started his count above the prostrate figure, Hagler commanded Watts to get up and continue fighting. "I wanted the guy to get up," he told his cornermen. "I hadn't punished him enough."

There was some controversy about the final knockdown. Hagler put Watts on to the apron with three seconds remaining in the second round. The fight's time-keeper, Francis 'Babe' Anderson, failed to sound the bell when the time had elapsed, which would have saved Watts because fighters are saved by the bell under the Portland Maine boxing rules. Sam Michael, the chairman of the Maine State Athletic Commission, admitted the mistake. Watts's manager Sylvia Brooker ended any potential controversy by admitting, "I am not sure that Bobby would have wanted to come back out for round three anyway."

In March, Britain's middleweight hopeful Alan Minter ventured to Las Vegas to confront Vito Antuofermo, who was returning to the scene of his disputed fight with Hagler, for the undisputed world middleweight title.

Bob Arum, who was staging the event at Caesars Palace, was concerned that the 4,500-capacity sports pavilion where the fight would take place would be sparsely populated. British fans had bought 1,000 tickets to support their hero but Top Rank executive Irving Rudd revealed that only 85 tickets had been bought by American fans so both fighters' camps were required to ramp up their attempts to generate interest.

Doug Bidwell, Minter's manager and father-in-law, blamed the poor reputations of previous European fighters in recent showings, especially Lorenzo Zanon and Alfie Righetti's dismal challenges to Larry Holmes' heavyweight title. "American boxing fans think that most British and European fighters have inflated reputations and are not worthy of world rankings," he reasoned, "but take my word for it, this will not be the case with Alan Minter. He is here to fight."

Freddie Brown, the grizzled veteran old trainer who had worked with Rocky Marciano, came to speak for Antuofermo. He favourably compared Minter to Hagler. "Minter is a southpaw who knows how to fight," said Brown. "There are a lot of southpaws who are awkward but Minter knows what he's doing. Although Hagler is a better puncher, Minter is smarter."

Both camps treated the other with generosity and respect. Minter in particular was circumspect in attacking the champion because of tragic events in his own recent history.

Bidwell trained Minter through a distinguished amateur career, in which he won 90 of 112 fights, 16 of the victories while representing England in international competition. It culminated when he won a bronze medal in the 1972 Olympics in Munich. Since turning pro in October of that year he had won 38 of 44 fights, 22 by knockout, and lost five. One ended in a "no contest" in the second round. "I got disqualified for not giving my best," he recalled. That was in 1974 against Jan Magdziarz.

"There have been some ups and downs," Minter said. "Some people wrote me off after that. I was also beginning to get hurt in fights. But I carried on and I carried on." And he brought himself back up. A year after the disqualification, Minter fulfilled an old dream by winning the British middleweight title, beating Kevin Finnegan over 15 rounds. He won the European title when he knocked out Germano Valescchi in Milan in five. "My ambition after turning professional was to win the British title," he said. "I did that. Then it was to win the European title. I did that." And then, by simple elimination, it was to win the world title. The quest left him a saddening legacy to live with. On 19 July 1978 he knocked out Angelo Jacopucci in the 12th round of their European title fight; the next day Jacopucci died as a result of a brain injury.

Bidwell had successfully reined in his eagerness to fight at full throttle. "The penny has dropped and he has become a more patient fighter," said the trainer. After the Jacopucci tragedy, Bidwell claimed, "It didn't change Alan's boxing style but you will never hear him say he hates a fighter."

Minter and his cornermen used two code terms to remind themselves of their strategy for beating Antuofermo – "CB" for clever boxing and "CA" for controlled aggression. And that is what Minter used to defeat Antuofermo. Through guile and grit and using his skills as a boxer to decisive effect, the 28-year-old southpaw took charge early, kept the champion off balance, controlled most of the fight and recaptured the initiative when it seemed that Antuofermo had seized it from him in the middle rounds.

Although the thousand Englishmen were in an uproar when the decision was announced, Antuofermo was stunned and silent – "What can I say?" – and many others ringsiders were at least mildly surprised over who the real winner was and why. The official scoring was no help. In fact, it only fuelled the dispute. The three judges, presumably observing the same fight, came to conclusions so sharply divergent that they might as well have judged it sitting under the ring, listening to footsteps.

The fight had familiar echoes to Hagler's match-up with the Italian. For most of the early rounds, throwing a left off his right jab, Minter kept Antuofermo at bay. The champion charged and bulled, trying to get inside but there the attacks would end.

Repeatedly the two men wound up in a lurching embrace, with referee Carlos Padilla, who had no vote in the decision under Nevada rules, stepping in to break them.

"The referee wouldn't let me fight," Antuofermo complained. "Any time I got on top of him, the referee grabbed me. With Hagler I was able to fight on top because the referee let me fight."

"I had to break them," Padilla said. "There should be no holding, no clinching, only hitting. What they were doing was not infighting. Infighting is not holding." With his inside attack weakened, and Minter sticking with the jab and popping hard lefts, Antuofermo had trouble getting off effective combinations.

Both fighters' reputation for bleeding easily was not tested and neither man was ever in serious trouble. Antuofermo dropped Minter – the only knock-down in the fight, in the 14th round – with one of his infrequent left-right combinations, but it appeared as much a slip as a decking, and the embarrassed Minter was quickly on his feet, unhurt.

Under the ten-point-must system, judge Charles Minker of Las Vegas scored the fight 144-141 for Minter, giving him nine rounds with one a draw. Ladaslad Sanchez of Venezuela scored it for Antuofermo, 145-143, with four rounds even, while judge Roland Dakin of England had it 149-137, giving all but one round, the 14th, to his countryman, with one round even. It was Dakin's scoring that caused the most furore.

Dakin himself took the fuss calmly. "Nonsense," he said, adding, "If it hadn't been for my scorecard in Monte Carlo, Antuofermo would not have been the champion. I was the deciding judge when he beat Corro. Didn't argue about that one, did he?"

None of this perturbed Minter, however. "It was a hell of a fight," he told Antuofermo when they met outside the ring. "You're a great fighter."

For the moment, Minter basked in his new celebrity, though he seemed curiously subdued. He sensed a winding down. What he had done was just beginning to dawn on him. "You dream of this day, and after it's all happened it's like an ordinary fight, isn't it?" he said. "I'm happy, so happy. I can't put it into words. But I don't show it, do I? I will." With his wife Lorraine clutching Minter's new belt – his championship belt – he left the arena and strolled through the hotel lobby to the cheers of his countrymen.

Hagler returned to Caesars Palace in May for his final fight before the proposed title shot. He was pitched against the experienced Mexican, Marcus Geraldo. Geraldo, whose birth name was Marcus Lopez, had been around the boxing scene for years and had fought a litany of famous names, including going the distance with both Thomas Hearns and Sugar Ray Leonard, who described him as "hitting harder than Hagler and Hearns put together".

He stood at 5ft 11ins and most significant of the ring statistics was that his reach, at 76 inches, was longer than Hagler's span. This weapon was a useful additional to the armoury which had stopped 30 of his 49 opponents.

It was a scrappy ten-round fight. Hagler adopted the strategy of launching searing body shots mixed with punishing right hand crosses aimed at Geraldo's head. The Mexican champion used showboating tactics to disrupt

Hagler's timing and make him miss often. When he was awarded the unanimous decision, a clearly relieved Hagler declared that it was "mission accomplished" as he turned his gaze across the ocean and on to the looming figure of Alan Minter.

Defending His World Championship At Home

HAGLER WAS determined that his official coronation as the middleweight king would take place back in Boston. His status however had done little to dim his ravenous hunger. "I'm a champion with a contender's mindset," he had told the press before he retreated to his self-imposed prison to begin his preparations for his first defence to Fulgencio Obelmejias.

He returned to Cape Cod's Provincetown Inn with his trainers and an assortment of training partners, and would regularly shriek "I'm still as mean as ever" as an affirmation of his monster's continued presence.

"I have watched other fighters win world titles and then lose the dedication that got them there," Hagler said. "They start training in majestic locations and gradually go soft. It was Joe Louis who said, 'It's hard to get up and run when you are wearing silk pyjamas.' I have no intention of going down that route," he shuddered involuntarily.

Hagler embraced the loneliness as an essential part of his mental training. He used the long periods of silence to channel his anger. "I remember everything they did to me. I'll never forgive them," snarled Hagler, referring to the WBA and WBC. "I want to stay bitter. I use it; I feed on it. That's why I put myself in jail like this to train for a fight. I want to be mean. All I want to think of is destruction. Then nobody can take from me what's mine. The only way they'll get the title from me is to kill me."

In January 1981, this rage was directed towards the number one challenger according to the World Boxing Association and the World Boxing Council, Fulgencio Obelmejias, a 28-year-old Venezuelan. Obelmejias had represented his country at the 1976 Montreal Olympics, where he was ignominiously despatched in the first round by Cuba's eventual bronze medallist Luis Felipe Martinez. A year later, he began his professional career, where he accumulated an array of knockout victories, his most notable scalp being the former World Boxing Council Junior Middleweight champion, Elisha Obed. Hagler was customarily unimpressed.

"How did he get to be number one?" Hagler wondered aloud before a blazing wood fire at the frozen tip of Cape Cod, 120 miles from Boston. "When I was working my way up the ratings, Obelmejias wasn't behind me," Hagler said, staring into the fire. "Nobody was jumping me over anybody, from seventh to fourth, or fourth to number one. But all of a sudden I get to be champ, and here's a guy from nowhere right behind me. I've got to figure somebody in the WBA or the WBC said, 'Hey, I think this guy can beat Hagler,' and they jumped him up to number one. And when I knock him out they'll find somebody else they think can beat me and jump him into number one. If that's the way it is, why even have ratings?"

While Hagler's voice was soft, his words were hard and his demeanour chilling. Goody Petronelli confirmed, "The title hasn't thawed him a bit. He can't forget the many lean years when others got the title fights he thought he deserved. He smoulders when he thinks of the fat purses, of the recognition that should have been his. Now he's the champion, but the hunger is still with him. That's why he sometimes screamed at the early morning sky, startling the gulls into flight, as he ran along the dunes."

In Boston, Obelmejias seemed to be training more for an exam in American history than for a fistfight. His first request upon arriving was to be taken to Plymouth Rock, and then he wanted to see the USS *Constitution*, which is moored to a pier in Charlestown.

He also trained, but not very well. Mornings, heavily bundled against the bitter cold, he ran along the Charles, from the Museum of Science to the Boston University Bridge and back. When he wasn't sightseeing or spooning up clam chowder, he usually stayed in his hotel room studying an English-Spanish dictionary or watching television. *Sesame Street*, with its Spanish/English lessons, was his favourite. On the Wednesday before the fight he caught a cold.

"Can he fight?" said Rodolfo Sabbatini, the Italian promoter, smiling at the question. Sabbatini had promoted Obelmejias's last three fights, all in Italy. "Yes, he can fight. He can punch and he can move his hands. The only thing I don't know about is his heart. I've never seen him in trouble because he never fought anybody who could get him in trouble."

The people Obelmejias fought to gain his ranking included George Lee, an American he knocked out in one round in November 1979. From 15 March 1979 until that November, Lee had four bouts, losing all four. From 17 November, when Obelmejias fought him, until 27 January 1980, a period of 71 days, Lee was knocked out five more times on three continents, in four countries and in five cities.

Still, Obelmejias's victory over Lee earned the Venezuelan a jump from number five to number four in the WBC rankings.

Then there was Carlos Marks of Trinidad, whom Obelmejias stopped in nine to win the Central American and Caribbean middleweight titles in 1978. It was Marks's eighth loss over a 13-fight span.

There wasn't a world-class fighter on the number one contender's record. No matter. The number one contender's manager was Rafito Cedeino, a force in Venezuelan boxing and a friend of both WBC president Jose Sulaiman and WBA president Rodrigo Sanchez. In the six months prior to this fight, no fewer than six of Cedeino's fighters had been in title fights; five lost. The lone victor was Rafael Orono, the WBC super-flyweight champion, who beat Jovito Regnifo, who was also in the Cedeino stable in Caracas. Cedeino not only had both fighters in that one, he was also the promoter.

But against Hagler, all Obelmejias's status did was earn him $100,000 and get him semi-killed. In fact, Hagler came closer to losing his title in a driveway on the afternoon of the fight than he did in the ring that cold January night.

The evening before, the champion had driven in from Cape Cod to Avon, a small town 20 miles south of Boston. Ten inches of snow fell overnight and the next morning, when Hagler went out to drive to the noon weigh-in, his rented limo was snowbound. It took six men to shovel the car free. At that, the champion was 47 minutes late. If he had been two hours late he would have lost the title without a punch having been thrown.

The inclement conditions didn't deter 10,000 fans from making their way to the Boston Garden. They witnessed two former outstanding amateurs, heavyweight Chris McDonald and welterweight Davey Moore, make their professional debuts before the main event.

Once the bell rang, Obelmejias had no chance. The anger Hagler stored up was kept under control. He quickly demonstrated his capacity to be the complete boxer, operating with the knowledgeable detachment of a surgeon, graceful and flowing, unleashing punches in ever-changing patterns, hardly ever in bursts of fewer than three, mixing his jabs and crosses and hooks and uppercuts until they became a blur.

"If he gets a man in trouble, Marvin will work to take him out quickly," explained Goody Petronelli. "But should the man escape, he will revert to methodically ripping his opponent apart piece by piece. Patience is his trademark," the proud trainer beamed.

In the first round against Obelmejias, Hagler did little, contenting himself with studying his unknown prey at close quarters. Then he put into play the strategy devised by his managers-trainers. "Pressure him," they ordered. "Stay on top of him and make him fight a full three minutes." Obelmejias didn't help his own cause by fighting a stupid fight. At 6ft 1ins, with a 72-inch reach, he should have stayed outside, where he could have been more effective but he elected to work close.

Badly battered from the second round on, Obelmejias, who could deliver nothing beyond a few uppercuts, fell in the sixth from a thunderous right to the head. Struggling up, he took an eight count and then survived a savage pounding to the end of the round. He answered Rodolfo Sabbatini's question about his fighting heart.

In the seventh, though Obelmejias tried desperately to pull the fight out with wild rights, he took more of the same. At the end, bleeding from the mouth and a small cut under his left eye, he returned to his corner on old legs. American trainer Al Nayer, who was assisting Obelmejias's trainers, struggled to offer any meaningful advice. "This guy is a beast," he observed. Early in the eighth round, Hagler drilled home a savage right to the head, and the number one contender reeled back into the ropes. "That's it," said referee Octavio Meyran of Mexico, waving Hagler off.

In his dressing room, Obelmejias held an ice pack against his right hand. "I broke my thumb in the second round," he said, "and I couldn't breathe. The cold, it bothered me. I want to fight him again."

Hagler declared, "Obelmejias will have to wait." The champion, who received his career-best purse of $500,000 for this fight, planned a May defence against former champion Vito Antuofermo in Boston.

Excited journalists looked beyond the immediate future and speculated about facing either of the big two: the welterweight champions, Tommy Hearns and Sugar Ray Leonard, both of whom had declared that they would like to move up.

"Which one, Hearns or Leonard?" Hagler was asked. The champion grinned. "Either one. I want to make $5m like everybody else."

Before Hagler's next defence of his crown could be announced, the champion was unwittingly drawn into a political battle between Bob Arum and local government officials.

Arum declared, "Marvin Hagler or not, it will be a long time before a world championship fight takes place in Boston again." His anger was directed at Massachusetts law, which insisted on levying six per cent tax on revenue from the sale of television and broadcasting rights to any fight within the state. This made Boston particularly unattractive compared to Nevada's three per cent tax and New Jersey's two and a half per cent.

Rip Valenti, the local promoter, supported Arum's grievance and explained, "The only reason Hagler staged his first defence at the Boston Garden was because he had made a commitment to the people of Massachusetts that he would and he insisted on keeping his word." He warned that, "Unless the tax situation changes, we will never see Hagler box here again."

Joseph DeNucci, the state representative and a former middleweight boxer, filed a bill to change the rate of taxation. He argued, "Hagler is a top attraction and represents Massachusetts's best chance to pick up major fights and the associated revenues."

The political wrangling meant that a two-month delay ensued before Arum was able to declare that Hagler would return to grace the city's esteemed fight venue in his next defence against Vito Antuofermo in June.

A Blood Bath In Boston

AS A mark of his increased self-confidence as a champion, Hagler trimmed his moustache down to a less
ferocious length. "I have to look more presentable,"
he laughed. But the head was still austerely shaved, and more
than a touch of bitterness persisted in his views of the fight
game. "I've paid my dues, haven't I?" he spat at reporters
who spoke about his last purse of just less than half-a-million
dollars. "Now I'm waiting for some big money."

He cast his eye over the list of possible opponents he
could have faced, and offered a withering assessment of each.
The undistinguished Syrian, Mustafa Hamsho; the WBC's
number one contender Dwight Davison ("they must have
kept that pretty quiet" he mused); Curtis Parker and Wilford
Scypion. "Antuofermo is a better draw than any of these,"
he concluded. "But I'm a million-dollar fighter, aren't I?" he
asked reasonably. "I deserve to be in the company of want-to-
be middleweights like Thomas Hearns, Wilfred Benitez and
Sugar Ray Leonard."

He lingered on Leonard in particular, casting a cold and
envious eye on the reputed $16m purses that came with the
Duran fights. "Leonard is greedy," he said. "One day I will get
what I am due. I am very patient."

During the political stand-off between Arum and the
state, there had been serious discussions after the Leonard-
Larry Bonds fight, that Leonard would be prepared to meet

with Hagler. "But we decided to take Hearns instead," said Pat Petronelli. "It is not beyond doubt, however, that Marvin might meet Sugar Ray next year," he said. "Hagler's title could be next on Leonard's list should Sugar Ray take the junior middleweight title from Ayub Kalule later this month."

During his self-imposed exile to the dank heat of Province-town, Hagler muttered, over and over, "Gonna swat that mosquito, Vito the Mosquito." In his afternoon workouts with Goody Petronelli, his trainer would simulate Antuofermo's whirl-away style and Hagler would counter, coming in under the hooks, constantly throwing combinations. "You got me where you want me," Petronelli would grunt from the ropes while Hagler, lost in a semi-trance of intense focus, would refine his craft.

"He's been on my mind a long time," said the champion. Since the draw in Las Vegas in November 1979, Hagler said he had thought about the fight and how "I was robbed every day since". He allowed the sense of injustice, the constant in every one of his training camps, to strengthen his resolve. "You won't get any working odds anywhere around Boston that I will fail to put Antuofermo away."

The evening before the fight, a prescient argument about the use of salve to tend to cuts erupted between the camps. Antuofermo's talisman Freddie Brown requested permission from the Massachusetts Boxing Commission to use a specially concocted salve that he had made up to protect Antuofermo's paper-thin skin. The Petronelli brothers objected, preferring that a weak adrenalin solution be employed instead. Brown threatened to withdraw his fighter and a solution was eventually found when the commission's Dr Blumenthal tested each sample and ruled that neither were harmful or iron-based.

Still, the end came as everybody knew it would: a bright, ragged blossoming of blood over Vito Antuofermo's brow that coursed down into his eye sockets and the fissures of his wrecked face. The only surprise was the speed with which it happened: barely 30 seconds into the first round of his challenge for Marvin Hagler's world middleweight title. An elemental howl from the crowd signalled that the cutting had started and that once again there would be no chance in the world that Antuofermo would finish the fight.

A flurry of rights from Hagler took him on to the ropes; then, as he straightened to escape, heads collided. An accidental butt, seemingly on Antuofermo's part, but suddenly the mask of blood descended. Blindly he hung on as more of Hagler's rights pounded him and, with the bell, just as blindly he stared out at the crowd, oblivious of the necessity for speed in getting the cut attended to. In his corner, assistant trainer Panama Lewis was screaming incomprehensibly and Freddie Brown, Antuofermo's veteran trainer, a cut man of extraordinary skills, was in the middle of the ring, shouting at the referee.

Brown contended that Hagler had butted Antuofermo and wanted referee Davey Pearl to stop the fight and rule it a technical draw. Nearly three minutes passed before the fight was resumed, an extra two minutes that Antuofermo and Brown desperately needed.

And then, coldly, precisely, Hagler went to work on the cut again, opening it once more with a five-blow combination that started with a right uppercut. "I don't care how I did it," the champion said later. "That's the game of boxing."

In the second round, Antuofermo was put on the seat of his red trunks. He gamely recovered but continued to blindly walk into the hail of punches fired at him. His face was a crimson death mask yet he attempted to will his way back into the brawl. Eventually, with the ring looking more like an abattoir, his own corner knew that the end was inevitable and despite his protestations, pulled him out in the fourth round.

In the aftermath, Antuofermo was adamant that the butt had been deliberate. He cited the pre-fight argument about adrenalin as evidence. "Hagler did it on purpose. My trainer Freddie Brown was so discouraged because he knew he couldn't stop it with the stuff we were allowed to use, so he stopped the fight."

Hagler was nonplussed by the debate. "I wanted to put Vito's lights out because I have been preparing towards this rematch for quite some time." He said that the victory had been a vindication. "I didn't have to box Antuofermo again. But I wanted to fight him on a personal level because I wanted to prove something to myself, and all the critics who thought I had lost the first fight. And it bothered me. But I shut up all the doubters in the return fight."

Mustafa Hamsho
v Marvin Hagler

MUSTAFA HAMSHO was the next opponent in line to challenge for the jealously-guarded crown four months after the Antuofermo scrap on 3 October 1981. In July, Bob Arum announced that the Horizon Arena in Rosemont, Chicago, would host 'Double Dynamite', the biggest fight night in the city's history since 1962. Hagler would share double billing with World Boxing Association heavyweight champion Mike Weaver, who was defending his title for the third time against Chicago resident James 'Quick' Tillis which was also being broadcast by HBO.

Hagler happily obliged Arum's requests for press access at the conference because he had gleefully signed the contract for his first million-dollar purse and he was only too happy to share his joyful news. "This is a dream I've had for a long time," said Hagler, smiling gleefully. "I remember taking lower money than I was due several times, just so I could get fights." He now boasted, "I have always said I wanted to be a million-dollar fighter."

He then turned his attention towards his opponent and his pleasant demeanour was replaced by his fighting scowl. "I now have to take care of business against Hamsho. I have trained harder for this fight than any other fight in my life because of his style." He paused before adding his menacing caveat, "If he wants a roughhouse brawl, then I'm ready. I love a good fight."

Hamsho described himself as "the gatekeeper to Marvin Hagler's middleweight throne" and his fight record offered compelling evidence to support this assessment.

His colourful life had forged a tough, durable character which served him admirably within the ring. He was born and raised in Latakia, Syria in 1953, where he became an international class amateur. He was just 19 years old when he arrived in New York as a stowaway aboard a Greek freighter in 1973. All he had in his possession was a crumpled piece of paper with the name of a distant relative who owned a diner in Brooklyn, a fierce work ethic, and an immeasurable desire to succeed.

It did not take him long to grow disheartened as he sweated over a kitchen sink, washing dishes for 12 to 15 hours a day. "I had come to America with a grand scheme, but not a grand plan, and it didn't take me long to realise the golden goose was nowhere in sight," he recalled.

He daydreamed about his amateur boxing career. Fighting for his native country, he had beaten a Bavarian in Bavaria, a Russian in Russia, and several Greeks in Greece. It was not long before Hamsho made his way to the now defunct Gramercy Gym on East 14th Street in Manhattan. On his first day there he asked to spar and wound up in the ring with 'Irish' Bobby Cassidy, a light heavyweight contender who was perennially rated in the top-ten.

"Mustafa was a tough, tough guy," said Cassidy. "Crude but tough. We were all experienced professionals and we still had difficulty slowing him up. He never stopped coming forward. He could take the punishment and really had a will to win and get better. It was obvious he wasn't a quitter. Once he showed up, he never left."

"I am not afraid of any man," said Hamsho, when it was first suggested that he would get a shot at Hagler's middleweight championship.

In the early days of Hamsho's pro career, this prospect could not have seemed less likely. In his debut, a six-round loss to Pat Cuillo in Binghamton, New York, in August 1975, he didn't even get paid. For his second bout, a four-round draw with Danny McNevin, exactly two months later at the same venue, he received all of $75. There was little he could do about it.

Like so many other illegal immigrants, he was convinced that immigration agents were lurking behind every ring post, so he fought with pseudonyms like Mike Estafire and Rocky Estafire. Depending on where and whom he was fighting, he usually passed himself off as either Italian or Greek.

After several years of mismanagement, the extraordinarily colourful Paddy Flood took over the reins and Hamsho's career blossomed. Hollywood couldn't have created a better character than Flood. "The only thing Paddy likes more than boxing is the horses," Hamsho laughed. Every day after the gym the young and impressionable Hamsho would accompany his mentor to Yonkers Raceway to bet on them.

There was no shortage of schemes that Flood employed in order to make Hamsho into a bona-fide contender. Bobby 'Boogaloo' Watts was victim to one of these tactics. Hamsho recalled, "Watts was looking for a tune-up fight, but the opponent was not supposed to be a southpaw fighter like I was. He wanted a picture of me before we fought and so Paddy insisted that we sent him a picture with me fighting in the conventional stance. Well, we get in the ring, and I go southpaw on him. Watts turned to his manager and said, 'I thought this guy wasn't a southpaw?' His manager turns to him and says, 'Too late'." It was, as Watts was stopped in six rounds.

Hamsho had enjoyed a four-year undefeated run of 27 bouts, defeating top-ranked fighters like Rocky Mosley Jnr, 'Irish' Pat Murphy, Leo Saenz, the talented Wilford Scypion, the formidable Curtis Parker and Rudy Robles, before he earned his world title opportunity by battling his way to a split points decision over former world middleweight champion Alan Minter. Minter later declared that Hamsho was "the strongest man I have ever faced – and that includes Marvin Hagler".

Hamsho, who was now afforded American citizenship, and lived in Bayonne, New Jersey, with his Irish-American wife and six children, recounted, "I was told by my trainer in Syria that in America, when you get off the plane you will see a dollar on the ground. That's bull." He continued, "I have never had an easy day or an easy fight in my life. But where else could a grocer's son jump off a boat and become the number one middleweight contender in the world?"

He announced, "I've been waiting three years for this fight and I have trapped Hagler. He has had to fight me and I'm not going to let this chance slip away." He offered the champion an insight into the tactics he would have to employ. "If he wants to win, he better bring a baseball bat into the ring because that's the only way he'll stop me. He's going to have to kill me," said Hamsho.

His trainer, Al Braverman, supported this assertion. "I'll tell you what kind of style he has," the grizzled veteran said before the bout. "He's got no style. He just wades in, throwing punches from any angle." He explained, "When he launches his attacks, he also takes with him an iron jaw and unslacking courage," attributes that had helped earn this $200,000 shot.

Goody Petronelli was unimpressed. "It will be like sending a pit bull up against a machine gun," he countered. "He can't fight a lick. The only thing we're worried about is

Hagler strikes a classic pose, early in his career.

A relaxed Hagler poses in a gym in his home town of Brockton, Massachusetts.

Hagler lands a vicious right hook on Alan Minter in pursuit of the world title.

Homecoming - Hagler is greeted by adoring fans in Boston after defeating Minter to win the world middleweight championship.

Trainer Goodie Petronelli discusses tactics with Hagler.

Hagler poses with his wife Bertha and their 3-month-old daughter, Charlee, at the New England premiere of the movie Rocky III, in Boston.

All smiles - Hagler poses with Sugar Ray Leonard five years before their 'Superfight'; Leonard had just announced his retirement due to a detached retina.

Venezuela's middleweight challenger Fulgencio Obelmejias hits the canvas after a deadly left hook from world champion Hagler, in Sanremo, Italy.

The champion prepares to defend his title against Texan, Wilford Scypion.

Hagler pounds challenger Roberto Duran in the 9th round of their title fight in Las Vegas.

Trainer Goodie Petronelli ties Hagler's glove during training.

Hagler and Hearns on the promotion trail, in the build-up to their classic encounter.

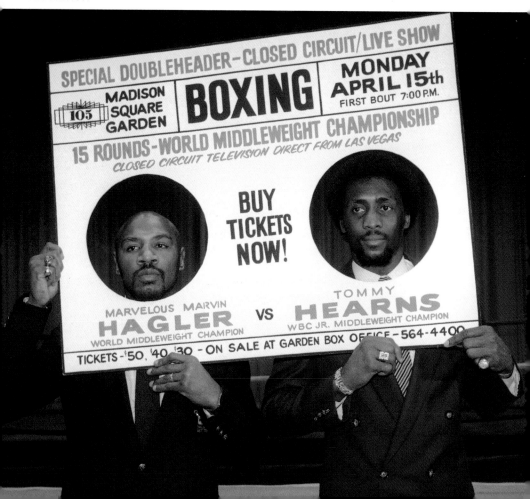

Hagler v Hearns: 'The Greatest Fight of All Time'.

Devastation - Hearns lies unconscious on the mat after being knocked out in the 3rd round by Hagler.

Defeat and jubilation - Hagler holds his arms aloft in victory as referee Richard Steele holds a shell-shocked Hearns.

A broken Hearns is carried out of the ring, as Hagler is raised aloft in celebration.

'Mugabi will fall'; Hagler prepares to fulfil his own prophecy.

Hagler grimaces during his fight with John 'The Beast' Mugabi. He went on to retain his title with an 11th round knockout.

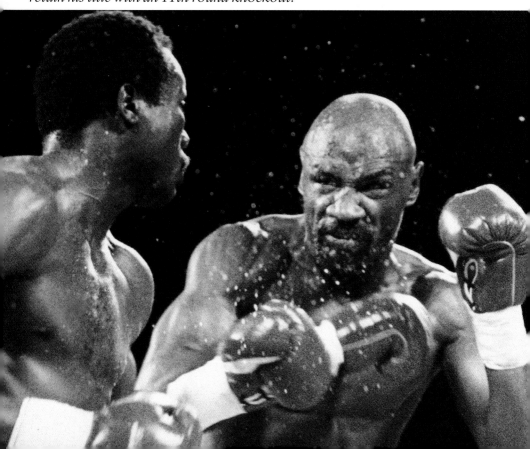

A confident Hagler gives the thumbs up, ahead of his 1987 'Superfight' with Sugar Ray Leonard.

Up close and personal - Hagler takes on Sugar Ray Leonard in the 1987 'Superfight', which Leonard won with a controversial decision.

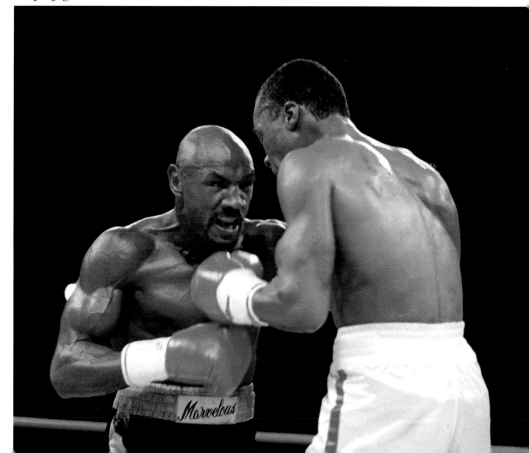

'Marvelous Marvin Hagler' is inducted into the Boxing Hall of Fame in 2011.

his head, which he uses like a billy goat, and his shots below the belt."

This was a concern that the experienced Petronelli brothers had devised a strategy for. It had been used to perfection during his previous fight. "In his last fight against Antuofermo, Marvin met him literally head-on," he explained. "The difference was that Hagler's head was better positioned during the close-quarter work. Antuofermo came out badly gashed and if Hamsho attempted the used the same tactics, he could suffer the same fate."

Hamsho entered the ring under the Syrian flag and the sound of his National Anthem buoyed him up to fever pitch. When the Mexican referee, Octavio Meyran, gave both fighters their final instructions, Hamsho was snorting like a bull, ready to charge at the gate. Hagler eyed him with a withering disdain. He had fed his monster continuously during his self-imposed prison training camp. "There is no love lost in this fight," he had told the press during his Provincetown exile. "I plan to keep him in the centre of the ring, pick my shots and make him look like an amateur."

Very early in the first round, Hagler introduced Hamsho to the evening's fare: two crackling jabs that almost snapped the challenger's head off at the neck. Hagler's jabs were like a combination of jackhammer and straight razor. Hamsho bullied his way forward, using his head with reckless abandon. Hagler was ready with his quick counters. As the first round ended, Hagler told Hamsho, "If you want to fight dirty, I'll show you how to play dirty and I'm going to hurt you."

In the next round Hamsho realised the Petronellis' worst fears and introduced Hagler to the top of his head. The champion went back to his corner with blood streaming from the cut over his eye. He sat calmly while Goody worked on the cut. "I've been there before," Hagler would say later.

"Goody's the best cut man in the world. He does his job and I do mine."

While performing his ministrations, Goody also persuaded Hagler to change strategy slightly: "Keep moving and jabbing. Tire him out. Don't throw anything else unless you got a good spot."

Hagler found a good spot nine seconds into the second round, nailing Hamsho with a straight right. Snarling, Hamsho fired back with both hands. He enjoyed his work. His punches came like buckshot; a lot missed, but those that landed stung. The champion's slipping and blocking of Hamsho's rushes and round-house punching was masterful. He would adroitly slip and slide from the wild punches before punishing Hamsho's carelessness with a stinging rebuke.

In the third, Hamsho butted his foe and drew blood from a cut over the right eyebrow. This offended Hagler, who fired back with a sharp hook which ripped open Hamsho's right eye but didn't slow him down. Late in the round Hamsho twice stuck his tongue out at the champion. Both licks missed.

The area below Hamsho's left eye was torn open in the fourth. After about a minute of the round, referee Meyran stopped the fight and asked the two ring doctors to look at Hamsho's cuts. "Why two doctors?" Braverman yelled. "The other guy is cut, too. Send one of the doctors over to look at him. At least give us half a chance."

Hamsho passed the physical, but the pattern was set. Hagler was a relentless sharp-shooter. By the sixth round Hamsho had dropped all pretence of boxing and was walking straight in, taking an awful beating, trying to land the one big punch. With blood streaming down his face on to his chest, he was rocked again and again, only to laugh at the beating and go in for more.

"I don't know what his corner was waiting for," Hagler said later. "The meat from his eyes was hanging down. But I can't let that bother me. I just have to think 'better him than me'."

In the tenth round, Hagler had the Syrian in serious trouble, attacking him with a volley of head punches which all landed on target. When he staggered back to his corner, his face looking like a grotesque mask, referee Meyran accompanied him and told Braverman he would permit Hamsho just one more round. Braverman nodded and told Hamsho, "This is your last shot."

Hagler came out firing. "I didn't want him stopped on cuts," he said. "I wanted him out." Hamsho tried gamely to fight back. In his corner, Patty Flood, Hamsho's manager, said to Braverman, "He's had enough. We've got to stop it."

Braverman started up the steps into the ring. Hagler fired four straight hooks and then a string of hooks and crosses as Braverman, a big man, struggled to get between the ropes. Finally he made it into the ring. Two seconds later Meyran took Hamsho into protective custody.

In the dressing room, Braverman tried to clean up the maze of cuts that weaved across Hamsho's face. "Butts," he said. "But I believe they were accidental butts." He tended to each wound. "This one, stitches," he said. "That one, stitches. This one, maybe stitches." The total amount of stitching required reached 55. The gregarious Flood, sitting alongside Hamsho, conceded that Hagler had given a boxing master-class. "I got to admit," he said, "I knew Hagler was a great puncher and he was strong, but I didn't know he was such a beautiful boxer."

Early the next morning Hagler sat on a hotel-room bed and reviewed his performance to the attendant press pack. He had just come from a hospital where five stitches had closed a deep slice above his right eye. The cut had come from the clash of heads in the second round. The bandages over the eye were partly concealed by sunglasses and a black hat pulled low.

"When I left the hospital, the doctors were still working over Hamsho," said Hagler with a glimpse of pride. "I thought that he would run out of blood before he ran out of heart." He said that he was most proud that he didn't allow Hamsho to win a round from any of the three officials.

On the officials' cards, where Hamsho had lost a point in the third round for butting, Meyran had Hagler ahead by seven points; judge Michael Glienna put him up by nine; and judge Al Tremari, who scored four rounds 10-8, had him winning by 15.

Hagler was irritated by the suggestion that Hamsho's swarming style would present him with problems. He felt moved to remind them of his pedigree. "This is my 57th fight and I've been in the ring with all types of fighters with different styles," he said. "He might give me problems for a couple of rounds, but after I have figured him out, I will sort him out like every other fighter I've faced."

Caved In

IN THE early months of 1982, promoter Bob Arum convened a meeting at which Steve Wainwright, Marvin Hagler's lawyer, and Emanuel Steward were present. The purpose was to agree a unique three-fight contract which would see Hagler fight three middleweights from Steward's esteemed Kronk gymnasium. First of all, the undisputed world middleweight champion would face the all-action Mickey Goodwin. Next he would take on William 'Caveman' Lee. Finally he would pitch himself against Thomas Hearns in the main fight of the trilogy.

The Goodwin fight was to take place in Italy in March 1982, with Arum agreeing that his friend Rodolfo Sabbatini would act as co-promoter. However, a month before the fight, Goodwin suffered a broken hand and 'Caveman' Lee, his tough, hard-punching but less-regarded stablemate, had to step up to take his place. This change of opponent also saw the fight moved from San Remo to Atlantic City, as it was felt the Italian public would not have the appetite for this match after a damning article appeared in the *New York Post* claiming that Lee had been knocked out by Hearns in a sparring session, a claim disputed by Emanuel Steward.

William 'Caveman' Lee was born in Philadelphia where he earned his fighting moniker from a childhood friend. He joined the professional ranks in 1976 and steadily built up a record of 21 victories against two defeats. In 1979, he was eager to step up to another level and moved to Detroit, where he joined the Kronk gym, initially as a sparring partner for Thomas Hearns.

He had been knocked out in a brutal fight with Frank 'The Animal' Fletcher in 1980 but won his next seven consecutive fights, including an emphatic defeat of Marcos Geraldo and a punishing war against John LoCicero in a fight that the commentator Al Bernstein describes as "one of the most exciting fights of all time", to earn a ranking of fifth by the WBA and tenth by the WBC.

Hagler was nonplussed by the late change of opponent and venue. He had shown remarkable tunnel vision during his training camp when Bertha gave birth to their daughter, Charelle Monique, his second child. Hagler refused to break off and visit them. Even when Goody and Pat Petronelli stopped in Brockton en route to Atlantic City, he resisted the temptation. "'I don't want to be kissing babies', he told me," Goody laughed. "'I've gotta stay mean for fighting'."

He didn't need to look too far for reasons to stay mean. He had been frustrated by his attempts to entice Sugar Ray Leonard into the ring with him. Mike Trainer, the attorney who directed negotiations for the golden boy of boxing, had an acrimonious history with Hagler's promoter, Bob Arum. When they did talk, Trainer would place obstacles in the way of the discussions. He insisted that Hagler must weigh six pounds under the official middleweight limit and seven pounds above the welterweight limit. He also decreed that Hagler must weigh 160 pounds when he stepped into the ring rather than at the official weigh-in, before gaining excess pounds afterwards.

The World Boxing Association further complicated matters by announcing that Hagler had an obligation to meet their number one challenger, the well-connected Fulgencio

Obelmejias, in a rematch before he could even entertain the thoughts of a super fight against Leonard.

As the negotiations repeatedly stalled, Trainer briefed the press that Hagler would have to deal with his mandatory challengers and would not be available to meet Leonard until 1984. "Ray will embark on a world tour and continue to progress his career," he declared.

Pat Petronelli saw it differently. "I don't believe that Sugar Ray Leonard really wants to fight Marvin Hagler. He can make millions fighting Bruce Finches and wants nothing to do with him."

Apart from the political machinations, Hagler's monster was given plenty to feed on by his immediate foe's behaviour. Lee, who had been scheduled to meet Buster Drayton before Goodwin's injury, outlined his intentions. "I plan to get him to move on to my dangerous right hand," he suggested. "I am thinking about turning southpaw in order to confuse Hagler."

"The last time I boxed a southpaw, he ended up with nearly 60 stitches in his face," Hagler reminded his cocksure opponent about the fate of Mustafo Hamsho. "I also cut up the southpaw Alan Minter in three rounds too," he said, before adding the chilling promise, "but you won't be around that long."

Interest in the fight was proving difficult to maintain and so both fighters agreed to stage a final press conference on the day before the fight. After answering questions, where Hagler warned Lee "the more you talk, the meaner I get", the fighters were requested to pose on either side of a heavy punch bag.

The amiable Lee, who had been described by Mickey Goodwin as "the only black guy I know who likes rock'n'roll and can swim", did his best to provide the cameras with some amusing publicity shots. He brandished a toy club and shaped to hit Hagler over the head with it. "I am going to beat you," he jokingly growled in a stage whisper. Hagler's gaze was contemptuous. "I've got a club, too," he said while raising his left fist. "If you don't shut up, I'll send you back to the Stone Age."

The brooding malevolence appeared to unnerve Lee. At the moment the fighters were introduced, it was apparent that there were at least a thousand things that he would rather be doing than stepping into combat with Marvin Hagler.

Less than a minute into the fight, Hagler threw a right jab which connected on Lee's unguarded face and the punch appeared to wake him from a trance and realise the enormity of the challenge he had taken. He froze before dropping on to the ring apron. Larry Hazzard, the referee, counted to five and the challenger clambered on to rubbery legs.

Hagler stepped forward and despatched a whiplash right hook to send Lee careering into the ropes before sliding to the canvas, obliging the referee to call a halt to the slaughter after 67 seconds. It was the first one-round victory in a world championship match for more than three and a half years, and included more than 275 championship bouts.

"I believe that I shook the world," said a smiling Hagler afterwards. "I took this fight for exposure," he explained. The fight was an opportunity to move on from the frustrating negotiations with Trainer and re-ignite interest in Thomas Hearns, who despite his loss to Leonard was the second-most marketable commodity in the middle divisions. "I wanted to finish it early as I didn't want Tommy to have too much to look at."

Lee, who was later to take up the comparatively safer occupation of bank robbery, was still dazed when he was back in the sanctuary of his dressing room and offered no arguments. "I wanted to be the first to dominate the fight but he got me first."

Three weeks later, Bob Arum presided over a New York press conference to announce that Thomas 'Hit Man' Hearns would challenge 'Marvelous' Marvin Hagler on 24 May in Las Vegas for the world middleweight championship. The figures that each fighter was due to receive were not as high as either could have earned against Ray Leonard, but they were enough to satisfy both. Hagler, as the reigning champion, would make $5m. Hearns would take home more than $3m.

Hearns was respectful towards the champion, who was six years older, heavier, stronger, more experienced and a formidable prospect. "Benitez won't fight me," he said. "Leonard won't fight me. Marvin's the only one giving me a chance to fight. I know what I'm capable of doing. My strategy is to go in there and box." His trainer, Emanuel Steward, chipped in that Hagler was actually a small middleweight and Hearns had all of the physical advantages. Hagler, however, reminded them that he had a nasty habit of rendering such arguments obsolete. "All you got to do," growled the intimidating champion, "is bring the tall man down to your size and put his lights out."

Hanging like a spectre over the fight announcement was the figure of Ray Leonard. He was on holiday in Mexico City when he was asked for his reaction. He disingenuously claimed that before he had announced his latest retirement, he had wanted to fight Hagler and suggested that he would have received $20m as his purse. The only stipulation he demanded was that Hagler would weigh less than 155 pounds, despite the middleweight limit being 160 pounds. When Hearns was informed of this, he was scornful, "Marvin Hagler is the world middleweight champion. Why should he have to come to the scales at 155 pounds?"

Emanuel Steward sensed an opportunity to win PR points and agreed that Hearns would be happy to accommodate Leonard's demands and come in at any weight he wanted. Hagler was privately delighted but refused to be drawn into the discussion about Leonard. He merely offered, "I'm just happy to see the fight materialise. It shapes up as by far the biggest payday of my career."

It was soon after this announcement that plans for the promotion started to go awry. While doing his roadwork, Hearns tripped, and he sprained a finger in trying to break his fall. He later reported that he "felt like needles were shooting through my arm" when he landed a right hand during sparring. Doctors instructed him to desist from sparring for at least 30 days.

When the news came out, Hagler was scathing. "Thomas Hearns is a sissy," he spat. "Boxers are used to fighting with pain. I suffer with sore hands all the time. In fact, all great fighters have sore hands. For a million dollars they could cut my finger off."

Emanuel Steward reassured the press that Hearns was in great shape and wanted the fight to go on. He also denied claims that they were delaying the fight to allow Hearns to put on more weight and improve his condition. Steward was angered by Hagler's lack of empathy and pointed out that Hearns had fully participated in all the public appearances during the nine-day, eleven-city promotional tour to hype the fight, in contrast to Hagler, who cited flu as the reason for his non-attendance, even in Boston, just 23 miles from his home town of Brockton.

Yet despite the positive news from Hearns and his team, promoter Bob Arum announced that the fight would be postponed. This was a contradictory message completely at odds with the fighter's own statements.

Hearns conducted a Detroit press conference to announce that the May bout was still on. Within hours, Arum issued a statement from New York declaring, "The fight was postponed indefinitely."

Arum claimed that the injury to the little finger on Hearns's right hand was the sole cause for the postponement. To support his actions he claimed he had consulted the three doctors who had examined Hearns and all three had attested that he should rest the hand for at least 30 days. This was in direct contrast to remarks made by two doctors who had appeared at Hearns's press conference.

It appeared that the real reason for the delay was more complex. In a Los Angeles federal courtroom, Judge Laughlin Waters had issued a temporary injunction on the bout, ruling against SelecTV and a pay television company which had the rights for a home telecast of the bout. Home Box Office, another pay television company, had filed suit claiming that Arum had granted it the rights for the Hagler-Hearns bout. The judge's injunction effectively precluded the fight from going forward. Court insiders told press reporters that Arum's contract for the fight expired on 31 May, after which the promoter had no rights to the bout, and more importantly, no financial liability.

For Bob Arum, the postponement of the fight beyond the contract expiration date allowed him to absolve himself of any financial liability which may have resulted in case of a judgement against him.

There followed several months of inactivity. In a routine training session, 'Boogaloo' Watts, now a sparring partner, broke one of his ribs in the gym and Goody Petronelli suggested that it was a good opportunity for Marvin to spend some time at home with his family. "It was the first break he had had in years," he said.

Hagler moved his young family to the exclusive Hanover neighbourhood, outside Brockton, where he had three acres and 69 pigeons to care for. He and Bertha shared the place with their four children, two of them, Jimmy, 12, and Celeste, 10, Bertha's by a previous marriage, and two of their own, Marvin Jnr, 6, and Charelle, seven and a half months. Hagler spent his summer with the kids, "mostly watching Charelle trying to figure out what her legs are for".

"I got the chance to see Charelle learn to turn over and begin to smile," he recalled, "to pull herself up on her feet on the side of the crib. I would've missed that if I'd been on the road."

He also spent time with his mother, who had re-married in 1976 at the house he had bought for her after the Antuofermo victory. She worked as a receptionist at Norris Industries, a Brockton company that manufactured kitchen disposal equipment, and was contemplating going to law school. "I always wanted to be a lawyer," she said. "If I hadn't had kids so fast, that's probably what I'd be today."

He also addressed an issue that had been the source of irritation for a while. Hagler had been frustrated that authorities had often refused to christen him with his preferred prefix of 'Marvelous' when he was introduced. The latest occasion had been after his knockout victory over 'Caveman' Lee. He was told that he could only be introduced by his legal name. He attended a probate court in Plymouth, Massachusetts, which ratified that Marvin Nathaniel Hagler legally became Marvelous Marvin Hagler.

The 'Marvelous' had been bestowed upon him by a Lowell, Massachusetts, journalist after Hagler had fought there as an amateur. "I had been trying to find my own identity," he explained. "I found that learning how to box was a very serious business, especially when you're trying to make it to the top. When I come in that ring, it's for real. There is no clowning around and this name change shows that."

The change also revealed a secret that he had hidden for years. He had added two years to his age as a young man, so he could start fighting sooner. When his real date of his birth was certified in court, Hagler told a reporter, "I'd appreciate it if you'd write that I am 30."

San Remo, Italy – Return With Obelmejias

Who do I want?
   Fully Oh-BELL!
   Make him work!
   Tire him out!
   Fully Oh-BELL's
   Gonna catch hell,
   At the bell!

In the dark, cold autumn morning before first light, Hagler's incessant chanting filled the air. During his run along the path and into the unforgiving sand dunes, the slap of his boots is like a mantra. "I think, 'Goin' through him! I have to be on the inside. Don't stay on the outside. Goin' through him!' while I am running," he said. When he ran into the mouth of a tunnel, he shouted:

   Get out of bed, Oh-BELL,
   I'm comin' at you,
   Gonna destroy you.
   Destruct and destroy!
   I'm the champ!

Hagler's routine since 1977 had varied little; sparring in a ring set up by the indoor pool, getting up before dawn to run with his sparring partners from the inn to the beach and beyond. Goody Petronelli described them as "the charge of the dark brigade".

"This is my self-imposed prison," Hagler described it. Among the scrub pine, goldenrod and rosehip, he served the harshest sentence of all, the one that he imposed on himself. The confinement was as solitary as he could make it. "I get mean here," he said.

Fulgencio Obelmejias had by now been restored to number one on the WBA list and was insisting on a mandatory challenge. The bout had originally been set for July but his rib injury delayed the fight until October. Hagler had knocked the Venezuelan challenger senseless in the eighth round the first time they had fought but decided to meet him again "and get rid of this guy once and for all".

His customary dedication belied a frustration that gnawed away inside him. "I have earned the right to ask for better opposition than Obel and should be earning millions of dollars," he complained. "I have been the undisputed middleweight champion for more than two years and defended the title four times." His purses for each bout were sizeable: Obelmejias ($500,000); Antuofermo II ($500,000); Mustafa Hamsho ($1m); 'Caveman' Lee ($500,000). "I am getting $500,000 for Obelmejias again but it is nothing compared to the $12m Leonard made for beating Thomas Hearns."

The validity of his complaint was upheld by a number of the sport's leading business operators. "He's right, he should be making a lot more money," said Jim Jacobs, the manager of Wilfred Benitez. "If you use the unified championship of the middleweight division as a gauge, should he be making less than Thomas Hearns or Wilfred Benitez? The unified championship is taken very seriously because there are only two unified divisions. To the networks it's invaluable."

This view was echoed by Emanuel Steward, the founder of the Kronk gym. He pointed the finger of blame squarely at the Petronelli brothers, "I feel sorry for Marvin. He has to be frustrated because he's getting some bad management." Dan Duva, who had staged the lucrative Leonard-Hearns match, agreed, "Marvin Hagler is one of the top six names in boxing, but he's not going to make the top purses until his business is handled differently."

Jim Jacobs offered some context. "Leonard, Hearns, Benitez, Roberto Duran, Larry Holmes, Gerry Cooney, Leon Spinks, Mike Weaver and Pipino Cuevas have each earned more than $1m for fights," he said. "Hagler belongs in this group. However, the thing that determines the fighter's value," he explained, "is the ability of the manager to negotiate a deal."

Hagler conceded that he sometimes doubted the wisdom of his managers Goody and Pat Petronelli along with his attorney Steven Wainwright. "Sure, my confidence does waver once in a while," he admitted. "But I still believe in them. Until I prove them wrong or until they prove me wrong, that's what you have to go with."

Pat Petronelli admitted that he had made mistakes but a lot of the frustrations had been down to the political minefield that boxing occupied. "We know we've got to fight one of the big names," he said. "But they don't necessarily want to fight us." He pointed out that the seven-month negotiation to fight Hearns had fallen apart in strange circumstances. Discussions to fight Leonard were obstructed by the myriad list of demands that kept being included and Jim Jacobs had categorically stated that Benitez would not consider fighting Hagler.

"The best deal we could get," said Petronelli "was Bob Arum's three-fight package that should earn him close to

$3m." The three fights included Obelmejias, Frank Fletcher ($1m) and an option for Tony Sibson ($1.4m). "The package, which was bought by HBO, was the only way we could sell the Obelmejias fight," he explained. Despite Hagler having defeated Obelmejias, the WBA demanded that he defend his title or be stripped of it. "It's important to have both titles," Petronelli claimed.

Leonard's attorney, Mike Trainer, was bemused by the deal. "What the Petronellis don't realise is that Marvin Hagler is bigger than the WBA or WBC," he said. "They can't strip him of his title and still be believable." Trainer believed that Hagler's second three-fight deal with Arum and HBO was a major mistake. "The contract prevents Hagler from shopping himself to other promoters," he said. "Marvin would be far better off as a free agent."

Dan Duva agreed. "I always thought that the purpose of being champion was that you can call your own shots and not be tied in with other people's difficulties," questioned Duva. "It takes Marvin out of competitive bidding. The Petronellis have security but as long as they have Marvin Hagler, what do they need security for?"

Jim Jacobs echoed this view. "Why should I talk to Hagler," he asked, "when he's tied up for three fights? How can I make a deal to fight Hagler for the middleweight title when I don't know if he's going to have it after his next three fights? I'll talk when he's available."

Emanuel Steward, perhaps the best placed person to comment on the Petronellis' dual roles as trainer and manager, still grudgingly admired their work. "No matter how many mistakes they have made managing Marvin," said Steward, "they've been good to him. They are good people."

This was the view that Hagler endorsed. "When I had my early fights as a pro – preliminary bouts for $300, $400

– the Petronellis declined to take their 33 per cent managers' share from my purses," Hagler recounted. "A lot of people back then would tell me they could move me better than the Petronellis. A lot of blacks would say, 'Stick to your own. The whites will take your money and, once you're all done, drop you.' I told them all, 'Forget you'."

He had granted them each one vote in their shared business, Marvelous Enterprises Inc., and accepted that he could be out-voted. "The business side of fighting frustrates me," he said "and so I leave that up to my people."

Hagler recalled that before he got his shot at the title, he had felt bitter and frustrated by the politics and packed his bags to prepare to leave the Petronellis and Brockton and move to California, to start his career anew. One night, he found himself knocking at Pat's door at 10pm to tell him, "I don't want to die in no man's gym."

"What I was saying to Pat," said Hagler, "was that I didn't want to be sitting here in Brockton forever. I had read about how old a man Jersey Joe Walcott was before they gave him a break." (Walcott was 37 years old when he knocked out Ezzard Charles in July 1951 to win the heavyweight title.) "I wanted to get out and see the world. Pat and Goody urged me to stay, saying, 'If we felt as though we couldn't do it for you, we'd be the first ones to let you find something else,'" he said.

After talking it over with Bertha, Hagler yielded. "So I took my bags back," he said. "But I was hurt. The rent had to be paid. The kids had to have clothes. It was tough. When people look at me today they say, 'Hey, you're a millionaire now, you got it made.' They didn't know me before I was a success and as a result they don't realise that everything I got I worked for. There hasn't been nobody giving me nothin'. Pat and Goody remember though because they were with me. Even though I haven't gotten the real big payday yet, that keeps me working, keeps me hungry."

Despite his frustrations, Hagler had Obel fixed in his cross-hairs. He had trained rigorously for this fight – for several weeks on the very tip of Cape Cod, before travelling to San Remo in Italy ten days prior to the fight – knowing how long a fall it would be if he ever slipped. He was getting $500,000 (to Obelmejias's $120,000), a pleasant taste of things to come.

"The way I look at it, this is putting money in the bank as well as keeping me active," Hagler said a few days before the fight. "There's no way I'm taking this guy lightly. I've had nine different sparring partners for this fight. I'm going to make sure I fight him even harder than I did the first time. I punished him then; this time I'm going to hurt him. I don't want this man back."

The politically well-connected fighter had risen to number one in the WBC and WBA. When Hagler whipped him, Obelmejias automatically dropped to number four in the WBA rankings, but he climbed back to number one by remaining undefeated against Norberto Cabrera, Chong Pal Park, and former WBA light-middleweight champion Eddie Gazo. In the meantime, two contenders above him lost and the other moved up to light-heavyweight.

Obelmejias complained that he had been suffering from a severe cold during his first fight with Hagler (although he never mentioned anything about his illness until after Hagler had won), and when he arrived at the balmy Mediterranean coast of Italy, he predicted victory. "It has been more than three months since I began training for this fight," Obelmejias said from his camp in Genoa. "I'm sure it will go completely different this time. If I hadn't been sick in Boston, things wouldn't have gone the way they did and I would have won and been champion. I'd never been in a climate like that. Now everything is okay."

Hagler seemed unconcerned about his own recent inactivity. Goody Petronelli said that he expected Hagler to expose Obelmejias as an artificial contender once again. "He's ready to tear him apart," Goody said. "He has been sparring a lot, his timing is nice, and he has no aches and pains. If Obel wants to come at Marvin, fine; he did that last time and ended up on the short end. If he wants to box, fine. We are ready for anything he wants to do." For years Hagler had trained by the motto "Destruction and Destroy" so for the San Remo crowd he added an Italian twist, wearing a shirt that said, "DISTRUZIONE E DISTRUTTORE".

Few things infuriated Hagler more than an opponent displaying disdain or contempt for him, and he simply couldn't abide sniggering. It violated the Haglerian canon of proper behaviour for a very serious enterprise between two men, one that can be settled only in the ring.

Obelmejias made his first mistake about 11 hours before the fight, when he kept smiling at Hagler at the weigh-in, raising his arms above his head and saying, "El campeon [the champion], el campeon. I fix Hagler, I fix." As they left the theatre Pat Petronelli said, "He's a punk." Hagler squinted, his eyes like beads. "That's how I like 'em," he said. "I'm gonna hurt him, Pat."

Whatever Obelmejias's plan was, it never really got off the ground. Hagler appeared cold in the first two rounds, losing both, but in the third he began to pick up the tempo and take the fight to Obelmejias, who was trying to catch Hagler with uppercuts whenever the champion came in. "As soon as Marvin threw the left, Obel threw the right uppercut to the ribs," Goody said. "We had trained for that. He was trying to catch Marvin when he was lunging in."

Hagler intensified the pressure in the fourth round, when he began to find a comfortable distance to fight from. Pat kept urging from the corner, "It's just a matter of time, Marvin. Keep pumpin'. Keep pumpin'."

Now in the fifth, Hagler began to tag his man – jabs, hooks, left hands. Suddenly, at the close of one exchange, Hagler reached back and let fly with that right hook. Obelmejias crumpled to the canvas. He rolled on his back, his mouth open, and stared blankly in the air as if studying the murals depicting medieval scenes painted on the ceiling of the theatre. At one point he struggled vainly to gain his legs, only to topple over again.

"Wasn't that a sweetheart of a punch?" Pat said.

"Beautiful," Goody said.

"I feel good, like a little boy in a candy store," Hagler said.

At 4.35am on Sunday, almost an hour after he had left the ring of the Teatro Ariston, 'Marvelous' Marvin Hagler walked along the Corso Cavallotti toward the Hotel Méditerranée. With his leather cap on his shaved head and a tote bag in his left hand, he looked like a workman heading home after the lobster shift. Which, in a way, was what he was.

His small entourage, including Pat and Goody Petronelli, trailed behind him as the last of the late-night revellers roared past in their Fiats. Hagler still had the adrenalin coursing through his body. "Oh man, I feel good!" he said. "Boy, this was an experience – fighting at 3.30 in the morning. Everything was on the money tonight. I showed Fully Obel what a professional fighter is. Everything was right. I felt like the real champion out there. Everything is looking up for me now."

The reason for the lightening of his mood was an incident that took place a few minutes after Hagler had dispatched Obelmejias. Leonard, who was at ringside doing colour commentary for HBO, was asked during the post-fight interview by Hagler, "Ray, if we're such good friends, give me a pay day!" To which Leonard replied, "Mike Trainer, sign me up."

"Did you hear what I said to Ray?" Hagler asked as he strolled back to his hotel. "Right in front of everybody. I put him on the spot. But I don't think Leonard wants any part of me. He's giving everybody a mirage to look at."

However, just moments after Hagler swept through the Méditerranée's lobby, Leonard appeared from a party in the hotel and whispered to Pat Petronelli, "Pat, after what I saw tonight, me and Marvin could make more money than anybody ever made in the history of boxing. I mean that."

Petronelli, who looked at Leonard and knew he wasn't seeing a mirage, felt a chill. "Right!" he said to Leonard. Earlier, Leonard had urged Petronelli to be in Baltimore for the big announcement about his career he had planned for 9 November, saying, "It's in your interest to be there." Now he was telling Petronelli about all the money that could be made from a Hagler-Leonard bout. "I thought, 'Could Leonard be planning to use his Baltimore forum to announce a return to fight Hagler?'" he said. "I'll be there," he promised.

"It would be conservative to suggest that we were looking for something around $10m or $12m to fight Leonard," Petronelli speculated. "We can struggle with those numbers. Sugar Ray will receive $20m."

Ever since Leonard had suffered a detached retina while training for a fight a year ago, his future had been the subject of widespread speculation. But aside from Leonard himself, no one had a greater interest than Hagler in whether Leonard would fight again.

Most boxing observers were convinced that Leonard planned to announce his retirement at the press conference, but the consummate showman continued to play it very coy.

When asked about his intentions, Leonard said that his eye doctor, Ron Michels of Johns Hopkins Hospital, had examined him and had given him a clean bill of health.

"My vision is 20-20," Leonard said. "Back to normal. Now it's a new thing. It was up to Dr Michels. Now it's up to me. I have to start to re-evaluate. I had made up my mind, but now that's changed … If anything happens, it will be a one-shot deal."

A week later Hagler and the Petronelli brothers flew to Baltimore for Leonard's announcement. Six thousand tickets were sold, which offered a timely reminder of the allure which Leonard possessed.

Many of the fans held up messages, pleading for Ray not to retire. Hagler was standing off-stage in his tuxedo, beaming with anticipation as he watched the sports commentator Howard Cosell conduct the proceedings, which included a highlight film of all of Leonard's major fights before Leonard sat in a corner of the ring and listened as everyone from Howard Cosell to his eminent eye surgeon Ronald Michels paid their tribute to him.

Leonard later admitted, "I didn't know what I was going to say. The majority of my mind was saying 'retirement'. But the Sugar Ray in my head was saying, 'Bring Hagler in, bring all the guys in, make this thing a huge event.' I was thinking more like a publicist."

"I took a few hits of cocaine before I went out," Leonard said. "I kind of thought I knew what I was going to say, but I wasn't 100 per cent sure. I was under the influence, so who knows what I was going to say?"

Hagler heard Leonard describe the dream match-up with him. He was, therefore, the most startled man in the building when Leonard nailed him with the dagger, "But, unfortunately, it's never going to happen."

Hagler later recalled, "He was looking right at me, and then that's when he came out with that, 'It will never happen.' I was like, 'Who does this guy think he is? He always had to act like a superstar.'"

Goody Petronelli was furious. "We had flown to Baltimore to be used as stage props in another Sugar Ray Leonard moment," he spat. Steve Wainwright, Hagler's attorney, couched his language in more diplomatic terms. "We were surprised and disappointed when he said what he said, because we had not expected it at all. It seemed pointless to invite us down there to announce that he had nothing to announce. He's a showboat. He just wanted to get some attention, satisfy his ego."

Charlie Brotman, Leonard's publicist, attempted to apologise to the Hagler camp. "I wouldn't have advised Ray to do it that way. It was mean-spirited," he said. "Nobody benefited from the way he did it. If you're going to have a news conference and sell something, the idea is for somebody to purchase what you're selling. Well, there was no product, no service. There was no winner."

Leonard later outlined the reasoning behind his decision in a *Sports Illustrated* interview:

> I have run out of challenges, but I have to admit again that Hagler was always in the back of my mind. Now here was one more mountain to climb, and if I hadn't had the eye injury, I might have gone for it. It would have been a fight on the same level as Benitez and Hearns and Duran II. I would have had no problem getting up for Hagler. And I would have fought him at 160 pounds. All that stuff about wanting him to fight at 154 was nonsense. We were just pumping up the fight. He'd have been foolish to fight me at 154.

I know he wouldn't have done it, because I wouldn't have done it if I'd been the middleweight. I know Hagler as a man and as a champion, and I always believed if we fought it would be at 160. But then came the injury, and I knew I wasn't going to fight Hagler or anyone else again. And once I made up my mind there were never any second thoughts.

I know no one will believe that I can leave the ring at the age of 26, in my prime, and not come back. I've looked at Ali, and I've looked at all the other great champions, like Joe Louis, who made comebacks, and they all ended in disaster. You know, people have a certain love for you and respect for your intelligence both inside and outside of the ring. And I believe that if you tarnish that, they'll hold it against you. I don't want that. Not for any price.

The final chapter of Sugar Ray Leonard the fighter has been written. The book has been closed. But for Ray Charles Leonard the person, there's another chapter just starting. And there will be many, many more. I'm leaving the ring, but I'm not leaving the world. So watch out.

A Winter's Night
In Worcester

HAGLER WENT back to work and was confronted by another mandatory challenger. Obelmejias had been the WBA's top gun; Tony Sibson was the WBC's and the match was made for the following February at the newly-opened Worcester Centrum, a middle-class town some 40 miles from Boston. The 13,000 tickets sold out within 36 hours after the fight had been announced.

Sibson had been a popular amateur boxer for the Belgrave Club in Leicester. He juggled his training with a hod-carrying job on building sites along with playing lead guitar in his own group, activities he continued to do even after turning professional at 18.

His training base was as unprepossessing as Sibson himself. His trainer, Ken Squires, was a building site foreman who operated out of a gym in the quiet suburb of Syston, which he had built himself. Sibson had been taken to the gym by his father and his all-action style established a reputation as a successful and popular boxer. When he discovered, at the age of 18, that he could earn the equivalent of a month's wage on the building sites in just one fight, he quickly converted to the paid ranks.

Sibson had become the WBC's number one contender by accumulating a record of 47 victories, three defeats and

122

one draw. His defeats had come at the hands of the African light-heavyweight, Lotte Mwale, an exceptionally powerful fighter who twice became the world number one contender in the light-heavyweight division, and Hagler victim Kevin Finnegan. Sibson admitted that his preparation for this fight had been poor, including camping out for seven weeks in southern Spain. Since then, he had committed himself to the fight game and won his next 14 consecutive fights, winning the Commonwealth and European titles.

It was the manner of these victories that helped elevate his world ranking. He had been the only man to knock out Alan Minter, the only time he had been stopped by anything other than cuts. He had also KO'd the well-regarded Bob Coolidge on the Hagler-Minter undercard as well as handily defeating Dwight Davidson.

When Hagler fought Obelmejias, British fight commentator Reg Gutteridge invited Sibson to supply inter-round commentary and the Leicester man readily agreed, believing that he would have a chance to closely watch the champion and determine how he could defeat him.

When he was introduced to Hagler, Sibson showed due deference and respect, eager not to give Hagler opportunity to feed his monster. "I told him that I had sympathy for not being given the credit he deserved when he won the world championship in London. I also told him that I had an argument with Minter, who had worn a blatant plug for a truck company on his boxing trunks, causing the BBC to blackout the fight," Sibson recalled. Hagler remained steadfastly unimpressed.

"He's got a big mouth," Hagler snarled, venting his self-induced fury. "This is the last of the cocky Irishmen [sic]. The British people want nothing more than to take him home a hero. They've led him on, and they've led him to destruction.

But he's courageous. That's good. I won't have to look for him."

Sibson was mystified at the outburst. "I don't know where he got that from, unless he's just using it to psych himself up," Sibson said. "All I've said was that I'm excited about fighting him because I think he's the best middleweight, probably since Sugar Ray Robinson. And I say that even though Carlos Monzon was my boyhood idol."

Sibson had only fought outside of England once before, when he had successfully defended his European title against Andoni Amana in Bilbao.

When he arrived in Worcester ten days before the bout, they were greeted by heavy snowfalls and stinging blizzards, which disrupted their training. Sibson couldn't do his road work so ran inside the sports hall, which he had been allocated.

Fight observers were shocked, however, when Ken Squires announced that his charge would not be conducting any sparring session before the fight. Sibson explained, "I'm too damn friendly. I can't bring myself to hurt little people." He claimed that he couldn't knock his sparring partners out then take a shower with them afterwards. "That's just not me," he concluded.

When Hagler, who was holed up in Provincetown, was informed about Sibson's unusual preparation, he admitted being surprised before adopting his customary wariness. "I have never, ever, underestimated any challenger and I'm not about to start now," he said. Goody Petronelli was more dismissive. "Sibson could spar from now until doomsday and the result won't be any different. Marvin will destroy him."

By the time of the weigh-in, Hagler had stoked his internal fire to boiling point. When he was obliged to pose with his challenger for the pre-fight shots, Sibson playfully prodded the champion's chest. "Get your fucking hands off me," snarled Hagler. "I'll drop you where you stand."

It had long been Hagler's lament that he laboured in the suburbs of greatness, while fighters of lesser merit basked in metropolitan limelight. So when ring announcer Nuno Cam neglected to introduce Hagler before the fight, Hagler stored it as another source for his rage. As he had pointed out a few days before the fight, "If Sibson wins, he'll go home a national hero. If I win, I'll just go home."

In the first few rounds Hagler established a punishing jab. And he mystified Sibson by switching from southpaw to an orthodox stance and back even more than usual. "I couldn't find him for the first two rounds," Sibson said later. "I figured I'd find him sooner or later, but I never did. I asked myself, 'Where did he go?' But I know he was there because he kept hitting me."

In the third round, under orders from his corner, Sibson tried to trade jabs, but Hagler had began to throw combinations, digging hooks to the body and whipping overhand rights to the head.

In the fifth round Sibson, who had never been cut before, had his face split like a melon. There was a large gash over his left eye, a smaller one over his right. Blood dripped from his nose and mouth. In the sixth Hagler stiffened Sibson's legs with a straight left and then dropped him with a right hook and a left off the top of his head. Sibson took a standing eight count from referee Carlos Padilla, then turned away from his corner and pulled down his trunks.

"Good Lord," said Mickey Duff, the British promoter who was working in Sibson's corner. "I thought, 'What's he showing us his arse for?' Then we realised he was trying to tell us he had split his protective cup. We sent someone to the dressing room to get another."

It wasn't needed. Sensing it was time to take his $1.1m and go home, Hagler moved in and put Sibson on the deck again with three straight right hands. He looked like a man hammering a large stake into the floor. Shaking his head, Sibson, who received $557,000, pulled out his mouthpiece and regained his feet. Blood was pouring down his face. Padilla took one look and told Sibson to take the rest of the night off.

In the post-fight analysis, Hagler was questioned by BBC commentator Harry Carpenter. Hagler explained his destruction in the language of the craftsman he was. "I was just dipping into my tool box," he said. "I was enjoying my work." Carpenter was breathless with admiration but attempted to obtain some kudos for the British fighter. "But wasn't Sibson's bravery impressive, Marvin?" he prompted. Without missing a beat, Hagler gave a wolfish grin and replied, "Oh yes. Have you got any more men like him over in Britain who I could fight?"

HBO's Larry Merchant was less awestruck by the champion. In his interview, Hagler revealed the confidence which had developed enough to risk placing himself within the sport's pantheon of greats. He suggested that he was the greatest middleweight of all time. "Others would have to sit in judgment on that," Merchant said. "Well, at least the greatest since Monzon," Hagler said, backing off a bit farther than necessary.

Goody Petronelli was more circumspect in his analysis. "At this stage of his career, Marvin could already be rated among the ten best middleweight champions ever, and he's improving with every fight. His punching power rates with the all-time best, and he's a textbook boxer: He never drops his guard and never loses his head, and he's always in position to punch. And he has never been knocked out; indeed, it's doubtful that any middleweight in history could have KO'd him."

Sibson was magnanimous in his assessment. "I never believed that anyone could do to me what he did," he marvelled. "The man was an artist, a master. He put me in a cage, locked the door and threw away the key." The British man's face was a mass of ugly lumps and a maze of seventeen stitches zigzagged across his face to close his cuts. "I didn't realise that it was such a jump up in class," he said. "But that class is really just a class of one man."

Entered The Ring Frozen – The Woeful Wilford Scypion

TWO WEEKS after Hagler's fight against Obelmejias in Italy in November 1982, a pall of tragedy enveloped the sport when the South Korean lightweight Duk Koo Kim was knocked out in his attempt to capture Ray Mancini's WBA belt. Koo Kim slipped into a coma and died four days later.

Soon thereafter, Jose Sulaiman, the head of the WBC, made a decision that from 1 January 1983 all WBC championship bouts would be limited to 12 rounds. His rationale was that if the Kim-Mancini fight had ended after 12, Kim would still be alive. The critics pounced, accusing Sulaiman of applying compassion rather than logic in his assessment, pointing out that if you applied his logic retrospectively to 1918, of 645 documented fight-connected deaths since then, only 13 would have been prevented. The other 632 fatalities came in 12 rounds or less. And of those 632 fatalities, 190 were amateurs, who fight for three rounds or fewer. The WBA resisted following Sulaiman's lead and mandated that it would continue with the 15-round limit.

In the case of unified champions, of which there were only two, Hagler and light-heavyweight Michael Spinks, the two groups agreed that they would take turns acting as the 'host' organisation for title defences. The other would merely take their sanction fees.

For Hagler's fight with Tony Sibson in February, the WBC provided the officials and the supervision but the bout was scheduled for 15 rounds because the contracts for a fight of that length had already been signed. Problems started to unveil themselves just two days after the victory over the Englishman when Wilford Scypion, a tough fighter from Port Arthur, Texas, upset the odds and defeated Hagler's proposed next mandatory challenger, Frank 'The Animal' Fletcher, on a unanimous points verdict.

Soon after, Scypion's reward, to meet the middleweight champion, was agreed for Providence, Rhode Island, on 13 May. This was later re-scheduled for 27 May when Hagler injured his left knee when conducting his brutal road work sessions.

On 11 March, Bob Arum, co-promoter of the bout, received a telex from Dr Elias Cordova, the chairman of the WBA championship committee, informing him that the Scypion fight would have WBA officials and be for 15 rounds and that "only under these conditions, the bout will receive the WBA approbation".

Subsequently, however, using the argument that Scypion was the WBC's number one contender but only number two according to the WBA, Sulaiman convinced Gilberto Mendoza, the president of the WBA, that the WBA should pass up its turn in the spotlight. Dr Cordova refused to play along.

This dispute between the alphabet kingdoms meant that Hagler became caught in the crossfire. No matter which way he turned, one organisation decreed that they would strip him of half his championship.

After weeks of wrangling, a backroom deal appeared to be struck. In exchange for the control of Hagler's next two defences, the WBA agreed to let Sulaiman direct the Scypion match. "Twelve rounds," Sulaiman said happily.

Hagler objected. "Fifteen rounds," he replied.

Obviously distressed that a champion would dare speak up, even to a rival organisation, Mendoza then decreed that the WBA would sanction only a 12-round fight. It mattered not that this was in direct contravention of the WBA's 15-round rule. Nor did it matter that Sulaiman had agreed to ignore his own new rule by allowing Hagler to fight 15 rounds in each of his two defences following the Scypion challenge.

Enter the United States Boxing Association, or, more correctly, its hastily put-together offshoot, the USBA/ International. "You are our world middleweight champion," said the USBA/I, an organisation that had Scypion as its United States middleweight champion. "If you want to fight 15 rounds, we'll sanction it." Bill Brennan, the USBA/I's championship committee chairman and former president of the USBA, said that its intentions were honourable. "We'll be okay if we can keep our people honest and keep their hands out of other people's pockets."

Hagler was more than happy to have the USBA/I's blessing. He said, "I won the title in a 15-round fight, I've defended it six times in 15-round fights, and I'm going to defend it this time in a 15-round fight."

Pat Petronelli was more direct, "We're fed up with the WBC and WBA dictating terms to us. How can they sanction this fight for 12 rounds and the next two for 15 rounds? It's bad for the sport. We're taking a stand right now. Marvin is disgusted with both organisations. They keep saying, 'We're going to strip, strip, strip you of your title.' And we're saying to them, 'If you want to do it, go ahead and do it.' Marvin

Hagler will still be the world champion regardless of what they say."

Mike Jones, Scypion's co-manager, supported this standpoint. "When you get down to the nitty-gritty, one fact stands out: Marvin is the undisputed middleweight champion. How could any governing body deny that? And when Wilford wins the title, he will be the undisputed champion of the world."

On 18 May, Sulaiman wired Mike Malitz of Arum's office, "WBC emergency committee voted certification of Hagler-Scypion 15 rounds based on contractual agreement. Our officials will be Arthur Mercante, referee, and judges Tony Perez, Tony Castellano and Mr Fishenbaum."

Mr Fishenbaum was Stuart Kirschenbaum, the chairman of the Michigan Athletic Commission, who had already been appointed a judge by the USBA/I. Along with Kirschenbaum the USBA/I had selected referee Frank Cappuccino, and judges Larry Hazzard and Joe Cortez. A telex went back to Sulaiman, "Suggest you contact Robert W. Lee, president of the USBA/I." In other words, mind your own business!

As a last resort, Sulaiman tried a direct appeal to Hagler. He placed a call to the champion's training camp in Provincetown. Goody Petronelli answered the telephone. "I'm confused," Sulaiman said. "Why is Marvin saying all those terrible things about me? Why is Bob Arum telling me to stay home?"

"Don't believe all that stuff you read in the papers," reassured the trainer. "A lot of it is getting blown out of proportion." "I want to talk to Marvin," he requested. Petronelli was firm. "No, not now," he said. "You're a fight person. You know I don't want to get his mind all messed up over this 15- and 12-round stuff. If you want to talk to him after the fight, he'll be glad to talk to you." "I understand," said

Sulaiman. "Tell him I have always respected him and I think he's a great champion."

Wilford Scypion's surprise victory over Frank Fletcher was the culmination of a long, successful amateur career and a professional record that had started brightly before being tainted by tragedy. He knocked out all of his first 12 opponents before facing Willie Classen in New York. He demonstrated his increasing power and knocked Classen unconscious. Classen never regained consciousness and died in the hospital five days later. "It was the dark boxing nightmare that looms above every fighter," Scypion later said, "The black crow perched in the rafters of every stadium on fight night." He seriously considered retirement.

He eventually returned to the ring and saw his progress halted by Mustafa Hamsho, when he was disqualified for not getting back into the ring quickly enough after being knocked through the ropes. He would gain some career momentum before Dwight Davidson and then James Green brought it to a grinding halt. By the time he faced Fletcher, he had won five consecutive fights and this, combined with a career-best purse of $350,000, gave him a confidence that he could cause Hagler problems.

Scypion's trainer, Kenny Weldon, outlined the plan to capture Hagler's crown. "We will put him under continuous pressure," he said. "Hagler projects the image of being the ultimate macho fighter but we have never seen him mix it up." He then continued to poke at Hagler's reputation by dismissing his claims to be ranked among the greats. "Hagler should never be compared with Sugar Ray Robinson, Jake LaMotta or Mickey Walker. He is nowhere near."

At the press conference, Scypion supported his trainer's claims and voiced his own confidence, suggesting that he had the power to trouble Hagler. "I just need to get lucky once," he said. "A hard shot connecting at just the right moment on just the right spot on Hagler's chin and he won't recover."

Hagler scorned the idea of luck. "I rely on hard work to decide my fights," he sneered. "Forget the fuss about the number of rounds; I don't intend to let this fight last for 15 rounds. He has made the mistake of overdoing his chat and so I will finish him early."

During the introductions, Brockton jazz musician Dick Johnson played a saxophone rendition of the National Anthem. As he started to play, the people at the Civic Centre provided a backing track for him, a more classic rendition with a big, sweeping orchestra. The noise that it created, two melodies attempting to jam together, was a dissonant mess.

The same could also be said of the noise that played in Wilford Scypion's head as he bounced on the spot. Despite his confident assertions about his own prowess, when he stepped into the ring, he looked distinctly uncomfortable, like a man knowing that the gallows waited. "He was frozen with fear," his manager Mike Jones later revealed.

Hagler appeared to smell it and immediately hit him with a short but power-packed left hook which caught and staggered the challenger, turning his legs into jelly, and saw him barely conscious. As Scypion staggered backward into a corner, Hagler went after him – and then uncharacteristically backed off. "He was fighting back out of instinct, and that's the time you can get hurt," Hagler said later. "I figured I had 15 rounds, so there was no hurry."

In the next two rounds, Hagler toyed with his foe, switching back and forth from southpaw to orthodox and making the Texan reach and then miss with his intended punches. At times, Scypion must have felt he was fighting a mirage.

In the fourth round, the champion decided 15 rounds was 11 too many. Early in the third minute of the fourth round, Hagler unleashed a volley of punches – the first being a jarring overhand right – and when he was done, Scypion was down for the count. Just which punch had put him there was unclear. Even the HBO replays couldn't provide the answer.

When Jones saw Scypion fall, he decided he had taken enough. As Cappuccino counted eight, Jones was starting through the ropes, and at nine he was inside the ring. Even if Scypion had made it to his feet, and indeed he gamely tried, he would have been disqualified because his cornerman was in the ring. Officially the result was listed as a knockout at 2.47.

When the formalities were over, Bob Arum declared that Hagler's next fight was scheduled to be against the WBA's top contender, Juan Roldan, who had decisioned Teddy Mann on the undercard. "After that," Arum suggested, "it could be Roberto Duran, should he win the WBA junior middleweight title from Davey Moore or possibly, Wilfred Benitez, the former WBC super welterweight champ."

A few moments later, Hagler, in the bored manner of a veteran mountain climber who has scaled all the Himalayas, poured cold water on Arum's fire and said he was seriously pondering retirement. "I've beaten everything that's out there," he said. "There are no big-money fights for me, and I don't feel like just hanging around waiting for somebody to knock me off. I'm going home for a long rest. I'm going to be with my wife and my family, and I am going to think about it."

This surprise announcement reignited the interest of Thomas Hearns, who was watching on television. Since beating Benitez for the title, he had re-established his star credentials. Despite the fact that he had signed to fight Hagler once, before his hand injury curtailed the plan, the Hagler camp believed that Hearns wanted no part of him.

"Not so," said Mike Trainer, the attorney for Hearns and his manager, Emanuel Steward. "That is the only big-money fight for Marvin. But not yet, although I'll sit down and talk with them about it tomorrow if they want. First Tommy has to defend his title. And then he has to move up and meet a few middleweights to make this a credible fight. Hearns is the only opponent Hagler has who can make him a lot of money. Roldan's a joke. And you can forget Duran and Benitez, because Benitez has beaten Duran and Tommy beat Benitez. If Marvin wants to make a lot of money, he has only one choice – Hearns."

Another man who demanded the opportunity to talk to Hagler was Jose Sulaiman. "I believe the people with Hagler have abandoned the WBC title," Sulaiman said. "But I want Hagler to tell me this himself. I respect him; I like him. I will go anywhere to meet with him. I will pay my own way. Only then, after I have talked with Marvin, will I make up my mind whether he's still our champion or has abandoned us. And if he has, we'll find somebody else. At this moment he is still our champion."

Goody Petronelli said, "Sulaiman is welcome to sit down and talk with the world champion anytime, but my brother Pat and I will be there, too." He dismissed Hagler's talk of retirement, suggesting that the political wrangling had tired him as much as Scypion. "Marvin is going to take the summer off. He's worked long and hard, and he deserves a long rest. He's going to get it. In the fall he'll be a new man; he'll be raring to go. Then we can talk about his future."

The Build-Up To The Duran Confrontation

DURING THE summer months, Hagler took stock of his financial affairs and declared himself happy with all but one factor. "I don't like Bob Arum telling the press how much money I get for any of my fights," he said. "It changes people's reaction to me."

It also made him a target for chancers. "Last year, an 18-year-old boy arrived in Brockton and claimed he was Marvin's half-brother," said Pat Petronelli. "We put the kid up in a hotel for four days and had the police check his story out. The kid had looked straight in his eyes and claimed, 'Your father had an affair with my mother.' It was lies."

There was little obvious evidence of Hagler's wealth, apart from his home in the well-appointed Hanover district and his 1983 Cadillac. He retained a number of his frugal habits, such as travelling to New Jersey to buy cut-rate pigeons for his collection and continuing to take his mother to budget restaurants for lunch. "He claims that he never got to eat his food because of the fans interrupting," Goody Petronelli laughed. "So why waste money at a fancy place?"

Although he had bought a house for his mother after defeating Antuofermo, he insisted that others had to share his own work ethic. His financial adviser, Peter Mareb, revealed, "One of Marvin's ambitions is to own a chain of laundromats, in order to provide jobs for members of his family."

"I want to make sure that my brother and sisters have something to do," Hagler explained. "You want to work, fine; you can earn your money. I can help them instead of me just giving them things. It's also my way of saying 'thank you' for standing by me."

To protect his interests, Hagler had founded Marvelous Enterprises Inc. He and the two other shareholders, Pat and Goody Petronelli, met monthly with Peter Mareb to discuss investments and strategy. "At first, Marvin was self-conscious at the business meetings," Mareb recalled. "He had to overcome his basic cautiousness because he was afraid of not being considered smart." Mareb worked hard to challenge this, "I assured him that some very sophisticated clients understood no more than he did initially." Pat Petronelli marvelled at the speed of his development outside the ropes. "There's a wide gap between education and intelligence. Marvin isn't educated, but he's intelligent. He probably would have done well even if he had not made it as a world champion."

Hagler's income has been funnelled into a profit-sharing plan, a pension plan, a custodial trust account and educational trusts for his children. The champion received a relatively modest monthly salary, "about the same as someone earning in the high five figures", Hagler once explained. "He's not like many athletes," said Mareb. "He's stayed conservative in his needs. He's not compulsive about spending. He feels nervous about debts. He won't run them up."

Despite the comfort, Hagler worked hard to stave off complacency. "My security isn't guaranteed," he said. "I still have to work. This can be taken away from me."

He referred back to the struggles of his own career: "I worked in a Brockton leather factory for two dollars an hour and then when I worked for Goody and Pat, they paid me four dollars an hour." The purses he had recently received had been hard-earned too. "I was supposed to get 50 dollars for my first fight but the promoter Sam Silverman kept ten dollars from that."

"When I boxed Antuofermo, I got the best purse of my career, which was $40,000," Hagler bristled, "which is the same amount Sugar Ray Leonard received for his professional debut." He couldn't help comparing himself against Leonard. "I am an undisputed champion," he said, "so if you can pay Leonard and Hearns, who have only held one championship belt, eight to ten million, when is my turn gonna come?"

This rhetorical question obliged Hagler to look at some creative answers. In the past, the conservative element of his nature tended to win out. He would fight for a guaranteed purse. For future fights, he decided that he would accept a smaller guaranteed purse but would instead take a percentage of the gross profits. "I'm trying to be smarter than before," Hagler explained. "If I go out and bust my butt, I want to get my share of the money on offer."

The potential rewards made Hagler's decision to consider retirement a moot discussion. "It makes me want to fight more," he said. "The money means that I can now strive for other things, like my pride. When I finish, I won't ever have to ask anybody to lend me money to feed my family. That is a big achievement."

―――――

Don King was screaming, and Roberto Duran was weeping. During his long and largely illustrious career in the ring, Duran many times had been as plump as the Christmas goose, but through the force of his talent and will he had been able to summon what he needed to produce victory. Now, on 4 September 1982, at the age of 31, his skills and spirit apparently eroding, the game appeared finally to have caught up with him.

A few minutes earlier, before a crowd of some 5,000 people in Detroit's Cobo Arena, Duran had lost a split decision to Kirkland Laing, a club fighter from Jamaica. Laing had fled from a lunging Duran for two rounds, before he gradually gained control of the fight and steadily beat Duran to the punch as the battle wore on and Duran wore out. It was seemingly the last chapter in the Duran story. Almost eight months earlier, he had lost to WBC junior middleweight champion Wilfred Benitez, and six months before the Laing fight his weight had ballooned to 185 pounds.

"I was weak," he says. "I had to lose too much weight [he fought Laing at 155 pounds]. I was completely dilapidated. I was demoralised. I didn't care about Kirkland Laing."

He was with his wife, Felicidad, crying in a corner of his dressing room when King burst in, having stomped out of the arena and toward Duran in a fury. As Duran's regular promoter since 1975, King had made millions from him. After a particularly notable performance, Duran's biographer, Christian Giudice, recalled, "King would grandly whip out a sheaf of $100 bills, fan them like a deck of cards and hand them to Duran at the press conference as they smiled at the cameras." But those days now seemed as far gone as Duran's once immense talent.

King burst through the door of the dressing room, waving not $100 bills but a large cigar to punctuate his obscene, vituperative spiel. Someone locked the door behind him, but outside the room his large voice could be heard booming like cannon fire for ten long minutes.

Between curses and condemnations, King told Duran that he would never again promote a Duran fight, that Duran ought to retire. The game was over, and Duran knew it. After all those years, he was washed up. "I was finished, ruined professionally in boxing," Duran said.

He told Felicidad, "I'm going to retire. Everything is finished. I don't have the same feeling for it that I had before." His wife listened intently and then had her say. "You can't retire," she told him. Then she pricked him with this needle, "If you had any pride you would demonstrate to Panama and the whole world that you are not finished. You have to sacrifice yourself! One year." Duran admitted that her words had stung him. The way back had begun.

The final, humiliating encounter between Duran and King occurred in New York two days after King's tirade in Detroit. "King lets you know how brightly you shine in his firmament by how long he keeps you waiting in his outer office," Giudice explained. Roberto and Felicidad arrived at 1.30pm, seeking the purse for the Laing fight. When King hadn't called them into his presence by 4pm, Duran left. "I'm not going to be humiliated by anyone," he said, leaving his wife with the lawyers who had accompanied them. She finally saw King around two hours later.

The following day Duran walked the 20 blocks to the office of King's arch-rival, Bob Arum, who with King had co-promoted the first Leonard-Duran fight. Even before the Laing fight Duran had asked Arum for the chance to fight his young, inexperienced WBA junior middleweight champion, Davey Moore. Arum had agreed to make the fight, which led to a clash with King that ended abruptly after the Laing fight. King then didn't want Duran anymore. "I figured I wouldn't hear from Duran again," Arum said.

When Duran called, saying he was on the way over, Arum asked his match-maker, Teddy Brenner, "Do you think there's any future there?" Brenner said, "The guy hasn't taken any punishment. It's all mental. And he doesn't take care of himself."

When Duran arrived, Arum recalled, "He looked as if he'd been crying." "I was going with only one idea," Duran says. "To get away from King and fight for Arum, so that King could see that without him I had someone else to represent me." He told Arum he had learned his lesson. "If you give me the opportunity, I will work very, very hard," he said. "You have only yourself to blame for what's happened," Brenner told him.

Arum acquiesced to Duran's bidding and offered him $25,000 to fight 27-year-old British hope Jimmy Batten on the Aaron Pryor-Alexis Arguello card. Duran resented the offer, pocket change for him. "I thought Arum treated me a little harsh," he says. "I was going to tell him to shove it, but I held off. Arum was very hard, but he gave me a chance."

After signing for Batten, Duran called his old friend Luis Spada and asked him to be his manager. Spada had been the match-maker for some of Duran's early fights while working for Carlos Eleta, Duran's aristocratic Panamanian manager. The Argentine had once told Duran that if he ever needed anything to just call, "even to carry the spit bucket in your corner", and this was not forgotten by the great fighter. "You're not going to carry my buckets," Duran told him.

Spada, a one-time intelligence officer in the Argentine Navy, owned a gym in Panama and had managed three champions – Duran, light-flyweight champion Hilario Zapata and Rigaberto Riasco, the junior featherweight champ. He told Duran, "I'm not Mandrake El Mago [the popular cartoon magician] and I'm not a Chinese doctor. You have to train, you have to work."

For Batten, Spada felt that his programme, which included a high-protein, low-starch, low-sugar diet, monthly blood and urine tests and regular hour-long runs, hadn't started to take full effect. Duran agreed that he wasn't yet ready. "I didn't want to fight before the main event but, rather, after it," he said, figuring that the press would be interviewing Pryor and Arguello as he was dancing with Batten. The fight emptied what was left of the house. Duran won by a decision, but he was slow and awkward.

A few days later, Duran signed to meet former WBA welterweight champion Pipino Cuevas in Los Angeles on 29 January 1983. Spada agreed to fight at 152 pounds, Cuevas's ceiling, but for two days Duran resisted, thinking he couldn't make that limit. "If you don't get this fight, you better just fool around in boxing," Brenner told him. Then Arum held out a big carrot: beat Cuevas and Davey Moore, who had won the light-middleweight championship in only his eighth professional fight, would be next. Duran signed and meekly asked Spada, "Is it okay if I make 153?"

Duran trained rigorously for Cuevas and made the weight easily. What Felicidad saw in those days of training in LA was something she hadn't seen since the days before the Leonard fight in Montreal. "The enthusiasm came back when they told him he was going to fight Cuevas," says Felicidad. "From that point on, I began to see the same Roberto Duran as before – happy, joyful, the one that liked to joke around. I recovered him. He was back. He was the same Roberto I once knew."

Cuevas may have been a spent bullet, but Duran moved like the Duran of old, chasing him like a ferret around the ring and looking sharper than he had looked since Montreal. When he had Cuevas in trouble, he finished with fire. Cuevas didn't have a chance, losing by a knockout at two minutes and 26 seconds of the fourth round. Nor five months later did Moore have a prayer. Despite the layoff, Duran had no trouble making 152.5 pounds for Moore. "Making weight for a fight is a preoccupation with a boxer," Spada says. "It's his subconscious bothering him, making him restless. Twenty days before the Moore fight Roberto was 153. This gives the boxer breathing room, relaxation, calmness."

In Madison Square Garden on 16 June, Duran used every skill he had learned in his 79 professional fights. Moore had been in only 12. Duran closed Moore's right eye with a thumb, bullied him here and there, spun him around, jabbed him, pounded his body, hooked him up and dropped him with a straight right hand in the eighth that had the sell-out crowd of 20,061, most of them Latinos, doing handsprings in their seats. Duran was the new junior middleweight champion of the world. "I was born again," he said.

Ricardo de la Espriella, the President of Panama, invited Duran to come back home. Duran was hesitant, given the abuse he had received after his no mas declaration against Leonard. "When I spoke to the President, he asked me to please come, and because of him I finally went to Panama," Duran said. "He said he'd send an airplane. I went to Panama to see those people humble themselves beside me, applaud me and all those things."

On the ride from the airport into Panama City, crowds estimated at 300,000 to 400,000 lined the streets, cheering him as he passed. Less than three years before, he had been a prisoner in his own house in this town, and now the people were greeting him as they had greeted Pope John Paul II three months earlier.

"When I was in the car, during the parade, I laughed and laughed at the hypocrisy," Duran says. "I was saying to myself, 'Look at all those hypocrites, today applauding me, saluting me.'"

In May, Hagler was supposed to do a boxing skit with Leonard at Bob Hope's birthday party at the Kennedy

Center in Washington, DC, but Leonard had to drop out at the last minute to undergo surgery for a hernia. Duran was summoned from his training camp in New Jersey to replace him. He left in such a hurry that he arrived wearing two right shoes.

In his earlier days, Hagler had admired the Panamanian fighter, who, in his fiercely direct approach to boxing, embodied traits that Hagler himself coveted.

That should have been an occasion for two formidable champions to become acquainted. But Duran made a fatal mistake. After meeting Hagler and observing that he was about as tall as him, Duran said to his manager, Luis Spada, "I almost tall like Marvin. I fight him." When Hagler heard that, he treated Duran to the narrow-eyed squint he directed at opponents and, turning his back to him, would speak not a word more.

Arum and Spada couldn't believe it. "They're about the same size." Hagler, at 5ft 8.5ins, was actually one inch taller but it got the two camps thinking. When Duran stopped Moore, Hagler was among the first to get to the ring, and he ended up giving most of the interviews.

A month later, Bob Arum, who had controlled the middleweight title since Carlos Monzon, announced that the fight between 'Marvelous' Marvin Hagler and 'Hands of Stone' would take place on 4 November. He was considering staging the contest in either Las Vegas, Atlantic City, Miami or New York's Madison Square Garden. He finally agreed on Las Vegas's Caesars Palace.

Arum ignored Hagler's protestations about revealing his likely earnings and announced that each fighter was likely to earn $10m. Both men had agreed to accept a guaranteed purse of $5m each but share some of the gross profit, which would inevitably arouse huge interest on the closed-circuit sale. Goody Petronelli revealed, "Marvin's delighted. He feels really good about this fight." Luis Spada simply remarked, "Victory for Duran means an unprecedented fourth world championship. He intends to take it."

Both fighters actively participated in the publicity campaign across several major cities. "I'm very happy he has achieved what he has," Hagler said of Duran's rebound. "It gives me a chance to make my big pay day." However, he remained steadfastly unimpressed by the news of a newly revitalised Duran. "I really don't care about all that stuff," he said. "I saw him knock out Davey Moore and he looked very impressive, but Moore had only had 13 fights," Hagler reasoned. "When he's fought real good fighters, he hasn't been able to put them away."

Duran attempted to keep his strategy a mystery. Spada claimed that his 16 years' experience of trench warfare was the way to victory, "To win this fight, he is going to fight inside." Charles Boston and Bruce Starling, Duran's sparring partners, revealed that he would remain evasive. "You watch the fight," Duran said through an interpreter. "It's not going to be very easy for him to hit me."

Hagler countered that he was prepared for any tactic. "I expect him to come out moving his head from side to side and doing things like that," he explained. "He'll be moving, but he'll go back to his old habits once he gets hit a few times." He issued a chilling warning, "It would be a big mistake if he tries to outbox me."

The intriguing match gripped the fight community. Alexis Arguello, who had held titles as a featherweight, junior lightweight and lightweight, speculated that the step up in weight may neutralise Duran's famous advantage. "Duran might have hands of sand as a middleweight," he said. "I jumped three divisions and when I went for the fourth one against Aaron Pryor, my punches didn't hurt him but his punches certainly hurt me."

The boxing sage Ray Arcel, who had worked with a record 20 world champions, issued a warning to Hagler, "If he's determined to win, he could take it all." Arcel, who had enjoyed an eight-year association with Duran which had lasted until the 'no mas' fight with Leonard, praised Luis Spada's scientific approach. "He's going to be the first man to win a fourth title," he claimed.

"There's no script for this fight," offered Mort Sharnik, CBS-TV's boxing consultant, in summary. "Anything could happen. It could be a war, with Duran attacking as he attacked Leonard in Montreal, taking the fight to Hagler from the get-go. It could be a long, boring boxing match in which two superior boxers make intermittent contact between disengagements. Or a combination of the two."

Hagler retreated to his usual training camp in Provincetown with two sparring partners, Bob Paterson and John Ford, who imitated Duran's style. As usual, he trained like he was meeting the Creature from the Black Lagoon. During his stay, Pat Petronelli was asked why, as the fight approached, Hagler would go to bed earlier and earlier at night.

"He's such poor company and becomes so unpleasant," Petronelli explained rather matter-of-factly and in all seriousness, "that he likes to get to bed early to cut down on the time he has to spend with himself."

"I respect Duran," Hagler said. "He's a very experienced fighter. When guys are dangerous, don't play with them. My motto for this fight is: don't play with him – bust him up. I think this fight will bring out everything I've learned. It will all come out that night. I'd like nothing better than to end Duran's career."

Hagler did concede that he was concerned about the bout going the full 15 rounds, since the WBA, which had designated the ref and judges, was controlled politically by Latin Americans could be tempted to favour Duran. "I can't leave it up to the judges here," Hagler said. "I have to go in and do the job. If Duran goes 15 rounds with me, he's going to be busted up."

Duran opted to train in Palm Springs, where he revelled in Spada's discipline. The Argentine trainer granted Duran permission to spend a night with his wife. "Are you crazy?" Duran cried. "I didn't see her for eight weeks before Davey Moore and you want me to see her six weeks before Marvin Hagler?"

Despite this impressive self-discipline, Duran had never seemed looser before a fight. When he was getting a haircut at his Palm Springs hotel barbershop, he serenaded the attendants with a medley of Cuban songs. He told joke after joke, night after night, as he moved about Palm Springs, and he laughed loudest of all at them. He punished sparring partners during his daily afternoon sessions. He saw Arum walk by the ring one day and said, "Hi, Bob." Arum glanced over, and Duran stuck out his tongue.

"The problems Hagler presents don't interest me," Duran said. "When I'm in condition and I train, I'm not interested in anything like that. Nothing bothers me when I become hot-blooded; let him come any way he wants. I can fight inside as well as outside. If I'm not there, he won't hit me. I will have a lot of movement for him. I will go to the body. I should be frightened because he's a higher weight than me? You're crazy. Now it's time. Now he's going to fight someone with quality."

As the fight drew closer, the boxing community wavered between the two combatants' likelihood of success. "Hagler has never been in the ring with a fighter of Duran's quality," suggested Sugar Ray Leonard. "I pick Hagler, but I could see Duran winning the fight. He could win by a knockout. Ask Moore. Duran's a finisher. If he feels he has shaken Hagler, forget it. Boxing is 90 per cent in the head. If he sees it's within his grasp, he'll seize it. He soars. If he hurts Hagler, he'll be on a high. Here is a guy who can move, think, counter and fight and is motivated by more than money. He was an outcast."

"I give Duran a hell of a shot," Arcel said. "Boxing's a very strange business. God didn't make the chin to be punched."

Freddie Brown, Duran's chief trainer, was certain about who would win, "I got to pick Duran. I got confidence in him. I know how much guts he's got, how hard he can punch and how much ability he has. Very smart. You can hit him, but you're going to get hit back. And you'll know you've been hit." Like others who picked Duran, Brown remembered the 1979 draw between Hagler and then-middleweight champion Vito Antuofermo, in whose corner Brown was working.

"Hagler had trouble coping when Antuofermo pressed him and eventually lost control of the fight. Vito got right on top of him, pressing him, facing him, making him fight," Brown said. "Hagler doesn't like that. That's why Vito gave him all that trouble. Duran's a better in-fighter than Vito. He's as strong as Vito. Duran's a harder puncher and not as easy to hit. Vito was easy to hit. This is a real good fight for Duran."

By the time they both arrived in Las Vegas they were ready. On the morning of the fight Duran weighed in at 156.5 pounds in front of some of the 2,000 Panamanians who invaded the city, Hagler at a pound more.

"I'm in the same shape I was when I fought Leonard the first time," said Duran, referring to his WBC welterweight title victory in June 1980. And he was additionally armed with a strategy, devised by Spada, that called for Duran to box – to move rather than attack – and induce Hagler to miss.

Hagler was dismissive of the hype. "How ready can you get?" Hagler asked. "I want to get it over with. After a while, all the talking gets to you. Now he's going to have to fight."

The 'Bore' Against Hands Of Stone

TALK THEY eventually did, though it took Hagler a while to learn the strange new language Duran brought into the ring. And Hagler's discomfort with the relatively passive Duran showed in long, inexplicable lapses of his own originality and will, until he became aware that his title was truly at risk.

It was a strange fight, with small eddies and currents that made it difficult to score, but fascinating for what it revealed about the personalities of its leading men. Duran was an imaginative actor on stage, an original who created ring drama by the mere feint of his head. Hagler was stoic, without creative urgency or flair. He was a stalker, conservative and cautious, almost insecure, whose ring presence could be likened to that of a mechanic in a garage – speak softly and carry a big wrench.

The pre-fight preliminaries were unusually long, waiting in the cool evening air for over 20 minutes, and while Duran remained relaxed and looked to be savouring the atmosphere, the delay seemed to have a detrimental effect on Hagler. This showed during the first round, which was a sleepwalk. "I knew that Hagler was waiting for me to get inside to fight with him," Duran said afterwards, "so he could get his punches in with force." There was nothing doing.

When Duran didn't attack in the second, Petronelli began to worry, "I thought, 'What's going on here?'"

Not that much, really, which was the source of Petronelli's concern, though the fighters did mix it up somewhat more than they had in the first round. Hagler caught Duran with a solid right jab, a punch Duran would feel throughout the fight, and he scored uppercuts to the body and head when they fought inside. But Duran was making himself a difficult target and finding the range with his straight right hand, the punch that eventually took him as far as he went.

"Duran was fighting the smarter, more composed fight," one of the judges, Ove Ovesen of Denmark, would later say. "He made Marvin miss and countered on his own. I made those two rounds for Duran, but not by much." The fight was going as Duran and Spada had planned it. "I fought him at half-distance," Duran said. "I was waiting for him to unload so I could score on him. Whichever hand he unloaded, I was ready to counter. He didn't confuse me with anything. I was beating him without mixing it up too much."

Petronelli's foreboding deepened. "Duran waited and waited and waited for Marvin to lead," he said. "We had to change our tactics and go on the offensive, which isn't really Marvin's style." So at the end of the third, Petronelli told Hagler, "This ain't going too well. Put the pressure on him."

Through the uneventful fourth and fifth rounds, Hagler showed a harder jab but to little effect. "He'd slip and counter, slide back and wait for me," Hagler said. "When you're trying for a knockout, it's the hardest thing to get. That's what I was after, but you have to let them come. He wasn't there. Duran is too crafty to go after for a knockout. You leave yourself open, and he takes advantage of it."

Duran, meanwhile, was using every trick picked up in his 80 pro bouts (of which he had won 76) to keep out of harm's way; gliding left and right, then facing Hagler straight on, now giving him angles, then slipping and bobbing under punches, picking them off with his hands and arms, even turning his head to avert Hagler's savage uppercuts. "They were strong," Duran said. "I turned my head to be careful of his right because it's his most dangerous hand. His left is dead. The hand he most relied on was his right."

Hagler had trouble with Duran's hand speed, and he often couldn't find Duran's head. "I wasn't getting my jab off the way I generally do," said Hagler, who was more effective when he switched from a lefty to a righty stance, which brought him two feet closer to Duran. "It seemed everybody was disappointed that I didn't knock him out. I felt that way myself. But he wasn't that vulnerable to a knockout. It was hard to hit him with a solid punch. I didn't catch him with a solid shot."

He did, especially in the sixth, when he tagged Duran repeatedly and heavily with lefts and rights to the body and head and appeared to have him on the ropes. Duran needed his chin of stone to survive the sixth, but the fight was clearly Hagler's if he would only reach out and grasp it. And now Duran had another obstacle to contend with. In the fifth round he had driven a hard right to Hagler's forehead, and thereafter he felt pain in his right hand every time he landed it. Hagler never knew this.

Duran soon came to feel that his major protection against all-out attack, his cocked right hand, was so enfeebled that it left him vulnerable. "I was a little scared because he was coming in straight up," Duran said. "I could reach him with any right, but actually I was scared to throw the right hand." To survive, if not to win, Duran kept throwing it anyway through the rest of the fight.

All of this might have been moot had Hagler seized his advantage. But he didn't. Though Duran hadn't hurt him –

and apparently couldn't hurt him – one press report read, "Hagler fought from the seventh to the tenth rounds as if Duran were Larry Holmes."

"He came to tear my head off," says Duran, "but when he saw that I could hit him hard, with strength, he got scared and became a coward. That's why he didn't take too many chances and mix it up with me. Everyone was saying he was a destroyer, but when he hit me, he didn't do anything to me. His punches absolutely did me no damage. He got scared every time he threw a jab because I could get my right in under it. That's why he held off so much."

Why Hagler, whose general motto was "Destruction and Destroy", came so close to self-destructing became a central question following the 11th round, when he danced and let a tiring Duran back into the fight. What was he worried about? "I'm not a fool either," Hagler would say, "going in to get hit. You don't barrel in there on a guy like Roberto Duran. Why take unnecessary punishment unless you have to? I'd been effective and was winning the fight, so it isn't like I had to go in there and take the punishment to bomb him out."

Toward the close of the 12th round, Duran scored with a hard, straight right hand to Hagler's face, and just before the bell blood trickled from Hagler's swollen left eye, as Duran taunted Hagler by pointing to his chin and saying, "Hit me! Hit me!" Hagler, the undisputed middleweight champion, obliged with a hard right as he chased Duran into a corner.

The crowd of 14,600 in the stadium at Caesars Palace in Las Vegas was on its feet roaring long after the bell had sounded. But the 12th, which Duran won with such a flourish, was a mere prelude to what would happen in the next round. Duran brought the multitude up again, and again, and then it was chanting "Dooooran! Dooooran! Dooooran!" Spurred on by the crowd and driven by the force of his own furious will and considerable talent, Duran appeared to seize control of the fight.

Midway through the 13th, Hagler struck Duran with a mighty left to the face, but Duran countered to the body, jarred Hagler with a sharp right to the head, cracked him with another right and then a third, and followed with a left and a right. Now someone in the crowd was blowing a bugle, a clarion call, it seemed, for Duran. At the bell he landed a final right to Hagler's head, and Hagler smiled sarcastically as he went to his corner. It was Duran's round, and Hagler knew it.

Suddenly – and quite miraculously – there was a sense in the stadium that Duran, a 4/1 underdog who had been so roughed up in the sixth round it looked as if he would never make it to the ninth, had not only survived but might yet prevail; that the former lightweight and welterweight champion of the world was about to make history by becoming the first man ever to win four world titles; and that Hagler's middleweight crown, which he had won three years before and had successfully defended seven times, all by knockout, was in grave danger of being taken.

"'Marvelous' may be legally part of Marvin's name," said WBC junior middleweight champion Thomas Hearns, "but they should take it away from him now and give it to Roberto."

At the end of the 13th, Luis Spada told Duran, "You win the last two rounds, you win the fight. Throw punches. Make points. You have to win the last two rounds!"

Goody Petronelli told his man the same thing. He reminded Hagler that almost four years earlier in this venue, he had suffered his biggest ring disappointment, losing his first bid for the middleweight title with Vito Antuofermo. Now Petronelli feared a similar repeat. "I want a strong 14th and 15th," he told Hagler. "You can't make this fight close. You've got to win these last two rounds."

At that point judge Guy Jutras of Canada had the fight even, at 124-124, while judge Yasaku Yoshida of Japan, whose indecision had been such that he had called six rounds even, actually had Duran ahead 127-126, as did Denmark's Ovesen, 125-124. If many at ringside would later be astonished at the judges' cards – Hagler had certainly landed more and harder punches to this juncture – it was unmistakable that Duran had craftily fought within reach of victory in the 12th and 13th rounds.

That this was so, after what Duran had been through during the preceding year, and particularly in the previous 51 minutes, gave an otherwise routine evening a sudden sense of moment.

No matter. Hagler won the fight by heeding Petronelli's advice and battering an exhausted Duran for the last six minutes, finally shedding his caution when he had to and taking the fight to the challenger. He delivered two-handed combination punches which called on Duran to utilise all of his guile to survive. Hagler pinned the veteran in a corner and threw six slashing punches to his head and body and briefly, Hagler was marvelous again, but Roberto brought the crowd to its feet as he rallied and staged a punch-up as the bell rang to end the 15-round contest.

There was no show of appreciation towards one another. Duran dropped his arms and glowered at Hagler, disappointed that the fight was over. Hagler simply made his way to his corner. "If I could have had one more round, I would have knocked him out," he later said regretfully. "Sure, he caught me with a few right hands," said Hagler. "But my mind kept telling me that the only way he was going to beat me was to hit me with the ring post."

Duran didn't and Hagler escaped with a 15-round decision. Had the Panamanian nicked one of the last two rounds, he would have become the first boxer in history to rule four divisions. The judging was ridiculously close. Jutras scored it 144-142, Yoshida had it 146-145, and Ovesen scored it 144-143.

"The better man won," Duran gracefully conceded. *Sports Illustrated*'s William Nack captured the mood perfectly, when he wrote, "Despite losing, Duran came away with $4m and his reputation enhanced, while the winner stepped out of the ring with $8m and his image diminished. Hagler proved himself the best middleweight on the block, while Duran showed that he is a fighter for the ages and should again be the object of celebration."

Juan Domingo Roldan

TO SAY that Hagler never ducked anybody isn't exactly true. He kept a couple of would-be challengers at arm's length because they were so undeserving. In 1981, the Korean Chong-Pal Park was supposed to be in line for a title shot but, according to Bob Arum, "When we saw this guy on film he looked so awful we couldn't put him on television on an undercard." Park was stalled in the hope that somebody would knock him off. And, eventually, Obelmejias complied.

An Argentine middleweight named Juan Domingo Roldan posed a similar problem. Ungainly and bull-like, he had dispatched an astonishing string of South American opponents to advance to the top of the WBC ladder. At the same time he looked to be a tough sell for an American audience.

Roldan's insistence was tempered by offering him lucrative spots on four straight Hagler undercards, the idea being to either get him known or get rid of him. The latter was undoubtedly what Arum had in mind when he matched him against Frank Fletcher underneath Hagler–Duran. But Roldan upset the scheme by knocking Fletcher flying through the ropes with a massive right. Roldan could be staved off no longer.

In order to sell the fight, it was suggested that he was the Argentine equivalent of Hagler. He came from humble beginnings and maintained his down-home lifestyle to the detriment of his career. He grew up in Freire, a farming community in Cordoba Province, four hundred miles north-west of Buenos Aires. He wanted to stay there and resisted the possibility of moving his career along at a quicker pace by moving to Buenos Aires.

Now, at 26, he had a shot at the title which another Argentine, Carlos Monzon, held for a record-breaking 14 defences. Hagler had long declared that he wanted to equal or better that mark because, "That would prove I was the best, because Monzon was a great champion."

Roldan was no Monzon although he talked as if he would make people forget about Monzon. He said he had respect for Hagler outside the ring, "but inside the ring, I have no respect for him".

Apart from chilling Fletcher, his most notable battle was a mystery knockout over Reggie Ford in San Remo, Italy. Roldan took a wild swing and appeared to miss Ford's large jaw, but Ford went down.

He was well advised. His manager, Tito Lectore, had guided Carlos Monzon through the glory years. Even in Argentina, not many people knew much about Roldan, even well into his career, although Lectore did all he could to give his young fighter a reputation.

Lectore enjoyed telling about Roldan's greatest battle with a brown bear when he was just 17. It convinced Lectore, he said, that he had a future champion.

A carnival arrived in Freire. One of its attractions was a $200 prize – a huge sum in the neighbourhood – for anyone who could stay on his feet for three rounds against the bear.

Lectore said Roldan frustrated the bear for two rounds, then, in the third round, got beneath the bear and held on, rendering the beast defenceless. Roldan got the $200 and the bear, the story goes, was so humiliated, he never fought again. "I have pictures to prove it," Lectore would claim. The pictures had a studio look and the bear looked stuffed.

Nevertheless, Roldan arrived at the Riviera in Las Vegas intending to snap Hagler's dream of Thomas Hearns and Sugar Ray Leonard in super showdowns. "Let him think of Hearns and Leonard," he said, "Let him think of them. He has to get by me and that is to my advantage."

Unlike other fighters his size, Roldan had the muscular look of a football player, with great upper-body strength. "That is from growing up doing farm work," he explained. "I haven't been training for a 15-round fight; I have been training for a 20-round fight. I have been waiting for this chance for 18 months. I thought I had a chance before to face Hagler but they put me off. Now I'm ready."

Although he had been a professional since December 1978, he had been fighting since he was 13. He gave up school to fight and help his father on the farm. "There was never any other sport for me," he said. "I always wanted to be a boxer. It was important to me, but I found it hard to leave home to train. That's been the hardest part."

Now he left his wife and two children for six days a week to train in Buenos Aires, but on Sundays, he returned to Freire. "For the first time in my life, people outside Freire know who I am," he marvelled. "After I beat Hagler, people all over the world will know me."

His eyes were dark and malevolent – "the eyes of an executioner" claimed Lectore. "They sure aren't Bette Davis eyes," quipped Goody Petronelli. Roldan had practised his hate-filled stare for the moment he met Hagler but the champion was nonplussed. "I can feel him staring," Hagler said, "but I just glance at him. I figure that when the time comes, I'll do something about it."

Vito Antuofermo and Mustafa Hamsho had similarly tried to worm their ways under Hagler's skin, and to some extent succeeded enough to fail. Alan Minter suggested Hagler was a racist and found out that Hagler's only prejudice is against opponents. Obelmejias knew just a few words of English and those were a few too many. 'Caveman' Lee waved a club in Hagler's face and aroused his primitive instincts. Tony Sibson made the mistake of touching Hagler before the gloves went on. Duran tried to ruin Marvin's lunch but succeeded in appearing like he was out to lunch.

Psychology was something opponents tried to use against Hagler, only to find that his mind was a dangerous thing to play with. The idea was to shake Hagler's self-confidence, disturb his concentration, or otherwise throw him off his game. It never worked.

"It's all part of the game," reasoned Hagler. "You want to beat a guy before he steps into the ring. Those are the strategies but I'm too smart for that. I've been through all that bull. All it does now is make me that much madder so I can rip his head off."

"It all backfires," said Pat Petronelli. "They should save their psyches for the ring. Marv is a champion of that, too."

Muhammad Ali brought the psyche game to the modern era, Hagler pointed out, and Ali carried it off the best. Ali buried his opponents in a clever verbal barrage, and jousted in street clothes. "Everybody else has been a copycat," Hagler said.

"Some fighters are easily spooked," Goody Petronelli observed. He had developed a heavyweight named Steve Zouski, who had promise until he ran afoul of Marvis Frazier. "In the dressing room before the fight, he said his legs fell asleep," Petronelli said. "I massaged them and told him to relax but he couldn't. Some fighters bring it into the ring with them."

Wiford Scypion was visibly nervous and tight for most of the four rounds the fight with Hagler lasted. "He froze," Pat Petronelli said. "He couldn't function. He took one look at Marv and realised he was in the big time. It got to him."

Hagler was characterised as a master of intimidation. Promoter Butch Lewis, in an effort to build up his promising young middleweight James Shuler, said, "If you get past Hagler's menacing look, he isn't great. It's just that his body and bald head scare people half to death."

Hagler scoffed at the assessment, "What it all boils down to is I can fight. Forget that other stuff. You can look fierce and in tip-top shape, but if you can't fight, you're in trouble. I can fight and they won't give that to me."

But Hagler would admit to one psyche – his refusal to shake hands before a fight. Alan Minter's racially charged comment that "he won't touch white meat" missed the point. Hagler's policy held true for all colours.

"Marv hasn't got the greatest love in the world for opponents, especially before a fight," explained Goody Petronelli. "He's not a phoney. When he is in training camp, he builds up his loathing of them. He won't shake hands with a guy, that is not his style. After a fight, he always shakes hands."

At the New York press launch for the Duran fight, Hagler was asked to shake Duran's hand for pictures. There was a long awkward moment when Duran held his hand out and Hagler let it dangle. Finally and grudgingly, Hagler took it. "The only reason was that the guy was making me a lot of money," Hagler conceded. "There is no reason to be around an opponent so much. You're not marrying the guy. There's no reason to be saying 'Hi'."

Almost all of Hagler's challengers – or their handlers – had worked on him through the media. The general approach was to doubt one or another of Hagler's physical or mental qualities. Nothing gets past Hagler, an avid reader of newspapers and magazines and a devoted television viewer. "Nothing rattles him, either," reminded Goody Petronelli.

"Sure the Roldan people are saying that I can get hit by right hands because Duran did," he said. "They have to try to find that weakness. But I know that Duran had the hand speed of a welterweight, and all that experience. There is no comparison."

Antuofermo's ploy was to continually raise his first fight with Hagler and question his heart. "They also threatened to pull out of the rematch because they couldn't use a particular cut solution," he growled. "His handlers then tried to rattle me at the weigh-in when the maladjusted scales caused problems." This was the reason why Antuofermo remained his most disliked former opponent.

"It's just his attitude," Hagler said. "He still doesn't give me credit today. I'm the one who made him famous. Without that first fight, he wouldn't have been known for anything."

Hamsho irritated Hagler with his cockiness but it was Hamsho's manager Al Braverman calling Hagler "gutless" in a Chicago newspaper that made Hagler angry. "When he mockingly stuck his tongue out round after round, I decided to butcher him for his 55 stitches."

Although Obelmejias was quiet before his first go at the title, a year later he made the mistake of raising his hand at the weigh-in, claiming himself as the true champion. "Until then, Marvin had been having trouble sleeping, he was unusually passive," Petronelli said. "Marv returned Obel a stare and if looks could kill … He said, 'That's exactly what I needed – up to now I haven't been motivated.'"

Duran's attempts to goad Hagler two days before the fight provoked a different reaction. When he walked behind the podium to stand behind Hagler and predict his fifth-round knockout victory, Hagler, while keeping an eye on Duran, did not react. "That was his last spurt," Hagler said, "to get me upset. I coulda been bad and gotten up but then how would I have looked. I'd play right into his hands because then he's touched a nerve of mine. I said, 'I'll hold it. There's only two more days. You knock this guy out now and you ain't gonna get paid.'"

Although he propounds self-control in these situations, he admitted that he was sorely tired, "I'm getting increasingly tired of this crap. They think they can push me and I ain't gonna do anything but one of these days they're gonna be surprised."

The Petronellis were aware of Hagler's breaking point being close on the morning of the weigh-in with Duran. They had heard that Duran might slap Hagler near the scale, and debated with each other before deciding to let Hagler in on the rumour.

"It was the first time Marv froze," said Pat Petronelli. "He said, 'I promise, if he slaps me he's going to get hit so hard he'll never make the fight.'"

In consideration of that, and of the possible loss of a $5m purse, the Petronellis hit upon a plan. At the weigh-in, the two of them kept their bodies wedged between the two fighters. When Duran leaned one way, he faced Goody. When he leaned the other, he got Pat.

"My brother and I figured that we'd rather get hit than waste all of that money," Pat Petronelli laughed. "We won't get in the way of Marv when the bell rings against Roldan." Hagler was determined that he would suffer for his crude attempts to psychologically disturb him.

Roldan had won the first two rounds, mostly because Hagler chose to fight in reverse while trying to decode

Roldan's wild but fiercely aggressive style. The retreat was only the first element of Hagler's strategy. "It will take me a couple of rounds to figure him out," Hagler had said the day before. "After that, this is where he gets off the bus. He's been following me around for 18 months. This is the last stop for him. Now I turn on the red light."

However, it was certainly no part of Hagler's plan to wind up on the floor in the opening seconds of the fight. "It was a damn slip," the embarrassed champ, who hadn't been on the deck in 52 amateur and 62 previous pro fights, later protested. Referee Tony Perez ruled it a knock-down and, after shoving the seemingly puzzled Roldan toward a neutral corner, tolled the mandatory eight against an angry Hagler. "You can call it whatever you want," Perez said. "I called it a knock-down."

Roldan's glimmer of hope wouldn't last long – only until Hagler, having solved the riddle of Roldan's rushes, opened up in the third round with the guns that had carried him to his 58-2-2 record.

The Argentine threw all of his punches with singular purpose: to destroy. If he feinted, it seemed to be by mistake. The punches flowed in wide, angry arcs starting from the hip and against Hagler, who weighed in at the same weight of 159 and a quarter, he scored well early with a right uppercut. Roldan's ungainly style was used to his advantage and many of his most effective punches were thrown when he was off balance.

"He's so aggressive, you've got to drive him back," Hagler said before the bout. "He doesn't like it when people hit him back. This may surprise a lot of people, but I intend to hurt him. People think that just because I didn't knock out Roberto Duran that I'm ready to be taken. I'm going to show them that the monster is back. I went to school on Duran.

From him I got my master's degree. Starting now, I'm going after my Ph.D."

Hagler began serious work on his doctorate in the third round. After the second, he was told by trainer Goody Petronelli, "Slide back on this guy and catch him coming in. He's wide open after every punch." Earlier, Hagler had tried ducking inside some of Roldan's punches and had been tagged by an uppercut. Now, as Roldan punched, Hagler heeded Petronelli's advice to take a step back and, as Roldan's shots fell harmlessly short, countered with hard punches to the body.

Midway through the round, Hagler fired a straight right to the head. He caught Roldan at the end of the punch, just as his hand was turning over, and the knuckle of the tucked-in thumb caught Roldan in the corner of his right eye. "God, the pain was terrible," Roldan said afterwards. "It spread all the way across to my ear. I couldn't see anything."

Staggering backward in pain, Roldan slammed against the ropes and slumped down. With his right hand, he pawed helplessly at the injured eye. Jumping in, Perez waved Hagler off and began to count. The eye was swollen shut almost before Perez got to eight. "I'd planned on boxing him," Hagler said, "but I saw I was hurting him – I could hear him grunt every time I hit him in the body – and I wasn't about to make the same mistake I made against Duran. I forgot all about boxing Roldan. I knew I could take him out. It was just a matter of hitting him until he fell down."

At the end of the decisive third round, Roldan had told the people in his corner, "I can't fight anymore. I can't see him." Tito Lectore cut him short. "You've still got your left eye. You must have courage. You're beating him and you can take him out with one punch. You must forget the pain. You can be the world champion."

Roldan, described by Larry Merchant as one "rough, tough hombre", presented himself as a very awkward Cyclops but in the sixth round, Hagler ripped a cut over Roldan's terribly swollen eye. Perez became concerned, and after each round asked Dr Donald Romeo, the ring physician, to check the eye.

"Ask him if he wants to continue," Romeo said, as he made each examination, to Tito Alba, a translator who was covering the Roldan corner for HBO.

"Tell him he feels fine and wants to continue," Lectore, butting in, told Alba each time.

After the ninth round, Roldan again told Lectore he could fight no more. Lectore slapped him hard. Then he began to shake Roldan. "You can't quit," Lectore said. "You must have courage. Be brave. You can still win. Throw the big punch. Knock him out."

Roldan knew there was no big punch left. In the sixth, he had hit Hagler on the chin with a wicked hook. The champion withstood it without blinking. Still, Roldan answered the bell for the tenth round. Moving in quickly, Hagler shifted from his normal southpaw stance and caught Roldan with a straight right, fired two left hooks and then caught him with a right cross square on the injured eye. At 39 seconds into the round, Roldan crashed over on his back.

Sitting up, Roldan stared at the floor in despair. Then he climbed wearily to his feet and, shoulders slumped in defeat, turned toward his corner even as Perez finished the count. That's when Perez asked him if he wanted any more of Hagler, and Roldan said in Spanish, "No more. I've had enough."

Furious, Lectore threw a towel into the ring. Then, striding from the arena, he barged into Roldan's dressing room and belted a door from its hinges with a right-handed punch.

The following morning, Lectore, his hand badly swollen, said he hadn't thrown the towel at Roldan. "People shouldn't think I'm a criminal," he said. "I was just trying to give him courage. That's my job. But Roldan fought a very courageous fight. He fought the last seven rounds with one eye. I just threw the towel because of the bad luck. With two good eyes, Roldan won the first two and a half rounds. That's what's important. All the rest was bad luck."

Juan Domingo Roldan would go on to fight until 1988. A win over James Kinchen was the highlight because the next time Roldan stepped up in class to fight a true top-level fighter (for the vacant WBC strap) he was stopped in short order by Tommy Hearns. Hearns had decided before the fight that his best chance was to out-brute the brute, and as such went after Roldan in a way even Hagler had been reluctant to attempt, knocking Roldan down four times on the way to a fourth-round win.

He returned to Vegas just over a year later to contest the IBF middleweight belt with Michael Nunn. Roldan was knocked over again in the first round, and had lost six out of seven rounds on two judges' cards before the stoppage came. He retired with a respectable record of 67(47)-5-2 saying he was, "Proud to be remembered as the only man who ever saw Marvin Hagler get a count."

Hagler v Hamsho II

AFTER BEING sliced and diced in his 1981 encounter against Hagler, Mustafa Hamsho stayed away from the ring for a five-month period in order to let his physical wounds, which required 55 stitches, and his mental wounds heal.

The 'Syrian Buzzsaw', as he chose to be nicknamed, intended to honour a promise that he had made to his trainer Paddy Flood. After the fight, he had told him, "That bum couldn't beat you. You beat yourself." Hamsho told his friend, "There will be a next time."

When he did return, he had a renewed zeal which swept him past Curtis Parker, and then Gil Rosario in three compelling rounds. When he decisioned the highly regarded New Jersey protege Bobby Czyz, who had won his first 20 bouts, Hamsho felt that he was within striking distance of renewing hostilities with the Brockton powerhouse.

In March 1983, tragedy struck. Hamsho was left bereft when Flood, aged 46, died of a sudden brain haemorrhage. Three weeks later, his trainer Tony Canzi passed away and Hamsho considered retirement. Flood's widow, Jean, persuaded him to resist, reminding him, "You were a great team. In fact, you still are a great team and you can win the championship." She reminded the fighter of her late husband's rallying cry, "As Paddy would say, 'Up the Irish and the Syrians'."

Six months later, Hamsho agreed to fight Wilfred Benitez in Las Vegas.

After he beat the three-time world champion, he told ringside reporters, "Paddy was with me. In my imagination I saw him in front of me, pushing me, saying, 'This bum. Don't let him out of the corner.'"

This surprise victory elevated him to the position of Hagler's next mandatory challenger in a fight that was originally scheduled for Monte Carlo in June before being switched to New York in October 1984 on a bill that featured Mike McCallum and Sean Mannion facing each other for the vacant WBA junior middleweight title. Within a week of the announcement, 16,000 fans snapped up tickets to see Hagler's first foray in the city and the first middleweight title fight to be held there since 1975.

Hagler got ready for Hamsho in his typical Spartan style in Provincetown and didn't meet with the New York media until the day before the fight, when he announced, "I'm feeling especially mean." That condition was brought on by his acute antipathy for Hamsho, who had incurred Hagler's ire in escalating stages. First Hamsho said the Duran fight proved, "Hagler is a coward, he has no heart." The Roldan fight, Hamsho added, taught him that Hagler "knows how to thumb". Retorted Hagler, "Hamsho was better off when he didn't speak English."

Hamsho wasn't intimidated. Al Silvani, his trainer, claimed that lessons had been learnt after his loss to the champion and insisted that his fighter would "depend on a new style" that they had been working on for two years. In the past Hamsho's bullish tactics patented by Jake LaMotta, and featuring the liberal use of head butts and forearms, had given way to one that featured Hamsho "bobbing and weaving" and throwing hooks to Hagler's body.

The Hagler camp was suitably unimpressed. Dropping one style for another works "for as long as it takes to feel leather bop the cranium", Pat Petronelli dismissed. "Then he'll be his old self again."

Hagler was even more direct. "All he'll be doing is bobbing and weaving right into my left hook," Hagler said. "Once I've finished with an opponent, he ain't never the same again. Hamsho ain't right in the head to be talking the way he is."

For added inspiration, Hamsho revealed that he had a green and white robe made by Flood's widow, Jean, and the knowledge that the fight would be televised in Syria, which he left ten years ago.

Hagler was particularly dismissive of Hamsho's veneration to his trainer, "He can't keep crying Paddy Flood every time he enters the ring." He declared, "I do not want to see the man's face again after this fight. I do not want to hear his name ever again. I am here to eliminate him."

In the week before the fight, the issue of who will judge the two title bouts created a controversy which shifted the focus from the fighters to the list of possible officials, including several women.

John Branca, chairman of the New York State Boxing Commission, named Carol Castellano, who had judged 18 world title bouts, Eva Shain, who had worked 14 and Carol Polis who had adjudged eight as the three likely judges for the Hagler-Hamsho bout. This prompted a furious reaction from an irate Goody Petronelli, speaking on behalf of his charge, who declared, "There will be no fight. This is a man's game. The two title bouts should be judged by men."

"I think they are very qualified," claimed Branca, reminding him that they were all verified by the WBA and had officiated world championship bouts before. Petronelli was unmoved. "We're not buying that. The top bouts should be judged by men."

Hamsho recognised an opportunity to ingratiate himself to the possible officials and immediately issued a statement saying, "I think Hagler is plain worried, and sex should have no place in the appointment of judges."

At the rules meeting two days before the fight, Branca admitted that they "were still having challenges on the officials, but we usually don't announce who they are until the time of the fight anyway. In order to preserve the integrity of the game, we will not announce who they are until tomorrow. This is being done to avoid unnecessary pressure on so many people."

Pat Petronelli called Branca and informed him that Hagler, who was still in Boston, would not come to New York until he knew the names of the judges. Eventually, Branca conceded and named two men, Harold Lederman and Vincent Rainone, along with Eva Shain as the officials and Arthur Mercante as non-scoring referee.

At the final press conference before the fight, Hagler held two fists high above his head and said, "As far as the judges are concerned, I bring mine with me wherever I go. Their names are 'K' and 'O'. All I have in mind is destruct and destroy. Everybody wants to see blood. Everybody wants to see a KO, and that's my middle name."

The crowd gave Hamsho his first indication that it was not going to be his night when the two large Syrian flags that accompanied him into the ring aroused scattered booing, as did the playing of the Syrian national anthem. It is a long anthem. The crowd, tired of watching Mike McCallum beat Sean Mannion over 15 rounds, was on a short fuse. It booed until the anthem was aborted.

"Hamsho made a couple of dreadful mistakes in New York," reflected Hagler. "The first was showing up for a rematch. The second was making me mad." Lunging at Hagler from the opening bell, Hamsho committed a variety of fouls that appeared to be invisible to Mercante, although Hagler took great pains to point them out. Rubbing a glove over his shaven skull, the champion complained first that Hamsho was holding and hitting. Late in the round, he protested that the challenger was attempting to butt him.

Interspersed in the lecture were some piston-like jabs by way of punctuation. One of them opened a cut beneath Hamsho's left eye, on the bridge of his nose. At the round's end, which judges Eva Shain and Vinnie Rainone gave to Hamsho, Hagler did not return immediately to his corner. Instead, he stood in mid-ring and delivered an arm-waving lecture on the improprieties of boxing, "You want to play dirty, I'll show you how to play dirty. I'll hurt you."

The 11 rounds that the two men had shared three years earlier had convinced Hagler to anoint Hamsho as the "roughest and dirtiest fighter" in the middleweight division and he had vowed to dispense with the Brooklyn-based challenger faster this time. Now he may have issuing a quote from the *Fighter's Handbook of Tough Things to Say*, but Hamsho's approach quickly forced him to make good on his commitment. Back in the corner, Hagler notified Goody Petronelli that he was going to knock Hamsho out. "It sounded like a good idea to me," the trainer agreed.

"After he butted me, I decided these would be my judges," Hagler said, holding up his hands. "This is 'K' [he brandished his right hand] and this is 'O'. And 'O' sets up 'K' so I can put him away."

It took Hagler another round to collect his emotions and put punches together with his usual efficiency. Hamsho was bobbing and weaving, but a seemingly possessed Hagler was finding him with laser-like accuracy.

"Forty or so years ago, when the middleweight division was producing boxing's sweetest scientists, Marvelous Marvin Hagler's brand of controlled mayhem undoubtedly would have fired up the cognoscenti at New York's old Madison Square Garden," admired boxing historian George Kimball. "Hagler may not have been blessed with opponents or settings conducive to high artistry, but when he went to work on Hamsho in the second round, he was like a warrior from the golden era."

In the third round, Hamsho's desperate use of the head finally invoked a warning from the referee. Hagler remained calm and moved swiftly around the ring, baffling Hamsho with his combinations, thrown like lightning rods. He delivered two right hooks which put Hamsho down – for the first time in his 43-fight career – midway through the third. He went down as though shot. The force of the blow was so great that Hamsho sprained his ankle as he fell.

Somehow, he was up as Mercante's count reached eight and Hagler went back on the attack. Hamsho did all he could to hug and hold on. Hagler wheeled him into a neutral corner and patiently set him up for a sweeping, leaping, finishing right that looked like a mirror image of the catapult left hook employed by one of Hagler's idols, Floyd Patterson.

The ceasefire came with two minutes and 31 seconds gone in the third of the scheduled 15 rounds. It came with Al Certo standing over his fallen warrior, making the formality of a ten count by Arthur Mercante unnecessary.

The arena became Marvin's Garden for the night, a testimony to his four-year monopoly of a division. The adulation he received from the 16,000 fans, who had paid up to $100 for a seat, offset the irritation of the WBC stripping him of its version of the title because the fight had been scheduled for 15 rounds instead of the WBC-sanctioned 12.

It persuaded the oft-slighted Hagler to call the evening "the highlight of my career".

At ringside for the fight, Thomas Hearns, resplendent in a tuxedo, gold HIT MAN medallion and high-tech sunglasses that looked suitable for viewing a 3D movie, was besieged by autograph seekers. He was unimpressed by the win. "Marvin didn't show me anything new," said Hearns after the bout. "I can beat him any way he wants to fight. There was nothing for me to be concerned about other than Marvin winning the fight. He made me very happy."

For good reason. Promoter Bob Arum had been hustling to put together a $10m package that would make a Hagler-Hearns bout the richest middleweight fight of all time. The stumbling block was that the Hearns camp insisted that the purse be split 50-50; Hagler disagreed and demanded 55 per cent.

Hagler got $1.4m for beating Hamsho, "about as much as he could hope to make against anyone but Hearns" according to Arum. Hamsho got $300,000. Besides the money from a Hearns fight, Hagler had also set his sights on Carlos Monzon's record of 14 middleweight championship defences.

Hearns's manager, Emanuel Steward, contended that while Hagler deserves to be considered one of the all-time great middleweight champions, he was a fighter on the decline. "Anyone with any speed will now give Marvin trouble," Steward said. "Marvin doesn't respond to punches as fast.

"He was getting hit by short-armed, slow little Hamsho. Little Duran hit him with rights. Roldan hit him. Think what Thomas will hit him with. I think it will be a short night."

Not surprisingly, Goody Petronelli had a rebuttal. "Marvin is the most complete fighter in boxing today," Petronelli said, "and he has more guns now than he ever had. Hearns doesn't have Marvin's chin, his durability or his experience. As for Duran, he was in for a last payday against Hearns. I think Hearns needs a little more encouragement before he gets in the ring. When he's ready, we'll see who's king of the hill."

The Marvelous One
v The Hit Man

B ACK IN the early months of 1982, Bob Arum had convened a meeting at which Steve Wainwright, Marvin Hagler's lawyer, and Emanuel Steward were present. The purpose was to agree a unique three-fight contract which would see Hagler fight three middleweights from Steward's Kronk gymnasium. First of all, the undisputed world middleweight champion would face the all-action Mickey Goodwin. Next he would take on William 'Caveman' Lee. Finally he would pitch himself against Thomas Hearns in the main fight of the trilogy.

After Hagler clobbered the Caveman in less than a round, the rescheduled fight against Goodwin was complicated by the fact that the Kronk fighter struggled to recover from his injured hand, so Steward, Arum and Wainwright elected to go straight to the eagerly anticipated match-up with Hearns on 24 May in Windsor, Ontario. Despite the hype, the fight did not take place, to the frustration of both combatants, who spent the next three years facing a variety of opponents yet still demanding it.

Hagler made no secret, however, of the fact that Hearns occupied second place on his personal hit list behind Ray Leonard, who had teased the brooding champion before announcing his retirement in 1982, then re-emerging in 1984 to fight the limited journeyman Kevin Howard, who succeeded in knocking the showman down before he was halted in the ninth round. This lacklustre showing immediately prompted a return to retirement and caused Hagler to revise his sights and elevate Thomas Hearns to the top of his list of targets.

Hearns had rebuilt his stellar reputation after the loss to Sugar Ray Leonard and had recently dispatched Fred Hutchins and Roberto Duran inside three and two rounds respectively to defend his light-middleweight crown. The anticipation among the boxing fraternity was huge.

The official announcement that Marvin Hagler and Thomas Hearns would finally meet was made in December 1984 at the same Waldorf Astoria Hotel in New York which had been used two years previously to promote the same fight. As the sole promoter, Bob Arum oversaw the event and watched both fighters guardedly greet each other. Arum announced that both men would earn in excess of $5m. In fact, Hagler had won his first fight at the negotiating table and received $5.7m to Hearns's $5.4m purse.

In the New Year, the three central figures embarked on what Hagler dubbed the "magical mystery tour" as they visited 22 cities in just two weeks to promote their clash. The fighters insisted on travelling in separate corporate jets and would only meet at the press conferences.

Caesars Palace provided a state-of-the-art Gulfstream G-11, which Hagler described as a "flying hotel suite". He was accompanied by the Petronelli brothers and Bob Halloran, a former sports broadcaster now working as an executive with Caesars World. Arum also leased a second jet, a Falcon, which was slightly less luxurious. In order to satisfy the demands of the two egocentric warriors, it was agreed that Hagler would use the Gulfstream whenever the parties were flying west but they would switch planes when flying back.

During the hectic schedule, there was a three-day stop-over in Las Vegas,where the commercials for the fight were filmed. One image required Hearns and Hagler to meet head-to-head over a poker table and for the last time before they would meet, both men appeared to enjoy each other's company. "At one point, they were both straining to keep from laughing," recounted Joe Carnicelli, who was a former executive sports editor for the United Press International in New York before he established a sporting public relations company, which was employed by Top Rank to represent Hagler for the fight.

The evening before both fighters were scheduled to return to their bases, Carnicelli received an apologetic phone call from Pat Petronelli. "Joe, I know we are supposed to switch planes on Monday but Marvin has been pleased with the aircraft we have used," he said. "Marvin has looked at the plane which Hearns has been using and he's not going to use that one. In fact," Petronelli paused, "if Bob Arum makes us switch planes, Marvin is going home and the tour is over."

Carnicelli said, "Initially, I thought it was a joke. It would have been typical of Pat to do that. I slowly realised he was serious when he asked, 'Can you book us first-class tickets back to Boston because I have a feeling that we're going home?'"

Arum's reaction, upon hearing of the threat was not, according to Carnicelli's diplomatic phrasing, "What one would expect from a Harvard-educated Talmudic scholar." When he explained the situation to Emanuel Steward, he told Arum that Hearns would follow suit if he wasn't granted access to the same jet that Hagler had used. This impasse required Arum to lease an identical plane, so that both boxers could have identical modes of transport for the remainder of the tour.

Although neither fighter claimed to be a polished public speaker, Hearns, along with the rest of the Kronk boxing team, had received some tuition in speaking and elocution from Steward's resident PR adviser Jackie Kallen. A former entertainment journalist, Kallen had Hearns tutored to maintain eye contact with interviewees, to smile a lot and to avoid saying "man" all the time. She also taught Hearns to pause and digest questions fired at him before answering. This was evident in press conferences, where Hearns would now begin every response with the words, "Well, basically..." in order to buy himself some extra thinking time. "I think," supposed Boston sports writer Leigh Montville, "Jackie Kallen must have told him, 'Tommy, every time you want to say 'motherfucker', stop yourself. Then say, 'Well basically...'."

Despite this tutoring, Hearns still succeeded in angering Hagler every time he opened his mouth, with what Hagler claimed were blatant statements of disrespect towards him. Hagler's antipathy towards his challenger grew as every word he uttered about the fight built up a well of animosity between them.

Hagler's voice dripped with sarcasm when he recounted the failed fight of 1982. He told the press that Hearns was offered $2m for the fight but "complained about his little baby pinkie". He couldn't disguise the sneer of disgust when he asked Hearns, "Have you any idea how many people would have given a million dollars for that little pinkie? They'd have cut the thing off."

Steward tried to take the sting out of the simmering enmity by claiming, "Tommy's trash-talking is strictly business to increase the pay-per-view figures. People must understand just how out of character it is for Tommy to do that." This cut little ice with his shaven-headed rival, who sneered, "This tour has done me good. I may have had a little respect for Tommy Hearns before I spent time with him but now I only hate his ass." He promised to exact his retribution in the ring, "I'm going to do to him what I did to Alan Minter. He had that same kind of attitude."

Inevitably, the internecine politics of boxing attempted to intervene in the match-up. When Hagler's Madison Square Garden defence against Mustafa Hamsho was slated for 15 rounds, the WBC stripped him of his middleweight title. Hagler took the issue to court, where a federal judge ordered Jose Sulaiman to restore his championship.

Sulaiman opted for a new tactic and threatened to strip Hearns of the 154-pound title he had held since capturing a majority decision over Benitez in 1982. Officially, the WBC reasoned that Hearns couldn't box Hagler without first facing its top-rated challenger, John 'The Beast' Mugabi. Unofficially, Sulaiman let it be known that he would grant special dispensation on this matter, provided Hagler-Hearns was scheduled for 12 rounds and not 15.

While publicly expressing his respect for the traditional 15-round distance, Emanuel Steward actually preferred the shorter limit, which he figured would be to his man's advantage. However, the decision to lean on Hearns produced its desired effect. Rather than face another delay, which the Hearns-Mugabi fight would have entailed, Hagler reluctantly acceded on the issue and agreed that the fight would be the second one of his reign to be scheduled for 12 rounds.

Hagler ignored the wranglings and planned to stick to the training regime he had employed for his previous 25 fights, isolating himself away in Provincetown before moving to Palm Springs a month before the fight. Goody Petronelli managed to convince him to alter this plan and head straight to the Californian desert, where the Americana Hotel offered him the run of their premises and would allow him to adapt to the searing heat.

Although he agreed to a change of location, he maintained the same iron will and steely determination that had kept him at the top of his division. He sparred with Bobby 'Boogaloo' Watts and Jerry Holly, both tall, rangy fighters like Hearns. The Petronellis had also lined up a common foe to both fighters, Marcus Geraldo. When he failed to show, Larry Davis was brought in. He had to leave the camp after the first day of sparring when Hagler burst his eardrum with a left hook.

Hagler paid tribute to the quality of his sparring partners. "Bobby might have been a champion himself if I hadn't been there," he said. "He's smart. He knows who I am fighting. He'll lay against the ropes, throw overhand rights and hooks to the body, fight in spurts, do all the things Hearns is likely to do.

"And the other kid – Holly – watch him," he warned. "He's a younger, taller, bigger version of Thomas Hearns, plus he has got something Tommy don't have. He's got guts."

Hagler also based himself at Johnny Tocco's Ringside gym, a shabby, downbeat location which he claimed suited his philosophy. "This kind of place is where my roots are. It is the kind of gym where I started and where I belong. I don't believe in all that Rocky Balboa, rags-to-riches crap. My life doesn't change just because I am successful. You will never see me out there showboating, putting on a show for everyone, acting real cute and saying what you want to hear."

"He outlined his plans to cope with Hearns, a man whose lifestyle was in contrast to his own, and insisted that there would be no need to rely on any judges' scorecards. "I've brought my own judges," he said and held up both his fists.

One afternoon in Palm Springs, Hagler and the Petronelli brothers went for a walk around a nearby golf course. When they discovered a small grove of citrus trees, bursting with fresh fruit, Hagler couldn't resist.

"If I had ever thought about it, I knew oranges grew on trees," the child of the city streets said, "but here was all this fresh fruit that nobody had ever touched before."

He proceeded to scramble up into the trees and began filling up a sack with fruit. At that moment, a golf cart came puttering along. One of the occupants was Palm Springs' most famous resident, Bob Hope.

"He couldn't believe it," said Hagler. "Bob said, 'Marvin, what you doin' up there?' and I said, 'I'm just picking me some oranges, Bob. That alright?'" Hope, who had enjoyed a brief boxing career under the name Packy East, knew better than to argue. "Next thing you know, he invited me and Pat and Goody over to his house."

This brief flirtation with celebrity didn't distract Hagler, who ran a minimum of six miles every morning and then endured non-stop two-hour training sessions. He was leading his usual Spartan life and was all business in the training ring. "I'm not here to sign autographs or make appearances," he said. "In fact, I've heard people comment that I'm the hardest worker of any of the champions who've ever trained at this place."

In the final month before combat, Hagler spent much of his time between training sessions deep in seclusion, thinking about Hearns.

"Tommy is a dangerous opponent, and he's going to test me, but I know deep down in my soul that this man cannot whip me," said Hagler. "The thing is, I've been shook up, but I've never been hurt. Tony Sibson shook me up with a left hook I still remember. Even Roldan hit me with a couple of good shots, but that's where the conditioning pays off. I've been able to absorb those kinds of shots. But Hearns has been stopped and I ain't been stopped." He paused to enjoy the next line, knowing that it would sow a seed of doubt inside Hearns's mind, "I know he can go, but he don't know if I can go. That's what's going to be worrying him."

Hearns took up hammering his opponents when he turned pro in 1977, after a ten-year amateur career as a pure boxer. The rangy challenger punched with enough leverage to have knocked out 34 of his 41 pro opponents. He won the WBA welterweight title from Pipino Cuevas, in 1980, then lost that crown to Sugar Ray Leonard on a 14th-round TKO the following year. In December 1982 he won the WBC junior middleweight crown from Wilfred Benitez, and he continued to hold that as a hedge should he lose to Hagler. He was attempting to become the second 154-pound champion to win a 160-pound title (Nino Benvenuti was the first) but the Hit Man's credentials as a full-blown middleweight were regarded as questionable.

Hearns had fought five times as a middleweight. Three of his opponents – Mike Colbert, Ernie Singletary and Murray Sutherland – had all gone the distance and Jeff McCracken was still on his feet when the fight was stopped in the eighth. The only knockout had come against the hapless Marcos Geraldo, in a fight even Emanuel Steward called "an embarrassment".

"Usually a guy moving up in weight loses some of his punching power," said Goody Petronelli. "I don't think I've giving away any secrets by saying Hearns has had that trouble too."

Hearns chose to base his camp in Florida before moving to Las Vegas in the final few weeks. Most of his sparring was with a young middleweight named Vinnie Mayes, who supplemented his own boxing earnings with the daily fee of

$100 and brought his rugged style to bear. Emanuel Steward instructed Mayes to "let the tiger out of the cage" and he laced Hearns with power-packed body punches for round after round. Apart from avoiding Mayes's swings, Steward claimed that one of their biggest challenges was avoiding the number of people who tried to offer help and advice.

"You wouldn't believe the kind of people who are calling," he said. "They include voodoo doctors, an old man who wants to teach Thomas a special punch he claims to have patented in the 1920s, another who has offered a special mixture to soak his hands in, masseurs who believe they hold the key to unleashing his power, hypnotists and nutrition experts."

On relocating to Vegas, Hearns trained in Ballroom Four of Caesars Palace, a setting that was in stark contrast to the sparse surroundings of Hagler's chosen base camp. His routine also offered a contrast with his menacing foe. After starting with some light punching on the speedball, he engaged in sparring with Steward, who boxed in a southpaw style to imitate Hagler and allowed Hearns to aim punches at his open palms. Occasionally, Steward would lunge at Hearns and then sprawl forward to leave the impression that he had just attempted a wild swing and nailed nothing but air.

Occasionally, he sparred with southpaw middleweights Cecil Pettigrew and Brian Muller and a Kansas City-based light-heavyweight named Charles 'Hollywood' Henderson, while Gino Linder, a support member of the team, helped out with a drill designed to strengthen his midsection that involved Linder hitting Hearns repeatedly in the stomach with a medicine ball.

"I think the fight could be over very early because of Tommy's speed and punching power," Steward mused. "He's a much faster puncher than Marvin. However, should Hagler remain standing for the fourth round bell and beyond, it will come in the late rounds. At his age and with over 60 fights in his legs, Hagler can't handle the speed of a young man in the late rounds."

Steward claimed that he knew Hagler's plan of attack. "He must get to Tommy's body to prevail," he said. "That's everyone's strategy, and we know how to handle it." He dismissed Hagler's impressive roll-call of wins with a dismissive shrug. "Hearns has been meeting Class A fighters for years, such as Cuevas, Benitez, Leonard and Duran. Hagler has never been in against such quality." He conceded, "The only Class A fighter on his record was an overstuffed Duran, who still gave him plenty of problems."

Six days before the fight, Hearns halted his sparring. "We've learned from some of the mistakes we made with the Leonard fight," explained Steward. "We trained a little too hard for Leonard but we've learned to adjust."

Hagler continued to train behind closed doors. He explained that his decision was not a cloak-and-dagger operation. "We've not got any secrets," he said. "It's just that we're trying to be serious about business. Over at Caesars, every time you fart it winds up on television, and when the corner's trying to tell you something there's always a microphone stuck in your face."

ABC's *Good Morning, America* was in town, with plans to originate its programming from a remote location set up in the outdoor ring at Caesars on fight day and the day after, airing profiles of Hagler and Hearns, with David Hartman interviewing Goody Petronelli and Emanuel Steward on the morning of the fight.

The 89-year-old comedian George Burns was interviewed on the show and his indecision about the fight's conclusion mirrored the odds which had vacillated between one man and the other. "Hagler and Hearns are both tough," said the man who once played God. "I could pick a winner, but I wouldn't want the other one to get mad at me. I may be old, but I want to get older."

On the evening of Monday 15 April 1985, a strong wind blew through the tennis courts of Caesars Palace, where the ring had been assembled for the big fight. There were concerns that a storm was brewing and the 15,000 fans inside the arena hoped that the gathering cloud didn't indicate rain; they hoped instead for clouds of war. Bob Arum's promotional team had dubbed this meeting simply as "The War" and the atmosphere was charged by the time that Hearns, wearing a red robe with yellow trim over his customary gold trunks with his name etched along his waistband in red and the Kronk name along the bottom, had marched into the arena with the strains of 'Hail To The Victor', the Michigan University fight song announcing his arrival. As the challenger, he was obliged to enter the ring first and, as he dispensed with his robe, he looked in splendid physical condition and primed for action.

Customarily, the champion often uses his status as a final psychological ploy and keeps his opponent waiting for as long as possible before deciding to arrive in the ring. Hagler was too eager to taste conflict to engage in this kind of point-scoring. While he had sat sequestered in his dressing room, he could hear the whoops and hollers from Hearns's quarters down the hall, where it seemed as if the entire Kronk gym had gathered. "'That's alright,' Marvin told me," recalled Pat Petronelli, "'He can't take them all into the ring with him. It's just going to be me and him.'"

As soon as Hearns had entered, John Philip Sousa's patriotic anthem 'Stars And Stripes Forever' preceded his march into battle. When he stripped from his royal blue robe, his whole body and head gleamed with sweat under the ring's arc lights. He had thoroughly warmed up in the dressing room and was ready for a quick start. Hagler did not avert his gaze from Hearns throughout the preliminaries, including Doc Severinsen's trumpeted version of 'The Star Spangled Banner'. Even as Severinsen's trumpet notes were echoing through the stadium, Billy Hearns, Thomas's younger brother, taunted Hagler from across the ring. "I saw him," recalled Hagler later. "I was thinking right then, 'All you're gonna do is get your brother's ass kicked.'"

When referee Richard Steele dispensed his final instruct-ions, Hagler's beady eyes remained locked on Hearns. As the two physically splendid fighters faced each other mid-ring, Hagler snarled, "You better hope I don't bleed. It only makes me meaner."

When the bell signalled an opening to the hostilities, both men flew from their corners like dogs let loose from a leash. They eschewed any "feeling out" period and instead unloaded on each other with a wild abandon rarely seen in a boxing ring before. Within the first ten seconds, it had already become apparent that the judges' opinions weren't going to matter.

Hagler, usually the more cautious starter, opened hostilities with a looping southpaw right that Hearns ducked. They threw punches at each other as if they had only been granted a few seconds to do so and the dull thud of leather could be heard as the punches slammed into head and body. The crowd, initially awed into silence by the level of menace and commitment, exploded in a frenzy of undiluted excitement, as each fighter took turns to rock the other.

Emanuel Steward was similarly rocked by the level of intensity. He implored Hearns, "Just box him. Stick and move. Don't fight with him," but his pleas were in vain. Midway through this opening salvo, Hagler sustained a deep cut on his forehead, just above his right eye which caused blood to flow down his face like a running tap. The injury, which eventually required four stitches, was caused when he smashed into Hearns's shoulder in his eagerness to attack him. The crowd's bloodlust was heightened further and their noise made it impossible for both men to hear the bell chiming to signal the end of what *The Ring* later termed "the greatest round in boxing history".

HBO commentator Barry Tompkins was breathless with excitement. "This may be the most brutal, even round you've ever seen in boxing," he declared. Hagler had signalled his malevolent intent. "I wanted him to know who was the boss from the opening bell," he later said. "I knew I could take everything he had. I was sorry to see the round end as I hated to give Tommy a chance to go back to his corner and recover."

The fight doctor, Donald Romeo, went straight to Hagler's corner to examine the cut and the bruising which had started to swell beneath his eye. Goody Petronelli assured him that the cut could be dealt with and he returned to his seat. The real drama, however, was taking place opposite him. When Hearns retreated to his stool, he said, "My hand's gone. It's broken." This would not be mentioned by either the fighter or his camp in the aftermath. Instead, Steward attempted to calm him and beseeched him to remember their game plan of frustrating Hagler from long range. Goody Petronelli, meanwhile, was imploring his own charge not to change a thing apart from keeping his hands a little higher. "Don't change," he told the champion. "Just keep your hands up a little higher. Don't worry about the cut. Just keep charging and keep the pressure up." "Okay," Hagler responded. "I won't worry about the cut. If you go to war, you're going to get wounded."

Before the spectators had time to get their breath back, the bell sounded. Hearns was already off his stool and met

Hagler two-thirds of the way across the ring. Hagler again threw the first shot, a left cross, before Hearns started moving and spearing his opponent with his long left lead. Rather than quell the level of ferocity, the minute-long break had served to stoke it further and they greeted each other with an immediate exchange of heavy punches. Hagler, bleeding profusely, caught Hearns with a terrific right hand and Hearns replied with an equally venomous left, causing the blood from Hagler to splash into his own face. There were times in the fight when he waded in with such a two-fisted attack, it was impossible to tell which hand he was leading with.

"Box, Tommy! Box!" implored Steward.

"It's pretty tough to box when you're being attacked by a swarm of bees!" said Ralph Citro, Hearns's cuts man.

Hearns appeared to sense that a stoppage was imminent and upped the tempo further still, catching the champion with a series of vicious punches. One scything left ripped open a second cut under Hagler's right eye and made his face resemble a grotesque mask.

Hagler knew that his hard-earned crown was beginning to slip. He responded with a primal, untamed fury and made no pretence of finesse or tried to set his man up. Instead he threw a tidal wave of punches at Hearns in a bid to overwhelm him. Hearns refused to yield and fired back to Hagler's head and body but Hagler just ploughed through and continued to beat away.

The ferocity of the encounter threatened to overshadow the sheer range and quality of punches which were delivered by both men. Richard Steele continued to look closely at the injuries which turned Hagler's face scarlet and ringside commentators began to speculate that they would force him to terminate the contest. A deranged-looking Hagler ended the round by catching Hearns with a series of right hands which caused his knees to buckle, and as the bell sounded he turned to his corner on rubbery legs. Hagler looked back with utter disdain.

"This cut isn't bad, but it's bleeding a lot," said Petronelli, as he worked on Hagler's forehead. "Let's not take any chances. Take him out this round."

"He's ready to go," said Hagler, spitting a mouthful of water into a bucket. "He's not going to hurt me with that right hand. I took his best, and now I'm going to knock him out."

When they emerged for the third round, Hearns appeared to have taken heed of his corner's instructions and opened up with his snaking jab. Hagler was relentless and continued to bob and weave, never taking a backward step. Petronelli had been unable to stem the flow of blood and had only cleaned the cuts, which had continued to bleed profusely. Richard Steele halted the fight to call Dr Romeo into the ring to check whether the cuts were significant enough to stop the contest. He asked Hagler if he could see through the blood coming from his forehead. Hagler answered in the affirmative and would later claim that he sarcastically replied, "Well, I ain't missing him, am I?" This was a line that was almost certainly supplied after the fight. Tapes of the doctor's visit to his corner suggest that if Hagler did utter that now classic line, he was as great a ventriloquist as a pugilist. The doctor spoke to Steele and allowed the fight to continue.

Hagler knew that it was now or never. He dashed at Hearns and hit him with a right hook which sent him reeling backwards. Hearns's legs went into spasms and Hagler drilled home even more spiteful punches, eventually toppling his challenger to the canvas. Hearns dug deep into his reservoir of courage and clambered back to his feet before the count ended. When Richard Steele, who later said, "I've been a referee for 15 years and have never seen such intensity in a ring," assessed his capacity to defend himself further, he looked into the dead eyes staring back and threw his arms around the beaten warrior to signal the fight's conclusion. The most electrifying eight minutes of mayhem ever seen in a ring were over.

While Hagler, his face drenched in a mask of blood, cavorted wildly to celebrate his eleventh successful champ-ionship defence, some ringside observers were upset to witness the brave but beaten challenger being held up by one of his entourage like a baby and carried back to his corner. It was several minutes before he could stand on his own two feet and hear the official announcement of one of the sport's truly epic encounters.

Hagler delivered his immediate assessment in the same direct manner he had conducted the fight. "It was the only way to fight a guy like Thomas Hearns," he said. "I had to go inside and work him. I told you I'd cut him down like a tree and I did just that."

When he had opportunity to reflect, he was far more magnanimous: "I want to give Tommy all the credit in the world. He put up an excellent fight. He came out the only way he could if he wanted to take something away from a champion."

Emanuel Steward blamed the unprecedented intensity of the contest, "It was a more physical fight than we wanted and before the first round had ended, I sensed trouble ahead. They fought a 12-round fight in eight minutes and it was like starting a marathon with a sprint." He later cited the fact that Hearns had a massage prior to the fight, which weakened his legs and prompted such an aggressive opening salvo.

Other observers suggested that Hearns should retire with a reputation as a great fighter who fell just short of being classed among the greatest. Steward vowed to talk to his charge when they returned to Detroit. "I'm proud of him. He fought a great, great fight," he said.

Goody Petronelli treated with disdain talk of the loser retiring; he knew just how much Hearns had to offer the sport. "Hearns still has a beautiful future but maybe not as a fully-fledged middleweight," said Petronelli. "He has been a fabulously destructive welterweight but is not the same puncher at middleweight."

In the sanctuary of his dressing room, Hearns winced in pain as his right glove was gently removed. Dr Fred Lewerenz, the medical adviser for the Kronk boxing team, suggested that Hearns had fractured his hand. "The injury is to the bone leading from the knuckle of his finger," said Dr Lewerenz, and insisted that he have an immediate x-ray. Despite his agony, Hearns refused to mention his injury, sustained in the first round, during his post-fight interviews. He later said that he did not want to take anything away from Hagler.

Later, Hearns went into Hagler's dressing room where the trash talking of the last few months was quickly forgotten. "You've got a lot of class coming in here," Hagler told him. "We made a lot of money, but we gave them a good show," Hearns said. "Tell you what. You move up and fight the light heavies, and I'll take care of the middleweights."

Hagler laughed. "Sure. So you can move up and have the middleweights? You move up," he said.

After receiving four stitches for the cut in his forehead, Hagler went to a party in the Augustus Room at Caesars. He spoke briefly to the celebrators. Then, with his wife, Bertha, he watched a video replay of the fight. After seeing the knockout for the fourth time, Hagler smiled and applauded his own handiwork. He looked at his watch. It was midnight. "Let's go," he said to Bertha. His work was done.

The day after the night before, Hagler surveyed his middleweight kingdom with the glow of satisfaction from his latest achievement clearly in evidence. "This fight was the pinnacle of my career," he announced, "It was a must-win for me." He felt that the ripples from his comprehensive trouncing of Hearns would finally earn what he had long sought, "Respect as a great world champion. This is a feeling that I wanted to have a long time ago," said the 30-year-old title-holder. "I wanted to gain respect and have the eyes of the world focused on me."

He dismissed the suggestions that he may move up the weight divisions. "I began my career at 160 pounds, and it will end there," he emphasised. "I'm a legitimate middleweight." He refused to rule out the possibility of facing Michael Spinks, the undisputed light-heavyweight champion, providing "that he comes down to my weight". He reiterated his desire to better Carlos Monzon's record of 14 successful middleweight title defences. "Then," he said, "I will retire in peace."

This ambition was enough for Bob Arum to begin plotting the next several moves of Hagler's career. "While Hagler will probably fight John Mugabi and James Shuler next, there will be a fight bigger than last night," suggested Arum. "It will be the last fight of Marvin's career, his attempt to break the record. His biggest test will be when he faces Donald 'The Cobra' Curry." The fact that Arum promoted both fighters was a happy coincidence.

Hagler laughed at his promoter's incessant hype and insisted that before he planned his next moves, he wanted a well-earned break. His final words were intended to remind any potential suitors of his continued hunger and malevolence, "I've worked so hard, I don't intend to let anyone else wear my crown."

The Penultimate Fight – The African Lion

JOHN MUGABI had been born in Kampala, Uganda, in March 1960 and was raised by his maintenance worker father Tameel and his mother, Onec, during the repressive regime of Idi Amin Dada. Jack Edwards, a retired tea planter from London, had run a boys' club in Kampala which placed an emphasis on boxing. The one boxer he produced, Cornelius Boza-Edwards (who took the name of his mentor out of gratitude), went on to win the WBC junior lightweight championship. Edwards, however, remembered Mugabi well: "I had watched the lad since he started coming to the club aged ten. He had been a real spitfire even then."

Edwards recalled that Mugabi had been adept at wriggling through the kitchen windows of colonial bigwigs known to be giving parties and stuffing himself with pâté de foie gras. "But he was good-hearted; every time, he would come out with a shirtful of delicacies for the other kids," Edwards said.

He turned to amateur boxing and proved particularly adept, acquiring an enviable record of 190 victories, including 126 early endings, and just five defeats. He had won the silver medal at the 1976 Junior World Championships, losing to Herol 'Bomber' Graham. His final loss came in the welterweight final of the 1980 Moscow Olympics where he first came to the attention of the mercurial Londoner,

194

Mickey Duff, the manager, matchmaker and promoter who virtually controlled boxing in Britain for much of the 1970s and 1980s, not always to the approval of a large section of the sports press and the public there.

Uncharacteristically, Duff came close to being cut out of the action when the young Mugabi first attracted his attention at the Olympics. Duff had caught one of his early bouts on TV. "I thought he was an animal," and was impressed enough to "call the BBC to see when they were showing his next fight. I followed him through to the end." In the bout for the gold medal, Mugabi lost on a dubious decision to Andres Aldama of Cuba, rated number one in the world.

Even as Duff was scrutinising Mugabi's Olympic bouts, so was a West German promoter, Wilfred Sauerland, and he got to Mugabi first. Eventually the two men worked out a deal, giving Sauerland and Duff equal promotional rights. As a result, Mugabi fought seven of his early professional bouts in places like Gelsenkirchen and Kiel, where, to Duff's outrage, he was billed as the 'Brown Bomber'. Having explained to the Germans that this title had already been pre-empted, Duff suggested 'The Beast', a name Duff's trainer, George Francis, came up with after working with Mugabi. "Pound for pound, I've never seen a man who hits harder," the veteran trainer opined.

Following those early fights in West Germany, Duff brought Mugabi to the US and settled him in Tampa. In the next three years, The Beast ate his way through a collection of respectable American middleweight contenders. In one early fight, Duff matched Mugabi against Curtis Ramsey, a solid opponent, on an Atlantic City card promoted by Don King.

"I had to fly back to England on business, so I left Mugabi in the hands of George Francis, and told George to ring me the minute the fight was over," said Duff. "George called to tell me John had knocked out Ramsey in the first round. He hit him so hard that it had knocked Ramsey and the referee, Larry Hazzard, right out of the ring and on to the press table."

Before Francis could end his call, Don King sequestered the phone to add the weight of his opinion. "Hey Mickey," said King over the transatlantic line, "I'm in! That is the meanest motherfucker I have ever seen in my life."

King continued, "I had a little talk with Mugabi after the fight and he says he wants to go with me, but of course I told him you and me were in this together."

"I let him get it all out," Duff said. "And then I said, 'Don, if that conversation took place, then you must be fluent in Swahili, because Mugabi doesn't speak a word of English.'"

Nevertheless, Mugabi proved to be a hit in Tampa. When he fought at Tampa's Egyptian Temple Shrine, the crowd treated him like a favourite son. At one Sunday lunch held in his honour, Mugabi marvelled at his transformation from petty thief to guest of honour. "When I was a baby," he laughed, "I must steal my dinners. But now John Mugabi walks in by the front door. Oh, I like this place better than home."

Mugabi's father was killed in a car accident in 1979, leaving his mother to care for John's five siblings. "His death was very hard on John," said Francis Ntege, his close friend. "John respects his mother very much for the way she supported the family after his father's death. He wants to help her through his boxing."

This intention was frequently made difficult by the immediate distractions of his adopted home. "I love to go to the malls, spend a little money, get some nice karate video, or a nice hat or a saxophone," he boasted.

This brought a groan from Duff, who knew what trouble can follow a simple Mugabi mall trip. "He has no real idea of cash," his manager said. "He'll ask, say, for $500, he'll take a cab to a store, buy a big cowboy hat, just leave his wallet on the counter and walk out. He gets robbed all the time, he says, though probably he's just spent it or lost it. I'll say, 'John, you've spent $30,000 or $40,000 in the last three months.' 'No,' he says. 'How could I have put all this money in my stomach? I did not eat it. You take all my money. I do not want to be a boxer anymore.'"

The big trouble broke out, however, when Mugabi periodically decided that what he wanted most in the world was a car. "He came into my office one day when Mickey was away," recalled Phil Alessi, who promoted Mugabi's fights in Tampa, "and asked me for $18,000, like right now, to buy a car. I explained to him, as I always do, that he needed a driver's licence. I told him he could have a limo and a chauffeur if he needed to go somewhere. 'No,' he said. 'You buy me my own car, then you put a chauffeur in it.'"

Mugabi freely confided his number one dream. "I want to drive real bad," he said. "I want to go around. In America it is too far to walk into town to buy some food. Also I would like to go to the beach and have some barby-chew and dive in the water." He was not unaware of his licence problem. "I did not go to school a lot," he said disarmingly. "I know the road signs, what they mean. But they tell me, go read the book, go read the book. But the book is in English, and it is too hard. I must have a car. I like Mercedes best. Not sports car but a car for a gentleman. Maybe somebody can bring me a licence from Uganda, and I can change it for an American one. I want to drive real bad."

Mugabi's increasing awareness of the world around him was a cause of frustration for his boxing mentor, Francis.

"Normally, with a title fight, you'll block out everything extraneous and go ahead. With John, that would be a miracle. He has days when he won't do this, won't do that. He just can't block out the world. Honest to God, I wish he was a horse. Then I could put blinkers on him."

Francis believed that Mugabi's spending habits stem partly from the endless bloodshed that he had witnessed in his country. "What is the use of saving money," he would ask his trainer, "when people die so quick?"

Mugabi remembered despotic President Idi Amin as a benefactor of his sport, though personally a terrifying figure. "Amin liked boxing," Mugabi recalled. "He come into the Lugogo gym in Kampala when I am a teen-sized boy, play with the speed bag. He say, 'I am heavyweight, come on, come on, nobody want to fight me?' He say to me, 'Hey you, put on the gloves.' He is real big and mean and my hair feel tight and funny. But he just pretend to jab at me, bim, bim, bim. He says, 'How is your programme? What, you got no money? I must go and check with my bank to see if there is money for you.' He laugh.

"He sent a team of us to Japan in his private jet. He buy us equipment. When I went to Zambia to fight I am sorry for the kids there. My opponent has no gloves but rags tied round his fists. But when Amin run away he take the money with him, and in Uganda now the kids have nothing."

When Mugabi returned from a trip to his homeland in 1985, he feared it might have been his last. "A little bit sometimes I hear from my mother," he said. "I would like to see her again face to face. But I cannot go because they may think I am a big enemy. They have terrible killings, terrible killings. If the soldiers come to your door, you know you are going to die, but first they make you load their truck with what you got. They think their life is big party that God has give them. Their eyes are red, like animals. They are the beasts, not me."

By August 1985, Mugabi's record stood at 25-0 and he had risen to number one in the WBA's world rankings. Not one of his opponents had lasted the distance. Arum had initially pencilled the fight in for November but after Hagler had ruptured a disc in his back and had his nose broken during a sparring session, it was re-scheduled for Monday 10 March at Caesars Palace, where the fight would be shown alongside Hearns's comeback fight against James Shuler.

It was shortly after Christmas that Mugabi and Francis left Tampa for Nogales, Arizona, to resume heavy training for the Hagler fight, and the change in geography caused a change in the fighter. "When we were first training for the Hagler fight we were at the Eden Roc hotel in Miami," Francis recalls. "I said then I would rather train John in Alcatraz. Well, this is a deluxe Alcatraz, with no people underfoot and perfect weather."

And there were no shopping binges, perhaps because of the lack of temptation. That tended to be limited to the Casa de Video, where Mugabi would pick up Bruce Lee cassettes, and to the clothing store, where he bought some cowboy gear to wear on an excursion to Tombstone. "They all buried there, all the John Waynes," Mugabi said in wide-eyed wonder. He fast-draws an imaginary six-shooter and with magisterial inaccuracy yells, "Make me a day!"

It was on his first Sunday morning in Arizona that Mugabi noticed a man in the open door of a church wearing a maroon sweat suit, the back of which identified the owner as belonging to the Nogales Boxing Club. When Mugabi and Francis followed the man into church, they saw him strip off his sweats and reveal clerical garb. Father Anthony Clark was from Davenport, Iowa, but on loan to Sacred Heart with a special responsibility for delinquent boys on both sides of the border. Father Tony, as the kids in Nogales called him, recognised Mugabi at once. "I was tongue-tied," he said, "but I went over to him after the service."

The priest's motive was straightforward. Father Tony, who had been a high school boxer himself at 145 pounds, used the sport, as many have before him, as a means of rescuing embryonic criminals from the streets. Nogales is a city split as neatly as a restaurant avocado between the state of Arizona and the Mexican state of Sonora. Turn your back on the US, the K Mart and the Roy Rogers and pass through the border post, and abruptly you're in the Third World and the poverty which dogs it, about which John Mugabi knew much first-hand.

For that reason, perhaps, the fighter, as soon as he was asked, agreed to climb into the back of Father Tony's battered pickup and head over the border to talk to the kids. "We spent a nice hour," Francis recalls. "John showed the boys some moves, and they loved him." That nice hour, though, almost led to a second postponement of the Hagler fight, because when Mugabi tried to get back into the US, he was denied entry.

His visa, which had run out, was back in Tampa with his lawyer, being renewed. The problem might have been solved with a phone call, but Father Tony got in the way as he was a defendant in the 'Sanctuary' trial, in which priests and nuns were accused of sheltering illegal immigrants – refugees, the defendants call them – from El Salvador. "Father Tony started arguing with the immigration authorities," Francis says, "and I had to tell him to back off. Then John got mad."

"I am angry," recalled Mugabi, "because I have not had my dinner yet. I say, 'I am John Mugabi and I have come to fight Marvin Hagler.' They say 'fuck you'. I tell them I am a real people and I do not speak lies. They say I am threatening them. Four more men came running out. I do not think they could have put me in the jail, but I am glad Duff is there to call the lawyers up out of their beds. These policemen want to keep us all night, but in three hours they let us go."

The evening left Mugabi with an enduring respect for the turbulent Father Tony and the fighter insisted that he wanted to be baptised as John Paul Mugabi.

"His whole attitude has changed. I don't have to push him anymore," marvelled Francis, who eventually joined in the instruction sessions himself and was baptised as a Catholic alongside Mugabi. "I was worried that his relationship with Father Tony would make him a meeker person. He is more aggressive than ever. He is convinced that God is on his side, and also that Hagler is a fool to fight him."

The knockout of Hearns had underlined Hagler's claim as one of the greatest middleweights of all time. His appeal had also been enhanced by several television commercials. Pizza Hut included the strap line, "Marvelous Marvin Hagler: Pizza with anything he wants." It helped make him a familiar face to viewers who had never seen him fight and escalate him among the handful of fighters who had the ability to attract fans regardless of who they were fighting. "Muhammad Ali and Sugar Ray Leonard are good examples of this," said Bob Arum. "The Mugabi fight will ascertain whether or not Marvin has that same level of popularity."

Lawyer Mike Trainer explained further, "Hard-core fight fans will always support a good match, but it is the 'fringe' fans, those who only turn out when a fight becomes a 'happening', who can transform a promotion depending on close-circuit and pay-per-view revenue into a gold mine. In many respects, the health of the boxing industry will be gauged by the number of fans willing to pay to witness Hagler defend his trio of belts against a man known as The Beast."

Mugabi did his best to generate public interest. Mickey Duff argued that Hagler's own defence was hardly total. "Everybody who has fought Hagler has hit him," said Duff. "If Mugabi catches him, he'll go." And he added, devoutly, "Please God." Mugabi himself saw no problems. "I was studying him a long time, but not now," he said. "I know how he fights. He is a slow fighter. I am hungry for my title. I beat him up."

Hagler, the 3/1 on favourite, promised that he would "feast on The Beast". At his pre-fight news conference, he said, "I realise that this man Mugabi's got a dream. I had my own dream once, but these things are not easy to come by. I can see him eyeing my clothes and checking out my jewellery, but I spent a long time in this game before I could even put food on the table."

When Cornelius Boza-Edwards, serving as Mugabi's interpreter, suggested that Hagler's time had come and gone, the 31-year-old champion snapped back, "You better be nice to me. You keep calling me an old man but you're only gonna make me meaner."

Mugabi, resplendent in his latest cowboy hat, stood up and punched a hole in a huge poster of Hagler situated nearby. It was intended to warn Hagler of his expected fate. Hagler watched with a cold detachment before saying, "Punching a hole in the picture isn't me, that picture isn't going to be in the ring with you, I am."

It had rained for much of the day and throughout the undercard, obliging the 15,000 in attendance to wear the plastic bags that had been issued to protect their expensive clothing. Hearns warmed them up when he opened up with one big right hand to the jaw, counting Shuler after just 73 seconds.

The Hit Man was buoyed by the victory and the $500,000 incentive bonus Arum had offered if he knocked out Shuler in six rounds or fewer. "Now I want to sit and watch Hagler win, because I have something to prove," Hearns said during the wait before the Mugabi bout. "The next time we fight will be totally different. I'm a different man than when I fought him the last time. I didn't have any legs then. Everybody has seen round one, round two and round three, but they haven't seen round four. And round four will be just as exciting."

Even as Hearns talked of the rematch, Mickey Duff was busy in Hagler's dressing room doing his best to derail the champion. Duff was screaming that Hagler had exceeded the legal limits in almost everything, including the size of his protective cup.

"Duff had Marvin tighter than a drum," said Pat Petronelli. "He came in and made a big issue out of the protective cup just a half hour before the fight. He said the cup was too high and there would be no fight. He said the rules stated that the cup had to stop at the navel and that Marvin's was above that. It wasn't. Marvin was all taped, and here's Duff, screaming and ranting and raving."

Hagler looked at the Petronelli brothers. "Get him the hell out of here," he yelled. "I can't take this. I can't concentrate."

Duff departed only after the Petronellis promised that George Francis, Mugabi's trainer, could return with a Nevada State Athletic Commission inspector to check the cup. Francis came in five minutes later, took a look and said, "That's fine."

Hagler arrived in the ring to the strains of James Brown's 'Living in America', late, hooded and angry. The rain had stopped just a few minutes earlier, and steam rose eerily from the champion's shaven skull. "He was so mad he tried to knock Mugabi's head off with every punch the first two rounds," said Pat Petronelli.

Fighting right-handed except for the last five seconds of the first round, Hagler lost it to Mugabi, who dispelled the myth that he was as unfamiliar with the subtleties of boxing as he was with the written word.

"I needed the work, anyway," said Hagler. "And it was great. I love a good fight. I could see why he had 26 knockouts, and he's a very gutsy warrior. I figured I had to wear him out; I could see that was the way I had to go, because he was kind of strong and I had to take some of that punching power out of him."

Coming out for round two as a southpaw, Hagler quickly discovered that Mugabi couldn't handle his right jab, a devastating, head-snapping punch. And the champion was following his jab, moving to his right, causing Mugabi to reach in with his own right hands. "After that it was just a matter of time," Hagler said.

Mugabi's time almost came in the sixth, when he was rocked hard by right hands and almost out, only to be saved by referee Mills Lane, who stepped in and used eight seconds to warn Hagler for hitting low. The pause was enough to allow Mugabi to recover. When Hagler returned to his corner, with blood streaming from his nose, he told them, "It's all starting to come together." Goody Petronelli was furious. "You're getting caught with a lot of shots," he chided. He later expressed his fears to his brother Pat. "Although they may not be hurting him, he's taking shots he would have evaded with ease."

In Mugabi's corner, their concern was more evident. Francis said, "Mugabi came back and said 'My hand is very bad.' I told him he couldn't just give up because of a bad hand and he took a deep breath, nodded and went on." It later emerged that he had a hairline fracture of the right hand.

In the seventh round, Lane took a point from Hagler for a low blow and as the evening wore on with Mugabi still on his feet, chants of "Beast! Beast!" began to emanate from the crowd.

Although Hagler was landing his right jab at will, he was frustrated when he tried to set up the left behind it. Time and again, his sweeping left flew over Mugabi's head.

Hagler had The Beast on the run again in the ninth, but Lane halted the action and took Mugabi back to his corner for repairs on some loose tape on one of his gloves. Duff, recognising the respite as a fortunate break, told his man, "Congratulations, you just got back in the fight."

Feeling that Mugabi was weakening, Hagler began manhandling him inside, and further sapped his strength with short, wicked shots. By the end of the tenth, the challenger was exhausted and without hope. Not even the pleadings of Father Anthony Clark, the priest who had baptised Mugabi three weeks earlier and was working in his corner, helped. "We love you" were Father Tony's words as Mugabi went out to face Hagler in the 11th.

Hagler, whose right eye was nearly closed, knew that the war of attrition had taken its toll on his challenger. Midway through the round, the champion dropped him after a barrage of rights and Mugabi sat, arms on knees, and watched as Lane counted him out.

"If he had gotten back up and Lane had let him go on, the man could have been badly hurt," said Hagler when he was interviewed by Al Bernstein in the ring.

"What was so exciting about the fight was the way I done it," said Hagler. "I took the toughest opponent out there, a guy with all those knockouts, and I destroyed him. Him and Hearns, back-to-back. Now maybe all those doubters will shut up."

Hagler also suggested that the fight may be his last. "Aren't you going to miss me?" he asked the broadcaster.

Later that night the Petronellis met with their champion in his suite to discuss his future. "Right now, he's tired, he's sore and he hurts," revealed Pat. "He mentioned being ready for Hearns again in November but I told him, 'Hey, you're the one that's hurting right now. Goody and me, we ain't got a pimple on us, so you take your time and make up your mind.'"

"The guy's been fighting for a long, long time, and he was in one of his toughest fights last night," Goody added. "He has earned the right to do whatever he chooses."

With five days' distance from the gruelling encounter, Hagler had enjoyed some quiet reflection with his wife and family. Despite the protestations of his wife and mother, retirement wasn't discussed as an immediate prospect. "Just three more," he mused at his home in Hanover. "So far I'm on a great timetable. I don't think 31 is old. I'll be 32 in a couple of months and I think I still have one good strong year left. The record, [Carlos Monzon's 14 successful defences] that is what I am looking for."

Bob Arum had already started to dangle the carrot of a 23 June rematch against Thomas Hearns in front of him but Hagler had resisted. Goody Petronelli had questioned Hearns's wisdom. "Nobody should want to fight Marvin a second time," he said. "Look at the record: Marvin is devastating the second time around." In fact, of the 12 rematches he had fought, he had won all of them, ten by KO.

Hagler chose to question Hearns's desire. "Hearns don't want this fight," Hagler scoffed. "He's still trying to bluff the public. He's saying, 'I'm still a tough guy, and I want Marvin Hagler again.' Then everybody is supposed to say, 'Oh, my, you got a lot of heart.' Bullshit! He don't want me," he insisted. He summarily dismissed the dramatic victory over James Shuler. "Hearns knew Shuler had no chin and couldn't punch. He wins one fight and he's right back in a championship fight."

Hagler couldn't resist releasing his monster, which gave vent to his favourite topic: injustice. "If I had lost to him, it would have been goodbye Marvelous Marvin Hagler. They've been trying to get rid of me for years."

Despite the $5m he earned from the Mugabi fight, riches and a measure of respect had not softened his bitter memory of the years when champions avoided his southpaw cannons and – most galling – of the title. "Have I found peace? Not really," he said. "I'll put it this way: I'm happy but I'm not satisfied. I believe they really won't give me credit until I am done with the game. Because every time there is another opponent, somebody is going to say, 'This guy is going to take you.' Now they are talking about Donald Curry. It's like I haven't proved myself yet. What the hell do they want?"

There would be no second time for Mugabi. After his first professional loss, Mugabi had decided he was more suited to remaining a junior middleweight. "Marvin is very tough and very strong and a great champion," Mugabi said while nursing the bruises inflicted on him. They were too fresh. He didn't even hint at a rematch with Hagler.

Hagler - Leonard

MARVIN HAGLER and Ray Leonard seemed to have been born to define each other's opposite. Hagler was publicly cast as the long-suffering, steel-chinned relentless brawler, his face having stopped more leather than Leonard had thrown. He didn't win the middleweight title until his 54th fight. Leonard was, comparatively, a Boy Scout. The former welterweight and junior middleweight champion twice retired, twice un-retired.

Hagler was a left-handed fighter, although sometimes in mid-round he would suddenly switch and begin fighting right-handed. Leonard was strictly a righty. Hagler's body was sculpted, drastic. Leonard's was smooth. Hagler bloodied men. Leonard rarely chopped up men, only frustrated them.

Leonard's charm transcended race and sex. At his training camps, his workouts drew as many women and youngsters as they did men and many more whites than blacks, all of whom were let in free. Hagler's appeal was narrower. He trained before a crowd that was predominantly masculine, men who had willingly paid $5 a head.

Leonard liked camp to be cosy, like home. He often brought in his wife and children. His father was a cook. His brother and father shared his suite. When all of them gathered at his nightly supper table, he might as well have been back at his childhood home in Palmer Park, Maryland.

Hagler did not allow his wife or children in camp and liked to hear only good news from home. Phone conversations were short. He did not like company. He preferred to think of his Palm Springs hotel as "prison". While the rest of his camp entourage watched the Super Bowl together, Hagler watched it in the next room, by himself. In the last six weeks before this fight, Hagler had come to the phone only for the most urgent calls from home.

Leonard was the most fiscally fit fighter in the sport's history. His home in Potomac was sumptuous, with a wine cellar in the basement and a Rolls-Royce in the garage. In seven years as an active pro, he made 50 per cent more ($48m) than Hagler in 14 ($31m). Hagler was the last of the club fighters. He refused to shake the hand of a man he may have had to fight some day. He was said to have been so suspicious as to switch plates at dinner. He incited himself with slogans long on conviction if short on grammar. "Destruction and Destroy" was his favourite.

Leonard decorated autographs with a happy face. Hagler wrote, "I will knock him out." Leonard set up a video game room for his huge entourage. He read biographies and played tennis during camp. Hagler's entourage was small and was left to entertain itself. He ate most of his meals alone in his room, took a lunchtime walk by himself and traipsed the 300 yards from his hotel to his training tent carrying his own equipment bag. Leonard rode 100 yards in a van that dropped him at the entrance.

During workouts, Hagler played music constantly, rock music for most routines, but when he was hitting the speed bag it was rap exclusively, some of it written in his honour. "And I've heard it said/Hagler puts heads to bed." Leonard played only an occasional tune, happy ditties like 'Sweet Georgia Brown', when he was jumping rope.

Hagler loved the smell of the gym. Leonard endured it. "You hit Marvin," said one of his sparring partners, James Lucas, "and he just gets happier." Said Mike Trainer, Leonard's attorney and financial adviser, "Ray's not a fighter who loves to fight. What he loves is the mountain. He's got to be challenged."

In the ring, Hagler huffed and snorted and reprimanded his sparring partners, "C'mon! Let's go! Let's work!" Leonard said nothing. He was occasionally playful in the ring, cognisant of the crowd. Hagler seemed infuriated to have to share the ring with anyone. Leonard seemed to be inviting us to join him there.

Hagler summed up their positions with his usual clarity. "You know what they want, man. Either you're going to be the bad guy or the good guy. And I ain't never been the good guy."

He who had been cast as the man in the white hat, Sugar Ray Leonard sat at ringside, drinking beer with the actor Michael J. Fox as Hagler battled Mugabi. As the fight wore on, he noticed Hagler's once-searing jab seemed to sail wide of the mark or whistled over Mugabi's head.

"I was sitting there with Michael, and I'm watching Hagler get outboxed by a guy who is known as a slugger," recalled Leonard. "I said, 'Michael, I can beat Hagler.' He said, 'Yeah, Ray, yeah.' Everyone thought I was being a smart-ass. But I really saw a sign in that fight. I mean, I always felt I could out-box Hagler. If Mugabi can do that, I can do an even better job.

"That had the most bearing on my decision to go ahead with a Hagler fight. I felt he was at a point that he didn't have that same fire in his body or in his heart. He wasn't the same guy."

Leonard's assistant, Oliver Dunlap, recounted, "That evening, we were in Michael J. Fox's room at Caesars.

Whoopi Goldberg, Ray Leonard, and myself. The suite was crowded, so we ended up sitting in the bathroom – somebody was sitting on the toilet, a couple people on the side of the bath tub. Ray said to me, 'Call Mike Trainer.' I looked at my watch and said, 'You know, its three hours' difference. It's the wee hours in DC.' He insisted. 'Call Mike. Tell Mike I want to fight Hagler.' And we all kind of laughed."

"I thought it was the booze talking," said Trainer, "'Let's talk about it when you get home', I said. When he called me the next day, I realised that he really was serious."

There was still scepticism among Leonard's inner circle. Dunlap said, "You have to remember, Ray's social life after the surgery was kind of wild. We didn't take his comeback talk serious. He had some hard recreational bad habits. I never thought he would fight again, especially not against Marvin."

Nigel Collins, *The Ring* magazine's editor-in-chief, met Leonard shortly afterwards. "He didn't mention anything about a comeback," he said. Leonard did mention how excited he was about the new restaurant in Bethesda he had opened with Mike Trainer and said Hagler had been invited. Collins speculated, "With Sugar Ray involved, you have to wonder exactly how innocent the invite really was. The way things turned out, he was probably setting a trap."

Leonard explained, "The way Marvin thinks, if you're not a threat, he's cool with you. So we sat there at my restaurant, had a few glasses of champagne, and he just started telling me things. He said, 'I'm not motivated, I cut easy.' He was telling me things that normally a fighter wouldn't say, because I'm retired. He felt like I felt when I was retired. You don't have that same commitment in your heart, or that edge that we had from day one. I think you become civilised. You're not the fighter you used to be because now you're flying in private planes, you're staying in suites, girls tell you how cute you are.

That's not conducive to being a great fighter. He had one foot out the door, I think, after the Mugabi fight. He had all the fame he wanted, he'd made a substantial amount of money. There's not as much reason to keep fighting."

Hagler's words deeply resonated with Leonard. He had felt that when he retired at the age of 26, he had "died young as a boxer".

"Twenty-six years old and I was through with my career. It burned inside. It ate at me every single day. Jeez, I'm not finished yet," he recalled. "I'd go to the club with the fellas, and we'd get bombed all the time. It was like, 'Ahh, I'm not doing anything anymore.' But something deep inside me was saying, 'Ray, where's your vanity? Where's your respect for yourself?' I'd go on business trips, and first thing you do on a business trip is somebody says, 'Let's go get some booze, let's celebrate our deal.' You close a half-million-dollar deal, you're going to celebrate."

Then one day Sugar Ray saw Ray Leonard in the mirror.

"I saw no definition. Nothing. I said, 'Where are the arms I used to have? Where are the ripples I used to have in my stomach?' My wife laughed at me. The way she laughed, it hurt my feelings. It made me aware."

Leonard's ego was bruised. He explained to the *USA Weekend* magazine, "That when a man is a champion, he is so proud. You want people to say, 'Hey, champ, way to go.' You can sit there and listen to it over and over again. But it's always good to hear a different person tell you – that's why you walk across the street to another hotel. You want to fight the monsters. In doing that, your persona becomes greater. You become bigger. There are more lucrative contracts and phenomenal deals."

The following week from the opening of his eatery, Leonard began running, returning to the gym, sparring with

1984 Olympic light-middleweight silver medallist Shawn O'Sullivan. He put up a punching bag in his house and bought a stationary bike. "I saw a metamorphosis." Thus fortified, he prepared for his toughest fight, with his wife, Juanita.

"What would you say if I wanted to fight Hagler?" he asked.

"I'd kill you," she said bluntly.

His family and friends tried to talk him out of it but Leonard remained unswayed. "People didn't understand what I was proposing," Leonard said. "I am the American Dream: financially independent, living in an exclusive, wealthy area, two kids, a dog. That should be it, that's all Americans need, or think you should need. But I wanted more."

A few weeks passed before Trainer relayed a proposed challenge to Bob Arum, who duly passed it on to the Petronellis. There was no immediate answer.

Hagler was torn. Leonard was the one fight he had always coveted, but four years later he still resented the way he had been played at that Baltimore retirement ceremony. How could he be sure this wasn't just another ruse?

Two months later, in early July, Bob Arum convened a press conference at Christo's restaurant in New York. Dave Anderson, the sports editor for the *New York Times*, attended to hear the announcement. "All the boxing people knew what he was going to say," Anderson said. "He would defend his undisputed world middleweight title against Sugar Ray Leonard on 6 November on the condition that Leonard accepted $5m to his $10m and as long as Bob Arum was the promoter. If Leonard didn't agree to those terms, then he would accept Thomas Hearns as a challenger again."

Arum stood and introduced, "Marvelous Marvin Hagler. The greatest fighter of our time," before the champion, wearing a black suit with a red tie over a white-collared black shirt stepped to the microphone. After a career of destroying his opponents with his devastating punching power, he deftly delivered the most surprising punch of his career. "I have made no decision about a fight with Leonard or Hearns," he began. "I'm very seriously thinking about retiring."

With an emotional edge in his voice, Hagler talked about how "my mother, my grandmother and my wife have been looking forward to me giving up the boxing game and walk out a proud champion". He suggested that he "would like to see Leonard fight John Mugabi or Donald Curry" and how "Hearns didn't deserve a return match". Above all else, however, he desired to leave boxing "with all my health and faculties". Poignantly, he added, "When you get out, you don't want to be like Muhammad Ali." He referred to the former heavyweight champion who was suffering from Parkinson's Disease.

Anderson recalled, "In sports, retirements are always suspect. Especially boxing retirements. Ali once retired and un-retired within half an hour. Larry Holmes has retired and un-retired every few months in the last two years. So sceptics in the room immediately wondered if the middleweight champion was hanging Leonard on a hook, as Leonard had done to him in 1982 at his Baltimore retirement party."

Pat Petronelli disputed that Hagler was trying to make Leonard suffer. "That's not Marvin's style," Petronelli said. "Marvin thought Leonard had his chance to fight him two or three times. Now he has his family. He's got five kids. His mother wants him to retire; his wife, Bertha, wants him to retire."

Mike Trainer immediately announced, "Hagler's retirement would prevent Ray's comeback from ever starting."

Bob Arum admitted that he was shocked by Hagler's declaration. Just minutes before he had stepped to the microphone, the champion had called the promoter, who had paid him most of the $30m he had earned in boxing, into a side room. "I came here fully expecting Marvin to name the conditions for a Leonard fight," Arum said. "But he told me he had something that he wanted me to hear from him first. He told me, 'It's been great, you've been great, but the time has come when I want to hang it up.'" Arum paid tribute to Hagler's character. "It's easy to retire after a big score but retiring before one, shows what kind of a man Marvin really is."

Over the next few months, Hagler enjoyed playing off his menacing demeanour and fearsome reputation in a series of deodorant commercials for Right Guard in which Marvin, playing the genteel country squire, eloquently delivered lines like, "One wouldn't want to offend, would one?" and, "Anything less would be uncivilised."

Yet still, even behind the doors of his ten-room house with an indoor swimming pool, a sauna and sky lights, Hagler could not settle. Even as he enjoyed the spoils of his career, the figure of Sugar Ray Leonard would not recede from his thoughts. "Could Leonard be for real?" he asked his confidants, Pat and Goody Petronelli, who had been on the journey with him for 17 years. "Goody didn't believe it," said Pat. "Marvin didn't believe it either, but I was unsure."

Once the thought had entered his head, it continued to buzz like an irritating fly. "Marvin struggled to know what to do: to enjoy his riches and let Leonard go, or trade the pain for a $12m guarantee, his biggest strike." Goody Petronelli remained non-committal. "We said, 'Whatever you want to do, Marvin'," he said. "That's always been our approach, because he's gone as far as we thought most fighters could go."

It was Bertha Hagler who finally settled on a decision. "She told Marvin, 'I want you home with the family and the kids. We're wealthy enough'," Pat Petronelli recounted. "She thought he had fought enough but knew he really wanted to fight Leonard. Deep down in his heart he had always wanted to fight Leonard." She gave her consent.

Leonard would later suggest that the 109 days it took Hagler to change his mind and accept his challenge was an indication that the champion wasn't sure he wanted to fight him at all.

"Oh yeah?" Hagler bristled. "Well, how come it took Ray four years to make up his mind? He didn't want to fight me then."

Hagler agreeing to fight was only the first step. Months of negotiations ensued. Steve Wainwright recounted, "There were three things that ultimately were of importance to negotiations for the Leonard-Hagler fight: the number of rounds, the size of the ring, and the size of the gloves. The people negotiating for Marvin allowed Mike Trainer to dictate the terms because they were so confident that Marvin was going to walk right through Ray Leonard. So they gave up on the gloves, which is usually the prerogative of the champion, they gave up on the number of rounds, and they gave up on the size of the ring. Leonard got a huge ring with huge gloves and 12 rounds instead of 15."

Angelo Dundee, Leonard's head trainer, had been adamant about the ring size. "Whenever I had a fight with Ray Leonard, it was in the contract it had to be a 20-foot ring. I didn't want a bandbox or a telephone booth. My fighters knew how to move," he said.

Tony Petronelli, Pat's son, explained the rationale behind their acquiescence. "What you have to understand is we all thought Marvin was going to beat him," he said."You could have given them the whole parking lot to fight in. We just thought Marvin was too much for him."

Top Rank match-maker Bruce Trampler felt that Mike Trainer was starting the psychological games early and was doing his best to unsettle Hagler. "I always felt Trainer was fucking with Marvin. Once he sensed that Marvin did want the fight, he was going to make him pay for it. The gloves, the ring, everything. I always felt that he was doing it just to get Hagler's goat, to upset Hagler. But virtually every request that the Leonard camp made was granted, and it was pretty clear that the reluctant Hagler was now into it, like, 'Give 'em whatever they want, I don't care. I just want to destroy the guy.'"

Mike Trainer agreed, "I was willing to give them the things they wanted: for the fight to be in Vegas, for Arum to be the lead promoter, and for Hagler to get more money. And with that money, I bought three rounds."

It was just the third time in Leonard's career that he would be paid less than his opponent. Roger 'Pit' Perron, one of Hagler's training team, sensed that Leonard's willingness to focus on the conditions for the bout rather than the money was a cunning ploy. "Leonard had a lot of demands. Money wasn't one of them," he said.

"Leonard already had a couple hundred million in the bank, but Marvin had about $20m. And the concession was that it doesn't matter which kind of gloves they used, it doesn't matter if he went from an 18-foot ring to a 20-foot ring, and it doesn't matter if he went from 15 rounds to 12 rounds. Marvin conceded all that in exchange for the pay-per-view revenue from the whole country. The only two states Leonard had were Maryland, where he lived, and Washington, DC. And that's why Marvin made $21m and Leonard made $13m. The base pay was like $12m for Marvin and $11m for Leonard. Leonard didn't care about the money – he already made his millions."

Once the terms had been arranged in November, the two men embarked on a 12-city press tour, including an appearance with Bob Hope at Caesars, where the comedian plugged the bout as "a fight for the common man – two millionaires trying to beat each other's brains out".

Hagler began the tour and assumed the role of a boxing outcast. A man with blue-collar beginnings, who looked askance at the man he caustically dubbed 'Mr Politician', and 'Mr Middle-Class'. His distaste for Leonard's populist manner – the easy smile, the gracious ease before strangers – which he believed was hype, built on image-making rather than substance.

"He is a phony," said Hagler. "When Ali left boxing, they gave it all to Leonard. They guided Leonard. They gave him Ali's trainer [Angelo Dundee]. They gave him Ali's style, strategies. They transferred everything to Leonard. He's a copycat. He's a built machine. He doesn't even have his own name. They gave him Sugar Ray Robinson's name. He's been protected all his life. Besides, if he hadn't become a boxer, he could have done other things. Me? I had nowhere else to go."

Leonard ignored Hagler's jibes, choosing to praise him for the great champion that he was. Even these utterings left Hagler's emotional tank on empty. "At least Hearns said he was going to knock my block off," Hagler complained. Since the sweet talk didn't fit his programme, Hagler – midway in the tour – altered its content. He left.

Leonard later revealed his own strategy, which was to deny Hagler's monster the opportunity to feed on his words. He said, "My game plan on the media tour was to make Hagler think people didn't appreciate his boxing ability. I said, 'Do you think Hagler's going to run at me, fight me toe-to-toe? That's an insult to his intelligence.' I never once said anything that was derogatory, because I didn't want to feed that anger and aggression that he normally has when he goes to camp."

Leonard claimed that a key moment on this tour was when he chastised Hagler for turning up late for a news conference and Hagler said, "Sorry, Ray." Leonard said, "That's when I thought to myself, 'Gotcha'." Leonard continued, "I said, 'This man's a great man, he's a great family man, he's a legend.' I just said everything so when he got to the podium, he couldn't say, 'Ray's an asshole.' I didn't give him the chance to get angry."

This didn't stop Hagler trying. "Deep down I've been bothering him," he reflected. "Something about me is bothering him. He sees me all over, doing 'Punky Brewster' on TV, the commercials. That's me. I just keep doing what I do – winning and taking care of my family."

When the fight was formally announced in November 1986, Bob Arum predicted that the fight would gross $100m. At the time, most boxing people thought Arum's figure was heavily inflated to boost box office sales. After the publicity tour, it soon appeared that Arum's figure would be close. It eventually doubled the previous gross high of about $45m that the Larry Holmes-Gerry Cooney bout in June 1982 reportedly took in.

"It was an engagement that promised to be as much of an 'event' as the World Series, the Super Bowl, the Olympics, Bobby Riggs v Billie Jean King. When the 15,336 tickets for the 12-round showdown between the two great champions were put on sale in November by Caesars, they sold out within a month," said George Kimball.

Arum confirmed this view, "The bout has captured a constituency broader than boxing matches have known in the past." He proudly claimed that "the interest that women, for instance, have shown in buying tickets to closed-circuit outlets has been far greater for this fight than for the myriad other matches I have promoted, including Muhammad Ali's".

The diversity of the audience could be gauged just by looking at the closed-circuit sites in New York City. They ranged from the honky-tonk movie houses of West 42nd Street to the New York Athletic Club on Central Park South to the Palladium, the trendy nightspot on 14th Street.

On 21 January, Hagler moved to Palm Springs to enter his own private prison, spending ten weeks training for the fight, by far the most extensive period of preparation for any bout in his career. Hagler admitted that he would have preferred to have stayed home in Brockton longer but the Petronellis insisted as they were disturbed by the champion's hectic schedule and felt he would be able to concentrate on boxing here.

This was his fifth consecutive visit to the desert and the hotel he used, the Americana Canyon Hotel, was the setting. "I hope it's the easiest fight that's possible," said Hagler, with an unmistakable weariness, an image that was far removed from the "very ugly" mood, as Pat Petronelli put it, that his fighter would assume in the last weeks of training.

He opened up about the confusion he had felt before accepting this fight. "Before this fight, I was seriously thinking of retirement," he said. "I felt as though I had beaten everybody out there. I talked with my wife and my mother and my grandmother and I knew the way they felt. I also knew that I had accomplished everything that I thought I could do in boxing. And I thought I wanted to go out on top, and this was the right time. So there was a lot of confusion going on inside my head."

He admitted that his legacy mattered to him. "I saw how the press was really picking up on this fight and I don't want it said that I left the game of boxing and didn't give Leonard the opportunity. Basically, I think this is a fight that had to be," he said.

His training routine was set with military precision. He would pound six miles of road work out before breakfasting alone in his room. He would deliver his media duties at midday before starting training at 6pm every day. "I've done this before," he said. "I know what to do. What I have to do is block out these nice surroundings and pretend it's worse than it is. I have to deny myself. I have to think that this is just like a training camp elsewhere."

His ability to ignore the wondrous surroundings, which included the majestic, snow-capped San Jacinto Mountains and the elite Canyon Hotel, with its verdant golf and tennis resort also extended to his guests. The actor Sylvester Stallone visited Hagler's camp and was kept waiting for nearly two hours, being studiously ignored by Hagler until he had finished his training routine.

"This is Marvin's Olympics," explained Hagler's brother, middleweight Robbie Sims, to the Hollywood star. "This is his moment."

During the solitude of his camp, Hagler used the long hours to summon up enough bitter memories to feed his monster. "I'm a little scared about this fight," he admitted, "because Las Vegas is a gambling town." He cited the draw against Antuofermo as a prime example of how external factors could influence events. "I've kept the bitterness from that in my mind and in my thoughts ..."

For Hagler, these "forces out there" that conspired against him were constant fuel. "This one and that one that they keep thinking can beat me," he said. "Where do they find a guy like Obelmejias? Where do they find a guy like Mugabi? Where do they find a guy like Roldan? Where do they find these people?" He paused before musing, "They must have been looking under rocks." He proceeded to pause in front of a flat, circular concrete stone, before lifting it six inches off the ground. "Got to find somebody," he said. "Anybody under there?"

"They don't come up the rankings the way I did," he complained. "They just beat a guy, any guy. And next thing you know, they throw him to me. And I just keep drilling 'em down. 'Next.' Tall ones. Big ones. Hard-punching ones. Fast-hands ones. Ones can cut you up. All these people with different techniques. But I always find the strategy and technique to beat them. Now they got me going against 'The Brain', Ray Leonard."

"If he's foolish enough to step in the ring with me," Hagler told the *New York Times*, "I'm foolish enough to rip his eye out."

Leonard, in the meantime, was training on Hilton Head, a resort island just off the South Carolina coast. It started inauspiciously.

Mike Trainer determined that Leonard, having not fought since 1984, needed to have a couple of fights before he faced Hagler. Leonard met four challengers, who were permitted to wear headgear and fight in smaller gloves, over ten rounds in fights that took place behind closed doors.

Leonard later admitted, "Those first few weeks in training camp were just monstrous. These young sparring partners were kicking my butt. My face was not used to getting hit. It was used to having make-up put on it. My cardiovascular was not great."

In order to boost Leonard's flagging confidence, Trainer devised a plan. J.D. Brown, the match-maker for Leonard's Victory Promotions, was dispatched to go and spy on Hagler's camp. He recalled, "I disguised myself – my hair was black, so I dyed it gray. I put these horn-rimmed glasses on. And I went and sat in the back and watched him train for three days. I picked up a few things. He wanted to be in the center of the ring for all the sparring sessions; when a round would start and the guy would come out of the other corner, he'd be standing in the middle, waiting for him. And he got mad at his sparring partners, the Weaver triplets, because they weren't fighting him. They were boxing him. They were hitting him, moving, and he's like, 'Come on, stop moving. Fight me, you little bitch'!"

To prove his presence to Leonard, Brown waited until the end of the training session and posed for a photo with Hagler. When this ruse was later revealed, Hagler dismissed the idea that he had been duped. "I'll tell him what I'm planning," he growled. "I'm going to knock him silly."

Angelo Dundee usually arrived in camp three weeks before the fight but Trainer called him six weeks before and said, "Angie, you've got to come now. Please come now, the kid needs help. He's taking things too easy."

Dundee revealed, "Every day, we plotted strategy and tactics. Every day, we sat and talked about what he'd have to do to win. We then put him in rounds that were seven minutes long against guys like Quincy Taylor, who was a young hotshot. He fought both sides, like Hagler. And he could punch."

Leonard admitted that these sessions provided a tough learning environment. "I'd gotten so strong that I was breaking these sparring partners down. I was feeling so strong; I was going to fight Hagler toe-to-toe." His confidence was rocked, however, when Taylor knocked him down. "Just five days before the fight, I fell asleep for just a second and he hit me so hard. I was out."

Dundee remained confident. "It changed Ray's strategy," he said. Leonard agreed. "In the first months of training, my whole game plan was box, box, box. That's the logical thing to do against Hagler. But I kind of settled into being a middleweight. I was hitting guys to the body, hurting guys. I felt so strong. I became this beast who was going to beat Hagler up, open up the scar tissue over his eyes, cut him up. What a mistake that would have been. Thank god for Quincy Taylor. I should have paid him more. Best punch I ever took!"

Both fighters arrived in Las Vegas a week before the fight. After landing in the desert, trumpets blared and drums rolled along a red carpet that stretched from the entrance of Caesars Palace toward their limousines. They arrived nearly 24 hours apart, and the psychological distance between Sugar Ray Leonard and Marvelous Marvin Hagler appeared even greater.

The challenger came first. He wore his famous smile as he was showered by orchid petals from Roman maidens that flanked him. When he stood before the microphone, his charm offensive was on full beam. "I'm back home!" he declared. "I'm ready and I'm going for the big jackpot."

In contrast, when Hagler stepped out of his limousine, he ignored the costumed Caesar and Cleopatra and wearing a white cap that carried the moniker "NO MERCY" in red letters, he stepped before the microphone and spoke to the throng of 500 press and spectators that had gathered. "I plan on hurting Ray, and I want to hurt him bad." He paused before continuing his invective. "I want to smash his eyeball out. I want to knock his head off. I want to rip his brains out. I'm serious," he said, lest anyone doubted his chilling words.

His mood was fearsome in part because earlier in the day, the WBA announced that it did not approve Leonard as an opponent and ordered its title vacated. Hagler's attempts to bring an injunction to forestall the move had collapsed that morning. "So what else is new?" said Hagler. "They tried to take away my title before the Hamsho fight, and they tried to strip me when I fought Scypion."

Pat Petronelli was even more damning. "I'm sorry we ever got involved with the WBA," he said. "We've done them nothing but good, and they turn around and do this."

Hagler was adamant that the judgment would not have a bearing on the fight. "I won't be losing any sleep over it. Those belts can only be won or lost in the ring."

One of the more fascinating side-shows to the big fight build-up focused on the three men who would be in the corners on the night: Pat and Goody Petronelli and Angelo Dundee.

"I respect the Petronelli brothers," Dundee told a flock of reporters. "They go with their fighter like Charlie Goldman and Rocky Marciano, like Whitey Bimstein and Rocky Graziano."

Dundee, commonly described as the best trainer in the boxing business after quietly masterminding Muhammad Ali's victory over George Foreman in Zaire, repeated the feat when Ali won the title for an unprecedented third time by beating Leon Spinks in a rematch. He had also tutored Leonard to win his title back, with a dazzling array of tricks and cunning, when he outsmarted Robert Duran in their return fight.

The esteemed Mike O'Hara, the Detroit boxing writer, mused, "The corners will be crucial in this fight. The re-supply system in the 60-second span between rounds is where a fighter receives strategy, psychology, repairs, admonishment, a scouting report and sometimes nothing more scientific than a whiff of ammonia. Angelo Dundee has proven himself to be the best 60-second man in boxing. His record attests to that, with champions from Luis Rodriquez to Muhammad Ali and Ray Leonard."

Dundee, for his part, admitted he was excited but would check his emotions at the ring apron once the combat started. "I'm all juiced up and I'll be juiced up until the bell rings. When you lose your cool, you're no good to the fighter."

The arrangement between Leonard and Dundee was quite different to the relationship between the three men in the opposite corner. Mike Trainer explained that Janks Morton was Leonard's official trainer and Angelo Dundee only arrived two weeks before a major fight to fine-tune his charge. Dave Jacobs had also been with Leonard since he was a junior but he had subsequently left the team after the loss to Roberto Duran before healing the breach and returning.

"Angelo Dundee's role is clearly defined," said Trainer. "He is officially listed as Leonard's manager but he isn't involved in any negotiations or the business side of things. Janks Morton trains Leonard and gets him into condition before Angelo comes into camp. He then puts the finishing touches together and works the corner. When the bell sounds, Angelo runs the corner."

Each trainer claimed that their unique approaches would give their charges an edge. Goody Petronelli believed that his relationship with Hagler was based on a mutual respect forged through their early years together. "It's not that I might be a better cornerman. I think Angelo's effectiveness is diluted because Leonard doesn't listen to him. Marvin has the advantage because he has a corner he respects and he uses his corner. As great as Angelo is, I don't think he has that kind of input."

Dundee was non-committal. He laughed, "I respect Goody and this kind of comparison just juices things up. If it gets people talking about the fight, that's got to be good."

To demonstrate that there were no hard feelings, Pat Petronelli and Dundee agreed to meet for dinner after the fight with the loser picking up the tab and the winner choosing the menu.

At the final press conference, Hagler arrived wearing a bright red cap modelled after the French Foreign Legion's chapeau, replete with twin flaps hanging at the back of his shaven head. On the front, he had 12 gold stars to denote his successful title defences, which surrounded the words "WAR II".

Nearly 1,100 news media members from 31 countries watched the fighters engage in a role reversal. On past occasions like this, Leonard had been the star, tossing out amusing one-liners while Hagler stared ahead glumly. When it was his turn to speak, Hagler would give the verbal equivalent of a brandished fist and then be seated, with an expression that suggested he wanted to leave as quickly as possible.

Instead, Hagler arrived in good spirits. In place of the sullen game face that he usually brought was a ready smile and deportment which George Kimball described as "nearly as cheery as that of a television game-show host". Leonard conveyed a weariness, giving curt answers that seemed calculated to keep the news media at a distance.

Angelo Dundee attempted to needle Hagler about his age. "I accord all due respect to Marvin Hagler, the middleweight champion," Dundee said, "because he's a man of all ages." Dundee cleared his throat and took a comedic beat, waiting for the laughs. The laughs came, as did a big smile from Hagler, when Pat Petronelli waved his birth certificate. "It's signed, sealed, everything," he said. "Anybody who doubts its validity is free to come up and examine it."

What was noticeable was the absence of the barbed edge from Hagler's remarks, as well as the personal animosity he directed at opponents. At one point, he said that the public would see, "two geniuses at work".

"Ray has great boxing ability," Hagler said, "but I still feel I'm the best man."

It was in the comic mode, though, that Hagler was most disarming. When he made his initial remarks, Hagler first twisted the two flaps on his cap as if they were hanks of hair and, with a preening expression, wondered aloud, "Do I look okay?"

Later, when he was asked how he wanted to be remembered in boxing history, Hagler again played with the flaps of the cap and said, "As a guy with long hair, who beat Leonard."

When Leonard was asked, "If Hagler hits you in your eye, will you respond like Duran did to you and say 'No mas?'" Leonard retained his poker face and uttered, "I don't speak Spanish."

He finished the conference by admitting, "I'll have a lot of nervous energy, a lot of butterflies inside me on the night." He promised, "I will not let him dictate what's going to happen in the ring."

Ring The Bell

ON THE day of the fight, one poll in a Las Vegas newspaper found that 60 of 67 journalists covering the fight favoured Hagler. One of them was Leonard's longtime HBO broadcast colleague Larry Merchant, who picked Hagler in nine.

"There was a personal element for me, because Ray had worked with me at HBO as an analyst," Merchant said. "When we had our customary fighter meetings on the day before the fight, Ray asked what I thought, and I said, 'Well, I have to pick Hagler.' And I could see that he was disappointed – that he thought I had to be not just smarter, but more loyal. When I left I said, 'I'll be happy if you make me a liar.'"

Hagler had assumed his pre-fight impression of a caged tiger. Roger Perron recalled, "I can remember the day before the fight, getting in the elevator with him at Caesars Palace. We went up 12 floors and he never said one word to me. It was like he never saw me before, like he didn't know who I was. And I didn't dare open my mouth. The fight was fast approaching, and he was gettin' mean."

The capacity of the outdoor stadium at Caesars was supposed to be 15,236 but the officially announced attendance would be 15,336. Tickets, with a $700 top for ringside, had long since sold out, although 2,000 of the best seats were used specifically for the hotel's preferred gambling customers.

Nigel Collins recounted, "Being ringside was like being at the centre of the universe. It was like the normal stuff of life and death was temporarily unimportant. Nothing mattered except for the fight."

Al Bernstein agreed, "There was great energy in that arena. There's something about outdoors at Caesars that was just special. It was in a parking lot when you get down to it, but it just felt special. And the build-up to this fight was unbelievable. It was the quintessential promotion of that time."

His colleague Barry Tompkins described it as, "the most remarkable feeling I've had in 40-some years of broadcasting".

Behind the scenes, the atmosphere was building. The dressing rooms were adjacent to each other in the Caesars Pavilion. Dundee eschewed his customary cool to pound on the wall which separated the rooms, yelling, "We're gonna get you!"

On the other side, referee Richard Steele noticed that there was a subtle difference in the way Hagler was behaving. "When I was giving the instructions in the dressing rooms, I really saw something different about Hagler. He just wasn't himself. He had done something to his demeanour and something to the way he carried himself. I couldn't put a finger on it at the time, but during the fight I began to realise that he was trying to play a boxer instead of the fighter he really was. His 'destruct and destroy' mindset, that's what got him to be the great fighter he was, that's what got him to be the champion he was. But Leonard had won that mental fight, getting him to change his style."

Leonard was first to enter the ring, dancing his way in to Kool and the Gang's 'Victory', ducking between the ropes, dressed immaculately, in a short, white satin jacket with red flames at the end of the sleeves that was better suited for a sophisticated night out than the biggest fight of his glittering career. Leonard shadowboxed in the ring, spinning low and twisting quickly, and to that performance the crowd howled. Ray Charles Leonard was back. "Go get him, Ray!" shouted Dunlap. "You got him!"

Three minutes later Hagler ascended the steps into the ring, dressed in a purple top with a hood pulled over his head, allowing himself only tunnel vision. He threw punches at the cool night air while growling, "Let's go! Let's go!" as a final signal of his malevolent intent to start proceedings.

Before they could begin, MC Chuck Hull completed his introductions and the Pointer Sisters sang the American National Anthem while a pyrotechnic version of the American flag flew above the Caesars roof.

During the proceedings, Leonard scored an important psychological blow. "As we paced the ring in the minutes before the bout, I saw that at one point we were moving toward one another on a collision course. And," said Leonard, "I made up my mind I wasn't going to avoid it." When Hagler veered at the last second, Leonard's reaction was, "Gotcha!"

The pattern of the fight was established straight away. Leonard came out dancing and moving and making Hagler lunge and miss. In the early rounds he was the consummate boxer, firing combinations as he kept from harm's way. Leonard put on a show, twisting and turning and popping Hagler – here an uppercut, there a jab, at one point grabbing the rope in his right hand and mugging at the champion, at another point delivering a low-blow bolo punch sure to further inflame an already frustrated opponent.

"When the bell rang," Leonard recalled, "I saw Hagler in an orthodox stance. I wanted to say, 'Hold on. Stop this fight. You're not doing the right thing!' It was that blatant. I was like, 'What are you doing?' Then I thought, 'Well, shit, this is great!'"

He continued, "I had all this nervous energy, but when he did that, it settled me down. It occurred to me that he was a little bit more in awe of the moment than I was, and he was just as concerned as I was. That showed me a vulnerability that Marvin shows no one. When Hagler walks into that ring, he's a beast. But against me, he was more like a little lamb."

Hagler later refuted the claims that he had fallen into Leonard's psychological trap. "A lot of people think I made a mistake by fighting him right-handed," he said. "But you know, the strategy was that I know he fought another southpaw, but he looked good that fight. I knew that he knew how to fight southpaws, so I didn't want to give him that look."

Still, Hagler was having a devil of a time connecting with anything close to a serious blow. Leonard was getting off more quickly, consistently stealing a march on Hagler. Looking off-balance and disoriented, Hagler missed frequently and often wildly.

Whenever Hagler did get too close for comfort, Leonard would reach out and grab him around the back of his neck, pulling Hagler off balance. It was a tactic which Dundee had taught Muhammad Ali to employ to particular effect against Joe Frazier. "I told Ray, 'You're going to be able to move this guy. He's never been manhandled,'" said Dundee. Richard Steele was compelled to issue a number of warnings.

The wily Dundee remained unfazed by Hagler's change of plan. "I wasn't surprised Hagler came out orthodox. That was his power side. You go back and look, when he fought Tommy Hearns, he knocked him out with a right. So when he came out like that, Ray was prepared because of what I thought Hagler would do."

In contrast, the Petronellis urged Hagler to reconsider. Goody kept yelling at him, reminding him that when he was fighting southpaw he was doing better. Kenny Bayless, the chief inspector in Hagler's corner, believed that they were not emphatic enough in their demands. "They were so calm. I felt they should have been in Marvin's face, yelling and screaming and saying, 'What are you doing? You need to do this!' I thought that Marvin was giving up the early rounds. But they were calm. They were giving instructions. Everything was very professional. I just don't recollect them getting nervous or saying, 'Hey, you're losing these early rounds, you need to pick the pace up' or anything like that."

At the start of the fourth round, Leonard claimed another small psychological victory. "When the bell rang, I rushed right to the centre of the ring apron. I then did that in a lot of the rounds that followed," he said. "I had heard that one of Hagler's maxims was that the first person to the centre of the ring wins the fight, so that's why I would do it. It's just the little things that I did to play with his head. Anything to prevent him from doing what he wanted. This was a small thing, but it was big for him."

Later in the round, he caught Hagler with a bolo punch to the body. "It didn't hurt him, but it hurt his pride," Leonard recalled.

Leonard won the first four rounds outright, but by the fifth and sixth, Hagler was beginning to find the range and Leonard was no longer moving with his early verve.

"I still came on, fighting him on the inside, even trying to beat him with his own speed," Hagler said. "Everybody was looking for me to knock him out, but you know what? I just wanted to beat him."

He buckled Leonard in the fifth round with a meanly delivered uppercut. Goody Petronelli said, "There were a couple times where I jumped up and said, 'I think we got him!' Marvin landed his best shot on Leonard's chin, and I saw Leonard was hurt. I was like, 'Marvin, you got him hurt, finish him.' But somehow Leonard wormed his way out of it. Marvin started winning a lot of the rounds from that point on, but Marvin never got to put the finishing touch on him. Marvin was a great finisher. He got all these knockouts not by being a one-punch knockout guy, but he'd wear you down when he got you hurt."

At the end of the round, Hagler gave Leonard a contemptuous shove. Hagler later explained his reasoning. "People say his movement was giving me problems. Movement?" he spat. "You mean running? He tried to steal the last part of every round – that's amateur. Professional, you got to win the whole round, not 30 seconds."

Leonard's plan was to have Dave Jacobs yell out when there was 30 seconds left in each round. "I'd then know to throw those combinations and impress the judges." He later defended his approach. "I wasn't really 'stealing' rounds. I was keeping the round close, then winning the final 30 seconds. That was the plan."

In the seventh, a Hagler hook rocked Leonard and the challenger briefly sagged. Now, Hagler battled Leonard to the ropes, firing shots up and down. He had Leonard in trouble as the bell sounded. Before he retreated to his corner sanctuary, Hagler sneered, "Slow down, you little bitch. Fight me like a man."

Leonard returned to his corner buoyed by Hagler's words. "When you're talking trash, you ain't punching. I had Hagler's mind all messed up. If Hagler was talking, that meant it was going my way. I wanted him talking trash instead of punching."

But Hagler was beginning to catch Leonard on the ropes, and the challenger was growing weary. In the ninth, the best round of the fight, Hagler pinned Leonard in the latter's corner and was whaling at him ferociously with both hands, rocking the challenger and looking to finish him.

In an instant, Leonard retaliated with a flurry that had Hagler's head snapping left and right. Leonard then spun away and escaped. Hagler pursued, thinking he still had Leonard in trouble.

But when Hagler caught up, Leonard flurried again, drawing upon reserves he had no right to have. Throughout the fight, even with Leonard right in front of him, Hagler had problems solving his foe's rich boxing style. He couldn't seem to put combinations together, and whenever he seemed to have Leonard in trouble, he couldn't muster the savvy to put him away.

Dundee believed that this round was central to Leonard's victory. "Ray won the fight, in my opinion, in the ninth round. Marvin had him on the ropes, and Ray backed him off. And at that point, I felt like people were watching Ray rather than watching the fight. He backed up the beast. To me, that's when the fight turned. Marvin was getting back into the fight. He was making it close on the scorecards, and all of a sudden Ray took it away from him."

Leonard admitted that his exhaustion was almost complete. "I was dead. I couldn't have won without Angelo," he claimed. "He said the right things, just what I needed to hear. That's the value of Angelo. He does the right thing at the right moment. Like with Ali, cutting the gloves against Henry Cooper. Angelo's so cool under pressure. That's his magic."

Dundee dismissed Leonard's fulsome praise. "In the corner, between rounds, I'm yelling, 'Six minutes left!' Then, 'Three minutes for the title!' The guy who helped the most in that fight was Richard Steele, the referee. Before the 12th round, he said, 'Last round! 12th round!' I says, 'Next champ!' Ray jumped up, put his arms up. You utilise every little thing you can get."

The Petronellis remained calm in the eye of the storm. Hagler recounted, "They said maybe I lost the first three rounds but reminded me it's not how many rounds that you win – it's how you finish the fight. You can lose three rounds and make up the difference by the end. I think I did that. In the last two rounds, I really had him going. I had him hurt in the 11th and the 12th."

When the final round began, Leonard looked to be battling on will and instinct alone. There appeared to be nothing left. He had extended himself past his limit. But he had to survive one more round, three minutes of what turned out to be sustained fury that echoed his approach against Hearns. Hagler abandoned any finesse, channelling his ferocity in a hail of punches up, punches down, lefts and rights.

Desperate and sensing that Leonard was in trouble, Hagler opened the 12th by lunging and missing with a right hand. Off a left hook, Leonard caught Hagler with a three-punch combination that brought the crowd of 15,336 roaring to its feet. Then Hagler nailed Leonard with a stiff right and suddenly the two men were talking to each other. They had been doing that all night.

"They were using certain words in the ring that I would not care to repeat," said referee Richard Steele. "They were going at each other verbally as well as physically."

After the chatter stopped, Hagler caught Leonard with a sweeping hook, but Leonard bobbed beneath another, escaping, and began moving laterally and then backward as the stalking champion bulled in and finally caught him in a neutral corner. Here Hagler banged him with a sharp left hook, but he missed another left as Leonard dipped, then missed again. But Hagler still had Leonard pinned to the ring post, and he belted him with lefts and rights.

Suddenly, when Hagler seemed to have the tiring challenger where he wanted him, Leonard began throwing hard, flashing punches in a sustained burst that left Hagler bewildered and covering. It was the longest flurry of the fight, a dozen rapid-fire punches on Hagler's face and arms that ended with Leonard slipping free and now moving left and right. Once again Hagler advanced and trapped Leonard on the ropes, and once again Leonard summoned up a flurry, not only getting away but actually sticking out his chin and mugging at the champion, just as he had done when he forced Roberto Duran to surrender in the "No mas" fight of 1980.

It had been a Hagler crowd from the outset – Leonard was even booed at the weigh-in that morning – but chanting had been heard for Leonard in the middle rounds, and now, as the end drew near, the chants grew louder and more sustained, "Sugar Ray! Sugar Ray!"

Hearing that, Leonard began dancing to the left, out of reach of Hagler, circling the ring while raising his right hand in the air. Hagler moved in, raising his right hand, too, and manoeuvred Leonard on to the ropes again. He drilled Leonard to the body and then landed a crackling left that sagged the challenger. The bell then rang to end it.

Leonard's face, drained of expression, reflected the will, effort and intensity that he had brought to, and expended on, this fight as he embraced Hagler, who claimed that Leonard whispered, "You beat me, babe" in his ear. This is a claim that Leonard later vehemently refuted. "First of all, even if I felt he did win, I wouldn't tell him that. No fighter would ever say, 'Oh man, you kicked my ass!' All the way back to Jack Johnson, a fighter never says, 'I lost the fight; you won the fight.' I didn't say that to him. I said, 'Marvin, you're still a champion to me.' And I kissed him on his cheek. He misinterpreted what I said."

Leonard then sagged and collapsed to his knees. As he appeared about to swoon to the canvas, two of his seconds, Janks Morton and Ollie Dunlap, grabbed him by the arms, lifted him to his feet and helped him back to his corner.

Meanwhile, Hagler danced in his corner, eager to show that he still had energy to burn. "I was bouncing around the ring, all happy and everything," he remembered, "because he knew it and I knew it – that I won the fight."

Leonard later cited Hagler's behaviour as a sure-fire tell that he knew he had been defeated. "That was totally uncharacteristic of him. At the end of the fight, before the decision was announced, he was dancing! Hagler never does that crap. He knew ... he knew."

The fight was close and a difficult one to judge, but there were scattered boos from the crowd when ring announcer Chuck Hull declared that it was a split decision. After revealing that judge Lou Filippo had scored it 115 to 113 for Hagler and that judge Jo Jo Guerra had it a ridiculous 118 to 110 for Leonard, Hull then intoned that judge Dave Moretti had scored it 115 to 113. Goody Petronelli echoed Hagler's worst fears when he heard the judge's decision. "When Chuck Hull grabbed the microphone, I said, 'I'm worried, I'm worried.' And sure enough, when we heard, 'We have a split decision,' I said, 'Uh-oh'."

Leonard was more sanguine. "I wasn't sure which way it was going to go," he admitted. "They say you gotta take the belt from the champion. I felt that I did enough. He was missing more than he was hitting me."

Hull's next line made history and brought down the house, "The winner, by a split decision, and new middleweight champion of the world, Sugar Ray Leonard!"

Ecstatic, Leonard leaped up on the bottom ring rope, just as he had when he won his first world title on 30 November

1979, defeating Wilfred Benitez for the welterweight championship. Hagler was furious.

Judge Moretti later explained his rationale. "I don't believe
it was that hard to score. I had it 115-113 for Leonard. For
some reason I was just locked in that night. After the fight I
told Lou Filippo, who had it 115-113 for Hagler, 'I can't find
a problem with your score.' Lou was the type who preferred
harder punches. Well, they might have been harder, but they
just weren't enough – in my opinion, anyway. Lou said he
didn't have a problem with my score either."

Pat Petronelli had vicious words with Jo Jo Guerra after
the fight. "You'll never judge another fight as long as you
live!" he promised. The irony was not lost on him, however.
Before the fight, there were four judges available and each
camp had the option of challenging somebody off there. Pat
successfully argued for the removal of Britain's Harry Gibbs,
believing that Hagler's victory over Alan Minter would not
endear him to his countryman. Guerra was elected on the
panel instead. At the press conference, Gibbs later revealed
that on his own private scorecard, he had Hagler winning,
115-113.

The decision also split opinions among ringside
observers. Angelo Dundee was asked if he thought a margin
of two was a correct score. "Inches or miles?" he retorted.
"I've been around long enough that I don't care if we win by
a whisper." He was adamant however that, "Ray outhustled
Hagler. I thought he fought the better fight, but hey, it's in the
eyes of the beholder."

In contrast, Hagler's old attorney Steve Wainwright
argued, "Marvin deserved it. He was the one who took the
fight to Leonard. Leonard never took the fight to Hagler."

Fight commentator Larry Merchant, however, scored it a
draw. "I thought Hagler did enough to hold on to his title. But

Leonard was able, as I said at the time, to steal the fight fair and square. As an underdog, he won the drama and looked like he was able to impose his boxing style on Hagler. If you go back in history, there were other examples of this, where the great fighter got the decision because he was the fighter that the public loved. I think this was a very close fight, but I also think Ray pulled off a historic con job to get the decision – and I think he earned that."

Hagler looked on in stunned silence. His mind dragged him back to the previous occasion when he had relied on the judgement of others to determine his success. "I immediately thought back to the first Antuofermo fight. They gave him a draw, and I was told that a draw is like the fight going to the champion because you didn't beat him decisively. I had to live with that. Then I was hoping that someday, if the shoe changes, maybe I would get a break." His monster raged. "In the boxing game, I never got that break."

Leonard tapped the former champion on the shoulder. "I said, 'Hey, we're still friends, right? Still friends?'" Hagler, still trying to comprehend the injustice he had been dealt, stared blankly into space. He eventually replied, "It's not fair." Leonard pressed, "No, we're still friends, right?"

Because of the commotion and noise around the ring, Leonard claimed that Hagler merely replied, "Yeah, good fight, good fight." Leonard then claimed that he declared, "You're still the champ."

Hagler's apparent conciliatory tone could not have been further from the interview he conducted with HBO commentator Larry Merchant, "That flurry stuff didn't mean nothing."

He continued, "I give so much credit to the guys like Roberto Duran and Tommy Hearns and Mugabi. Even guys before that, Mustafa Hamsho, even the second fight with

Antuofermo, these guys came to take my title. This guy only came to survive."

The dressing room was a scene of devastation. Amid the wailing and gnashing of teeth, the fury aimed towards Judge Guerra was palpable. Kenny Bayless, the chief inspector, recalled, "It was very unpleasant in Marvin's dressing room after the fight. They kept harping on the judge that scored it wide for Leonard. They really blasted that judge."

Hagler's mother was distraught and when she entered the sanctuary, Hagler attempted to console her. "Ma, don't cry," he said. "They got sick of seeing me around. I ain't got a mark on me. I've had harder sparring sessions. They gave the decision to him, but I'm alright."

The tears in the opposing dressing room were a direct contrast. His wife, Juanita, was crying with happiness when she accompanied Ray Jnr into the room. "Son, your dad was tough tonight," Leonard explained. "You can go to school tomorrow with your head held high."

Angelo Dundee recalled that Leonard then went up to Mike Trainer and gave him a kiss on the cheek. "Mike said, 'Ray, you are a tough little shit.' Then they walked out the door together, and Ray said, 'You know what, Mike? I am a tough little shit.'"

At the press conference as he prepared to address the media, some old animosities surfaced. Leonard refused to sit next to Bob Arum. Trainer and Arum disliked each other intensely. "I don't want to sit next to that man," Leonard said. So, 20 feet away from Arum, he thanked Hagler for giving him "the chance to make history".

He then read out a prepared statement, relinquishing his newly acquired title. He said, "I hereby relinquish the middleweight title. I only wanted to show the world that I could beat Marvin Hagler."

"I was never interested in his title," Leonard later explained. "Just in beating him. I still think he's the undisputed middleweight champion of the world. Marvin never hurt me, but he shook me up. I felt his punching power late, but by then he'd given away six or seven rounds so he had to come on strong. My strategy was stick and move, hit and run, taunt and frustrate. I knew it would be a tough fight, but I beat him to the punch. He was calling me a sissy."

Then, abruptly, Leonard left. "I have no more to say," he said, and he was gone.

When Hagler appeared, he took a number of swipes against various factors that he believed had robbed him. Firstly, he complained bitterly about the scoring, calling to mind the day in Vegas in 1979 when he drew with then champion Vito Antuofermo and thus lost his first chance at a title. He was not gracious in defeat. "I feel in my heart that I am still the champion," Hagler said. "I hate the fact that they took it from me and gave it to Sugar Ray Leonard, of all people. I can't believe I have to go to sleep and wake up and have to believe all this again. The bell saved him three times. Leonard fought like a girl sometimes. His flurries meant nothing. I think he should have to beat me more decisively to take the title."

He then hinted at the malevolent forces of the city's gambling overlords. "Las Vegas is a gambling city. If I'd fought anywhere else in the world, I would have won the fight. Here," he said, sweeping his arm around the room, "there is always an agenda."

Six years, six months and ten days after it had begun on a rainy night in London, Marvin Hagler's championship reign had come to an end.

Aftermath

"SOME DAY you know you're going to lose, but what I wanted to do was retire as the undisputed middleweight champion of the world," Hagler said. "With all my belts. They didn't beat me. They took them from me. They took. That's what they did. They took. So that's the bitterness. I think time will help. That's all I'm asking. That's all I'm looking for. That's all I want, peace and time."

Over the next six months, he had the time he requested but peace appeared to be a far more elusive goal.

After he left Las Vegas, shorn of the title that meant everything to him, Hagler abandoned the monastic zeal with which he had conducted his life for the past 11 years and his old secure world began crumbling around him.

The fight's outcome was only one link in a chain that fell apart. The progression actually began a week before the bout, when Hagler's beloved mother-in-law, Anna Washington, died of heart disease in Brockton, leaving him and his wife, Bertha, to grieve together long-distance on the telephone. "He wanted to go to the funeral, but he couldn't," Bertha said. "It was hard. I had my kids but no husband to come home and hold me."

Still grieving, Bertha flew out for the fight and suddenly found herself mourning for Marvin, too, and his lost title. "These were not easy times for us," Bertha said. "One minute you lose your mother, and the next your husband loses his job. It was a bit much for any soul to take."

Bertha claimed that their once-solid relationship had begun to experience problems during the year after the Mugabi fight, when her husband had initially entertained the notion of retirement. "Women were throwing themselves at Hagler, so the stories went, and he was not throwing them back," mused local television anchor man John Dennis, a long-time friend of Hagler's.

Bertha believed that the sad loss of her mother and the loss of the Leonard fight would bring her and Marvin back together again. "Instead," she says, "it drove us apart."

When they returned home to Hanover, Hagler was an emotional wreck. "He cried a lot," Bertha said. "I got him to talk about it a little. He felt he did get robbed. He said, 'I'll never be able to get my life and marriage together until I get my belts back.'" In the end, she said, he grew colder and more remote.

"I was trying to get him to talk to me," Bertha said. "He'd say, 'I don't want to talk about it.' I'd say, 'You have to talk about it. You can't go on like this.' It was frustrating for me because I couldn't get to him. The more I tried, the more distant he became."

Hagler grew further from her, physically as well as emotionally. He spent more time away from home. "I thought, 'Maybe he'll wake up and find there's more to life than drinking and partying'," she said.

Bertha maintained that her husband's central problem was the outcome of the fight and that he remained angry with her and the Petronellis over it. "He's bitter toward all three of us," she claimed. "He's going to have to come down to reality. He knows the mistakes he made in this fight, and he has to deal with them."

The differences between Marvin and Bertha became public in late June, when Bertha filed an abuse petition in Hingham District Court that claimed, "Marvin threw me out of the house. He pushed me. He hit the car with a boulder. I am in fear of him." A judge issued a temporary order barring Hagler from their house and gave Bertha custody of their five children, for the time being. Hagler did not contest the order and moved to an apartment in Boston. "The incident was," she said, "the first and only time he had ever been violent with me."

The story made all the papers, which prompted a swell of stories, detailing Hagler's downward spiral. A few days later, sports anchor John Dennis of WNEV-TV in Boston reported that Hagler was involved in "widespread abuse of both alcohol and cocaine". Dennis went on to say, "Those closest to Marvin Hagler say it was that decision on 6 April that started him on the downward spiral. Almost immediately after his return home to Boston, they [friends and family] say Marvin's despair over the loss steered him toward alcohol and cocaine."

Hagler dealt with the reports in the same direct manner he confronted his opponents. On all counts, except for that of excessive drinking, Hagler pleaded his innocence. He refuted claims that he had abused Bertha. "Yes, we had an argument, and I did throw a rock at her car," he confessed. "I thought I was handling things in the proper way. I wasn't putting my hands on her or anything like that."

He did admit to drinking heavily but insisted, "I've put it back in moderation now." He was, however, adamant that he had never abused cocaine. "If I do cocaine, I can lose all those things I worked very hard for."

The recent troubles in his marriage were nothing to do with his loss to Leonard, he insisted. "There's no connection. Things were heating up before the fight. I don't see why people are making a big thing out of it. Because I lost the fight, they said I was going crazy. That's bull. Everything tumbled down on me at the wrong time. My mother-in-law's death, the fight, my marriage – everything was on top of me. I admitted I was drinking a lot more than what I normally do. It was me trying to understand what was happening with my marriage."

"Bertha and I need some time away from each other. We've been together since we were 14 years old. I love Bertha. I always will. If people were to leave me and Bertha alone, maybe we could figure out our own problems and maybe we could put it together ourselves."

Bertha had consulted Marvin Mitchelson, one of the country's most celebrated divorce lawyers, to begin seeking a legal separation. Mitchelson urged restraint, telling her not to act rashly.

"He could hear in my voice that I wanted to be separated but I didn't want to be separated," she says. "He said, 'If you're really sure what you want to do, give me a call.'"

Bertha confessed that she was torn. "I love him, and the kids love him, and they want us to go back together," she said. "I still have my wedding ring on. This is a cool-down period for Marvin and me."

Hagler, however, was more circumspect. "I don't know," he said. "I'm still undecided about a lot of things."

This indecision extended to his career. He did not go back to the gym during the preceding six months. "We saw him only sporadically," said Pat Petronelli.

Hagler explained that it was because he could still taste the bile in his mouth.

"It was unfair," he cried. "You can't take a champion's title away like that. Leonard didn't beat me. I can't understand the judging. There are millions of people watching and seeing what is happening, and they can do this right in front of television. I think it's really bad."

Hugh McIlvanney, the doyen of fight scribes, had attributed the Leonard result to what he dubbed as the "Schulberg Factor". "This phenomenon – a compound optical illusion – may not have been discovered by Budd Schulberg, the novelist and fight aficionado," McIlvanney explained, "but he receives credit here for pointing it out to a few of us who were asking ourselves how Hagler came to be so cruelly misjudged.

"Budd's reasoning was that people were so amazed to find Sugar Ray capable of much more than they imagined that they persuaded themselves he was doing far more than he actually was. Similarly, having expected extreme destructiveness from Marvin, they saw anything less as failure and refused to give him credit for the quiet beating he administered. What Ray Leonard pulled off in his split decision over Hagler was an epic illusion."

Hagler agreed with the assessment. "I think what happened to me is this: When I don't knock a guy out and he's left standing, everyone thinks, 'The guy did great! He survived.' That's what Leonard did. He didn't come out there to try to win the title. Leonard came out there to look pretty, and just to show he wasn't scared, and to get in the ring with me. But, hey, he didn't come out to try to knock me out. He knew he couldn't do it.

"I never talked so much to a fighter in the ring in my life," Hagler recalled with exasperation. "He was just running. This man was exhausted. How are you gonna win a title like that?" he asked. "I saw him look over my shoulder at his trainer Angelo Dundee, and Dundee wouldn't let Leonard quit. Leonard wanted to quit. I had him three times!" Despite his protestations, Hagler absolved himself of any blame. "I don't blame myself," he said. "I beat the man. He wants to talk about points? Why don't you give me points for aggressiveness? I think I scored just as much. I think I did very well. The only thing I didn't do was knock him out."

"In my heart," he explained, "I feel I won the fight. I know it was the judges who decided. I have to be a man about everything." Pat and Goody Petronelli did not find it as easy to forgive themselves. They had been criticised for accepting $2m more to make the fight 12 rounds instead of 15. Many experts had cited this crucial concession as a significant factor contributing to the loss.

Goody had also come under fire for his ring strategy of making Hagler more conservative.

"My fighter needed 15 rounds with Sugar Ray Leonard," said Pat Petronelli. "Marvin had told us, 'He's good and he's fast. I need 15 rounds to wear him out.'" Hagler dismissed their self-flagellation. "Leonard insisted on 12 rounds or there would be no fight. I would have fought him over six rounds if I had to."

Leonard, who had returned to retirement, had evinced a twinge of sadness in his reflections on the greatest evening of his life. "My heart goes out to Hagler," he said. "I swear to God it does. As much as I wanted to beat him, I wish there was a way I could have beaten him and could have said, 'Here's your belt.' That was the symbol and centre of Hagler's life. It represented all he had worked for and much of what he has ever had. I feel sad for him. I really do."

Leonard's sympathy was perhaps the most galling thing of all. "Marvin didn't like the media hype, the showboating," says Pat Petronelli. "The showboating drove him crazy."

"You know – pretty boy," Hagler sneered.

The very image of Leonard as the establishment's choice had driven Hagler to distraction in the years before the fight and had fuelled his intensity to the very moment he stepped into the ring against Sugar Ray. Hagler had fought brutally for the acceptance that had come to Leonard so easily and naturally.

To Hagler, Leonard was forever the showman – quick, pretty, flashy and glib – moving in the ring as he moved through life. To Hagler, he was a form without shadow, a shadow without form, and all Hagler had to do was reach out and catch him, if he could.

Hagler had caught everyone else, of course. He had dominated his division by the sheer force and discipline of his might and art. And though he was making mounds of money and though he eventually grew bored with the show, he never took his eye off Leonard. He seemed to sense that he would not be whole unless he beat Leonard.

Pat Petronelli dismissed that view. "He has nothing to be ashamed of after a long and distinguished career," he said. "I want him to walk away and not look back."

Bob Arum echoed this opinion. "I think he would be nuts to fight again," Arum said. "Why would anybody with that kind of money fight?"

Leonard had retreated back into retirement and the alphabet organisations had already begun to schedule three different middleweights fights to re-distribute the pieces of the undisputed championship Hagler once owned. Arum had hired Hagler to do commentary on the telecasts of two of them.

"If I were to walk out of this game of boxing, I'd hate to walk out with this bitterness," Hagler said. "But I'm going to take time out. I don't know if I'm gonna fight again. Leonard doesn't have anything I want right now, except the satisfaction of whupping him. But that ain't what I want. I want my belts that they took."

Retirement

URING THE next 12 months, the press attempted to draw parallels between Marvin Hagler and Floyd Patterson. Patterson was the last boxer to take a defeat so badly that he took to wearing odd disguises when he ventured into the public domain.

Following the domestic incident with Bertha, one newspaper report suggested, "What was supposedly happening to Hagler made whatever happened to Dr Jekyll look like a little mood swing."

They focused on the idea that as the working man's fighter he was all business in his preparation. Others around him succumbed to sudden riches but Hagler, remembering that it was sacrifice that got him where he was, retained the blue collar along with his championship belts. When others trained in casino ballrooms, Hagler toiled alone in a downtown Las Vegas gym. His stubbornness was not calculated, just ingrained.

His half-brother Robbie Sims recounted, "After winning his world championship belt, Marvin had a special case made for it. Nobody saw this case except once a year." Sims shared, "Every Christmas morning, the case would be under the tree. Marvin would open the case; look at the belt for a while before retiring the whole assembly for another season."

When Leonard immediately relinquished the title which Hagler had worked a lifetime for, the building fury was surely understandable. "It was quite a blow to him, naturally," said Goody Petronelli. "He felt he was jammed. And at first all he talked about was a rematch." But Leonard displayed the same will-'o'-the-wisp qualities he displayed in the ring to avoid it.

Pat Petronelli had said, "I had a feeling he was going to take it bad, but not this bad." Petronelli said that Hagler was obsessed with what he considered Leonard's unfair tactics. He thought that Leonard should have been penalised for holding. "Marvin would keep repeating these things," Petronelli said. "I said, 'It's history now. You've got to go on with your life.'"

The truth of the matter was that reports of Hagler's angst were exaggerated. Hagler thereafter retired to Bartlett, New Hampshire, 150 miles north of Boston, where he didn't even have a telephone. "He's not unhinged," said Bob Arum. "He's having a ball, from what I hear. He's adjusting to his new life as a bachelor. The people who run into him say he's not brooding. In fact, he's proven most charming."

Boxing writer Jon Saraceno tracked Hagler down in St Martin in the Virgin Islands. Hagler did not appear to be brooding in mid-July. "He sleeps until 3.30pm, then gets up and he walks to the pool bar," the hotel concierge told Saraceno. "Then he gets picked up by friends and he's gone until morning." Hagler discussed with Saraceno, in vague terms, doing "the movie thing. You know, there's another life out there and I've got to start thinking about it." Later Hagler was spotted in a local disco. Saraceno asked the waitress if she was working Hagler's table. "For the last four nights," she said.

"I knew he was in a difficult marriage," Arum said. "Before every fight, he'd have serious problems with her. Many times when he missed press conferences, it was because of fights with her. Now I hear he's living in a luxurious apartment in downtown Boston, a man about town."

Hagler's only confidant by this time – the Petronellis no longer saw him – was his attorney, Morris Goldings. Goldings also said that reports of Hagler's unhinging were "too extreme".

"As for his initial seclusion, well, that's average for Hagler," Goldings said. "Even after his great wins, Marvin went into isolation. It's part of his style. After he beat Hearns and Mugabi, he did the same thing. I don't think he was depressed after those fights."

Goldings admitted that Hagler took the loss, his first in 12 years, to heart. "He's disappointed in the officials and he'll let people know it," Goldings said. "If you ask him about it, he will speak about it. But that's not to say he's not totally with it. He's attending to business, believe me."

The next order of business was the domestic dispute. Goldings said that what the Haglers were going through was fairly routine for a domestic struggle, and that perhaps Bertha inflamed the press a little bit when she characterised Hagler's aggression as boulder-throwing. "I think he threw a stone at her car," Goldings said, vaguely.

In any event, given Hagler's lifestyle as a fighter, and her objections, it seems almost natural that somebody in that house would throw something. "This was not a traditional marriage," said Goldings. "Here the husband does not work a 9-5 job but goes into what even he calls prison to train for long periods of time. He holes up with the Petronellis. That can take a toll."

Goldings said firmly that drugs were not part of Hagler's lifestyle. He admitted, however, that Hagler had drunk a few cocktails, on the grounds that he deserved a drink after 17 Spartan years. Goldings said that Hagler was busy in the meantime, hustling for endorsements and keeping a "watchful waiting" as far as his fight career went.

He was apparently resigned to life without Leonard and may or may not have fought again. "And we're working on other things," Goldings said. "But I really can't say any more."

Hagler was working on getting the rest of his life together. Apart from some business ventures, including television commercials and endorsements, he finalised his divorce from Bertha and then left for Italy, alone, to become an actor.

The move to Milan was impetuous. He arrived not knowing a word of Italian. "I found out fast that if you don't talk, you don't eat," Hagler later recounted. He enrolled at the Berlitz language school, started socialising with the locals, rode his bike into town for cappuccino and "learned to discriminate among olive oils when I cooked", he laughed.

"I like the country, the culture, the people," he explained of his radical decision to move to Europe. "And I knew Milan had people who could help me get into movies.

"I needed a change in my life. People said I wouldn't last a week here, and, I'll tell you, this was a challenge. The first day I was here I got locked in my room because my landlady didn't speak English, and I had to jump off the balcony, and then I had nothing to eat and no lira, and I'm this black guy who doesn't speak Italian, and, you know, I stuck it out because I'm a survivor. Now I love it here.

"Eventually, I just fell in love with the whole country, the whole culture," he said. "The other day I was riding my bike and I saw an 80-year-old woman helping her husband put on a cashmere coat. He's not going anywhere, but he wants to look nice and elegant. That's Italy right there."

His Italian contacts landed him a role as an American marine in the Italian movie *Indio*. He acted alongside Brian Dennehy as well as Anthony Quinn's son Francesco. "While the film wasn't exactly Oscar-worthy," Hagler explained, "it lit a flame in me." He started taking acting lessons, aggressively going after roles, and he won parts in other Italian action films including *Virtual Weapon*, *Night of Fear* and the obligatory *Indio 2*. He tended to be cast as the bad guy. "But," Hagler explained, "I'm always looking to branch out."

During the filming of *Indio 2*, rumours began to circulate that Hagler would accept the opportunity for a rematch against his nemesis, Leonard. Witnesses on the set in Manila reported that he was pounding a heavy bag with real purpose and looked in rock-hard shape at 168 pounds, "Right where he should be before razoring down to a middleweight's 160," suggested fight reports.

Hagler denied that he was considering a comeback. "I was working out in the Philippines because Sergeant Iron has to be very strong," he explained. "That's my character. When my body's in top shape, my mind is, too. And the only way I know to get in shape is doing my regular routine. A fighter's routine."

When he returned to the USA as a commentator for the 1989 rematch between Leonard and Thomas Hearns, he was scathing about Leonard's motivation for continuing to fight.

"I'm laughing at Leonard," he said. "I used to be the old man, but now look at him – he's getting old. What goes around, comes around."

He expressed pity that Leonard continued to fight. "All because of his ego. He just wants to keep his name and face in the papers," he sneered.

For the first time in public, he appeared to have found peace about his last fight. "If I didn't understand what happened in that fight, then it would bother me," Hagler said. "But I understand they took the fight from me. I don't know if they paid anybody off, but I beat Leonard. I look at the film and think, 'What are these people talking about?' I almost had him out in the ninth, but the bell saved him. Hearns had him out twice, but didn't finish him. Hearns has never been the same since I finished him. None of my fighters are ever the same. And Leonard is not the same, either."

He expounded on his reluctance to return to the ring. "I have considered the $15m I could make by coming back but it doesn't come close to changing my mind," he assured. "Financially, I'm in good shape. My health is good, my brain is good. One more fight and you never know what might happen."

He was conservative with the roughly $40m in purses he earned and in Milan, "I live in a two-bedroom apartment and get by on $10,000 a month for everything."

He was embarrassed by the sad financial state in which so many former fighters had found themselves. "I saw Joe Louis at the door at Caesars Palace, just shaking hands, and that left a bad taste in my mouth," he recalled. "Then I saw Jersey Joe Walcott doing the same thing in Atlantic City. Great champions," he said while shaking his head. "The boxing game is over," Hagler said in a gentle tone.

He recounted the moment he knew for certain that he would not return. "I was shooting my last scene in *Night of Fear*. We had travelled to Russia for the filming, and my character, after getting ventilated by bullets, was supposed to die."

"The director says, 'Die'," Hagler recalled. "Believe it or not, it was the hardest scene for me. I mean, how exactly do you die? Hey, I've never died. I've only lived."

Epilogue

Hagler married Kay Guarino, an Italian woman, in 2000 and lives happily in Milan, Brockton, and Conway, New Hampshire.